Tiger, Tiger

For a complete list of books by James Patterson, as well as previews of upcoming books and more information about the author, visit JamesPatterson.com or find him on Facebook.

Tiger, Tiger

James Patterson

Little, Brown and Company
New York   Boston   London

Little, Brown and Company
Hachette Book Group
1290 Avenue of the Americas, New York, NY 10104
littlebrown.com

First Edition: July 2024

Little, Brown and Company is a division of Hachette Book Group, Inc. The Little, Brown name and logo are trademarks of Hachette Book Group, Inc.

The publisher is not responsible for websites (or their content) that are not owned by the publisher.

The Hachette Speakers Bureau provides a wide range of authors for speaking events. To find out more, go to hachettespeakersbureau.com or email hachettespeakers@hbgusa.com.

Little, Brown and Company books may be purchased in bulk for business, educational, or promotional use. For information, please contact your local bookseller or the Hachette Book Group Special Markets Department at special.markets@hbgusa.com.

Part-opener photographs courtesy of — Prologue: (left) Abaca Press/Alamy Stock Photo and (right) Augusta National via Getty Images; Part 1: (left) CBS Photo Archive via Getty Images and (right) Ken Levine via Getty Images; Part 2: Ken Levine/Allsport; Part 3: Steve Munday/Allsport via Getty Images; Part 4: Alexander Hassenstein/ Bongarts via Getty Images; Part 5: Andrew Redington/Getty Images; Part 6: Mike Ehrmann via Getty Images; Epilogue: Ben Jared/PGA TOUR via Getty Images

ISBN: 9780316438605 (hardcover) / 9780316572774 (large print) / 9780316582391 (Walmart edition)
LCCN: 2024934704

Printing 1, 2024

LSC-C

Printed in the United States of America

Contents

Prologue   Father and Son   3

PART 1   Prodigy   11

PART 2   Amateur   43

PART 3   Professional   107

PART 4   Superstar   105

PART 5   Family Man   229

PART 6   Comeback   347

Epilogue   100 Rounds   431

Notes   *440*

Tiger, Tiger

PROLOGUE

Father and Son

2019   1997

One

The 83rd Masters
Augusta National Golf Club
Augusta, Georgia
April 14, 2019

The dream begins in a fourth-grade classroom.

At the Benjamin School, in North Palm Beach, Florida, ten-year-old Charlie Woods sits at his desk wearing a blue-and-orange school uniform and staring down at a blank notebook.

What is your wish?

The answer is easy. He wants to stand on a golf green and—for the first time in his life—witness his father, the world-famous Tiger Woods, win a tournament.

Charlie's made this wish before.

On Sunday, July 22, 2018, Charlie and his older sister, Sam, were among the 175,000 spectators at Carnoustie Golf Links, in Angus, Scotland. The siblings looked nervously at the British Open scoreboard as their father's lead evaporated on the back nine.

But in April of 2019, Tiger, determined that he's not "going to let that happen to them twice," tries again to persuade Charlie and Sam.

You want to come up to watch the Masters?

"No way, unless my sister comes," Charlie says, deferring to eleven-year-old Sam. But after her soccer team is eliminated from the Florida state tournament, Sam and Charlie join their grandmother, Kultida Woods, on a last-minute trip to Georgia.

Tiger was twenty-nine years old in 2005, the last time he won at Augusta National Golf Club. That was fourteen years—5,117 days—ago. His forty-three-year-old body has undergone eight surgeries, four on his back and four more on his knee.

He's told ESPN, "I want to be healthy for my kids."

Today is for them.

And for history.

In front of the clubhouse stands the Big Oak Tree, planted in the 1850s and now more than 150 years old.

Back in 1997, when twenty-one-year-old Tiger became the first minority golfer to win the Masters, the tree was surrounded by an unexpected line of fans in white jackets—the waiters and busboys of Augusta National. Today, those fans emerge once again as Tiger competes for his fifth Masters, and fifteenth major, win.

Sam and Charlie stand just off the green with their grandmother Tida. Like his father, Charlie's dressed in a red Nike top and black ball cap.

The final-round lead shifts among six players, including Tiger.

His putt on the 18th is for bogey, but it's good enough.

He's the winner—by a single stroke.

"Ti-ger! Ti-ger!" the crowd chants for the now five-time Masters champion.

Charlie runs to his father and jumps into his arms, squeezing him "tighter and tighter."

Tiger reaches for his mom, and the two of them sandwich Charlie in another hug.

Sam cheers enthusiastically but hangs back a little as the cameras follow. "Sam, she doesn't like the spotlight, can't stand it," Tiger says of his daughter. He understands. "She doesn't have to say anything." He pulls Sam close as they embrace, and she buries her face in his chest.

"I'm so proud of you, boy. So proud of you," Tida tells Tiger. "You counseled with Dad last night, didn't you?"

She knows how incredibly proud Earl Woods, Tiger's dad, would've been if he were here.

In the interview room afterward, Tida sits smiling in a green club chair, listening to her son reminisce about his 1997 Masters win.

"It's been twenty-two years," she hears him say nostalgically. "Life goes on. But there's been one continuity through it all—my mom was there."

That evening, the tradition continues. Patrick Reed, the 2018 Masters champion, helps Tiger into the fabled Green Jacket, the same rye-green wool coat he's donned four times before.

"It fits," he says.

Two

The 61st Masters
Augusta National Golf Club
Augusta, Georgia
April 13, 1997

The dream begins in a Southern California living room.

In April of 1986, Earl Woods has the television tuned to CBS Sports coverage of the Masters. His son, ten-year-old Tiger, roots for his golf idol, Jack Nicklaus.

The forty-six-year-old "Golden Bear" faces long odds. Nicklaus's goal for his final round: 65. He posts 35 on the front nine, leaving him thirty strokes after the turn.

On 17, Nicklaus sinks a long birdie putt. He shoots 65 for the round and edges out Greg Norman and Tom Kite by a single stroke for his sixth Masters title.

Tiger's already got the itch. *I want to be where he is, doing what he is doing.*

Ten years later, he's at Augusta National, playing a practice round with Jack Nicklaus and Arnold Palmer, but twenty-year-old Tiger misses the cut.

The next year, Tiger qualifies.

His father is there, too — against the advice of the doctors who've been monitoring Earl's complicated recovery from recent heart surgery.

Nick Faldo, defending 1996 champion and Tiger's first-round playing partner, senses the significance of the moment. "It's the beginning of Tigermania, right?"

Tiger bogeys four of the first nine holes, then rallies and builds a nine-stroke lead after three rounds.

In the wee hours of Sunday morning, Earl and Tiger share a bowl of ice cream.

"It's going to be the most important round of your life, but you can handle it," Earl tells his son. "Just go out there and do what you do."

The CBS Sports broadcast draws forty-four million viewers.

"Tiger's the man, period. He's your man; he's my man," says Augusta National headwaiter, Henry Ashley, who joins twenty or so of his Black colleagues under the Big Oak to watch Tiger play.

Nearby, Earl is also watching and waiting.

Tiger sinks his final putt, besting the second-place finisher, Tom Kite — who'd also finished second to Nicklaus in 1986.

At age twenty-one, Tiger becomes the tournament's youngest-ever champion. His seventy-two-hole score of 270, 18 under par, is the lowest ever at the Masters, and his twelve-shot margin is the largest ever.

"We made it," Earl says, face streaming with tears. "We made it. We made it." Tiger holds on tight as Earl whispers into his ear, "I love you, son, and I'm so proud of you."

Inside Butler Cabin that evening, Nick Faldo passes the mantle — and the Green Jacket — over to Tiger.

Later, Tiger vanishes from his own victory celebration. "I ended up falling asleep, holding the jacket, cuddling it like it was a little bear," he says. "I woke up in the morning, still holding it, and said, 'Huh, I did win it.'"

PART 1

Prodigy

Chapter 1

Navy Golf Course
Cypress, California
Summer 1978

A call comes in to the sports desk at CBS Los Angeles.

Jim Hill picks up. Hill, a six-foot-two Black man who played eight NFL seasons at defensive back, has only been on the sports desk at Channel 2 for a couple of years.

"My name is Earl Woods," the caller announces. "And my son Tiger is getting ready to revolutionize the sport of golf."

It's not the first time Hill has heard a dad brag about a son's athletic ability. "Well, what else is interesting about this story?" he asks.

"You've got to see him to believe him," Earl says, then adds, "I'm a former Green Beret. Get your butt down here."

"Here" is Cypress, California. The Orange County city of forty thousand is twenty-five miles southeast of Los Angeles. Hill is intrigued enough to assemble a camera crew to film the demonstration Earl sets up at Cypress's Navy Golf Course.

"How much do you practice?" Hill asks the toddler.

"A whole lot," Tiger answers.

Using three custom clubs that his father has had cut down to child size, Tiger hits balls and sinks putts, one after the other. Hill is suitably impressed.

"This young man is going to be to golf what Jimmy Connors and Chris Evert are to tennis," Hill declares.

Soon after Tiger's appearance on Channel 2, a national TV show seeks him out. *The Mike Douglas Show,* a talk show newly relocated to Los Angeles from Philadelphia, is looking for local talent. The host sees Hill's piece on Tiger, and soon the producers book him for the season's premiere week in their new Hollywood location.

On Friday, October 6, 1978, Tiger and Earl—dressed in coordinating red-and-white outfits—arrive on the soundstage at CBS Television City's Studio 43 and greet Mike Douglas as well as beloved comedian Bob Hope and legendary actor Jimmy Stewart, who is cohosting with Douglas for the week.

In front of the live studio audience, Stewart oversees a putting contest between Hope—a serious golfer with a single-digit handicap and the longtime host of the Bob Hope Desert Classic celebrity golf tournament—and Tiger, toting his tiny clubs in the canvas golf bag he brings everywhere.

"You got any money?" Hope jokes. "You wanna bet a nickel?"

Stewart asks Tiger to putt first. When Tiger misses the hole, Hope gives him a mulligan, while the *It's a Wonderful Life* star encourages him to take a second shot. "Tap it right in there."

Earl sets up the ball. Tiger moves it closer, focusing his gaze under the brim of his red cap. After three tries, he picks up the ball in frustration and throws it into the cup.

The young golfer charms the audience, but he also has a complaint. The putting green is uneven.

"Mike Douglas knew it, too," Earl Woods says once the cameras are off. "All he could do was laugh. He couldn't believe that Tiger could see the break, also."

*   *   *

Earl survived two tours in Vietnam, channeling a combination of innate athletic talent and a calm, focused demeanor. During his second tour as a Green Beret lieutenant colonel, he daringly planted explosives behind enemy lines.

Once he retired from active duty in 1974, Earl and his second wife, Kultida Punsawad—a native of Thailand who met Earl in 1968, when she was in her twenties and working on a US Army base in Bangkok—moved to Cypress, California, where they purchased a home on a corner lot at 6704 Teakwood Street.

Earl spends his days working at the aerospace company McDonnell Douglas, his evenings hitting 5-irons in his garage, and his weekends playing at the nearby Navy Golf Course, open to active-duty and retired military personnel.

On December 30, 1975, Tida and Earl—already father to two adult sons and a daughter with his first wife, Barbara—welcome a baby boy: Eldrick Tont Woods. Tont is a traditional Thai name, but Eldrick is Kultida's creation, a combination of her and Earl's initials. Earl nicknames the boy Tiger in honor of his friend and comrade Vuong Dang "Tiger" Phong, a brave South Vietnamese army colonel who went missing during the war.

Based on his belief that "the next generation of great golfers are going to be those who were introduced to the game between six months and a year," Earl set out to instill greatness in his infant son by power of example. He'd place Tiger's high chair in the garage so his son could observe as Earl practiced hitting balls into a net while narrating "exactly what I was trying to accomplish." His tactics worked, Earl says. "I'd monitor him out of the corner of my eye, and he'd be staring at the club, his eyes like marbles, waiting for my next swing."

When Tiger reached ten months old, Earl changed it up. "I just unstrapped him out of his highchair. He picked up a putter, put a ball down, waggled and hit a ball into the net. First time."

Earl immediately noticed that Tiger's "first swing was a perfect imitation of mine," like "looking at myself in a miniature mirror."

"Honey, get out here!" Earl shouted to Tida. "We have a genius on our hands."

In 1980, around a year and a half after Tiger's appearance on *The Mike Douglas Show,* Tida takes the four-year-old over to Heartwell Golf Course, in Long Beach, a small eighteen-hole, 2,143-yard par-3 course that specializes in classes and camps for beginning and junior golfers.

Although Tida herself recently took up golf so she could spend more time with Tiger, both parents recognize that it's time for him to get professional instruction.

Tida walks into the Heartwell pro shop with Tiger and his bag of mini clubs.

"My son is very talented," Tida tells assistant pro Rudy Duran. "My husband and I are interested if you could give him some private lessons."

Like Earl Woods, Duran first fell in love with golf when he was in the military, in his case the air force. After spending time as a pro golfer, Duran now teaches around a hundred kids between the ages of eight and eighteen. But he's a little taken aback at Tida's request that he coach a four-year-old. *The little dude can barely see over the pro shop counter,* he thinks.

Still, he's willing to see what the boy can do. At the practice range, Tiger gets out his cut-down 2.5-wood.

They really did a nice job getting the club to fit him, Duran thinks as he tees up four balls for Tiger.

Then: four perfect shots in a row. Each around sixty yards, with a bit of a draw.

Next, they venture to the chipping green to hit some pitch shots. Tiger pulls out another sized-down club, a wedge this time, and asks Duran, "Do you want me to pop them up?"

Duran is stunned at the skills he's witnessing. "What would Jack Nicklaus shoot if he was 3-foot-7? That's what Tiger shot."

The two of them start playing together daily. Duran sets a distance-adjusted "Tiger par" of 67; within a year, Tiger's shot a 59 at Heartwell, where on Saturdays his opponents are teenage junior golfers. On Sundays, he, his father, and Duran play nearby regulation courses, where, Earl notes, "at the end of the day he was always under par. This is important: He never developed a complacency or a fear of going low."

Duran develops an easygoing relationship with Tiger's parents, whom he calls "lighthearted" and "really easy to be around," not at all pushy or demanding. "To me, the family was raising a child, not a golfer," he says. "The golf was just something he had an aptitude for."

But this is a kid who "popped out of the womb a Magic Johnson or a Wolfgang Amadeus Mozart. He had talent oozing out of his fingertips," Duran says. "Mozart composed finished music in his head. I saw that in Tiger. He was composing shots in his head."

"What he's accomplishing at his age is phenomenal," he tells *Golf Digest* magazine, which runs a small piece on Tiger in 1981.

"The kid's not exceptional," Duran says. "He's way beyond that."

Chapter 2

Universal Studios Lot
Universal City, California
October 12, 1981

O n the Universal Studios Lot, five-year-old Tiger is unimpressed by making his second national television appearance.

"After all," he remarks, "golfers get on television lots of times."

Taking the stage in a red-and-white striped polo and a Spider-Man cap, Tiger perches on the lap of NFL great Fran Tarkenton, who quarterbacked the Minnesota Vikings to three Super Bowl appearances and now cohosts ABC's talent showcase, *That's Incredible!,* alongside singer John Davidson and actress Cathy Lee Crosby.

Over footage of Tiger driving, chipping, putting—both on Earl's homemade driving range and on the Navy Golf Course—and dancing next to his father when he sinks the ball in the hole, Tarkenton says, "On a golf course, Tiger has the kind of poise and confidence that would be the envy of most golfers ten times his age. His knowledge of the game is truly amazing."

So are his sporting goals, especially for a kid just starting kindergarten.

"When I'm going to be twenty, I'm gonna beat Jack Nicklaus and Tom Watson," Tiger says as the words INCREDIBLE KID! flash across the screen.

After the filming of *That's Incredible!*, Earl watches a seventeen-year-old fan approach Tiger for an autograph.

"He didn't know how to write, so he printed," Earl says.

Not everyone is as confident in Tiger's future. After the taping, cohost Davidson puts the question to Tarkenton: "You think this kid will ever make it?"

"He has no chance," Tarkenton replies. "Because he's got one of these doting fathers who's going to drive him, and he's gonna end up hating golf and hating sports and you'll never hear from him again."

The headline of a small piece in *Golf Digest*'s People in Golf segment reads: 5-YEAR-OLD TIGER—HE'S INCREDIBLE.

The article makes it into J. Hughes Norton III's clip file. As an agent with Cleveland-based International Management Group (IMG), Norton makes it his business to identify potential rising stars in sports.

Norton, an 8-handicap golfer who played hockey at Yale, has been with IMG for around eight years, since 1972. He first learned about sports marketing as a student at Harvard Business School. The IMG founder and president, Mark McCormack—who started the company in 1960 based on a handshake deal with golf superstar Arnold Palmer and eventually went on to represent Jack Nicklaus and Gary Player—spoke to an entrepreneurship class Norton was taking. When McCormack returned to campus a few months later, Norton asked for, then landed, a job at IMG.

Norton travels to Los Angeles to meet the kid from the *Golf Digest* clip. In Cypress, he finds young Tiger riding his tricycle in front of the house on Teakwood Street.

Earl does the talking. "I believe that the first Black man who's a really good golfer is going to make a hell of a lot of money."

"Yes, sir, Mr. Woods," Norton says in agreement. "That's why I'm here."

*　*　*

The *Today* show is broadcasting "on location in Southern California" at Calabasas Country Club.

"Eldrick Tiger Woods," says anchor Bryant Gumbel, introducing his guest. "The most amazing five-year-old golfer you have ever seen."

Though Tiger, whose ball cap reads SUPER KID, is making his third national TV appearance while still in kindergarten, Tida insists, "He's just a regular kid that loves to go out and play golf."

Play to win, she means. "One thing he love most," says Tida, whose native language is Thai, "is competition. He love to have somebody to play with him. He love to compete with even his pro or his dad when, uh, they're playing putting."

The camera cuts back to Tiger.

"Would you like to be a pro golfer?" Gumbel asks.

Tiger looks off to one side, considering the question.

"Yes," he finally says.

Duran fits Tiger for more clubs, but the young golfer's set is not yet complete.

"You know what, Rudy?" Tiger says. "We didn't get a one-iron—I want a one-iron."

"A one-iron?" Duran says. "You're not gonna generate enough club-head to get a one-iron airborne. You'll just hit it into the ground."

Duran watches as Tiger takes Earl's full-length 1-iron to the range and rips the ball.

On his sixth birthday, December 30, 1981, Tiger tries out his new irons.

Before today's small exhibition match at Redlands Country Club, he draws an admiring crowd on the practice range. "Does he ever get upset?" a woman asks.

"Sometimes, yeah," Duran tells her, adding, "He gets a two-shot penalty when he throws a club, so he doesn't do that too often."

The birthday boy is completely focused on hitting the balls until his coach asks, "What do you do when you want to hit it low, Tiger?"

"Stay off the right foot."

"What kind of club would you use?"

Pause. "Five-iron or 4-iron."

"You know what's going on." Duran nods approvingly.

Tiger, Earl, and Rudy Duran pile into Duran's white Porsche for a trip out to San Jacinto, around eighty-three miles east of Los Angeles, where Soboba Springs Golf Course has extended an exciting invitation.

Six-year-old Tiger doesn't really grasp the significance of "playing the great Sam Snead." The seventy-year-old Virginia golfer known as Slammin' Sam, whose swing is "so sweet, you could pour it out of a syrup bottle," is the winningest player on the PGA Tour, notching eighty-two wins in a twenty-nine-year career.

They're playing the 17th and 18th holes of the desert course. On 17, Tiger's tee shot fades short. He wades into a creek to play his ball.

"What are you doing?" Snead yells.

Tiger looks up, confused. "I'm going to hit the shot," he says.

"Take it out and hit it again," Snead tells him. "Just pick it up and drop it. Let's go on."

It's a generous offer, but it doesn't sit right with Tiger.

"My dad always taught me you play it as it is, there's no such thing as winter rules," Tiger insists. Earl and Duran don't intervene as Tiger pulls out his iron, miraculously "playing it out of the water and making bogey."

The move impresses Snead, who shakes his head in admiration even after Tiger bogeys again on 18, giving the duo a final score of par-par and 2 over.

The champion, in his trademark Stetson Madrigal coconut-straw porkpie hat, offers to sign Tiger's scorecard.

In return, the boy in the cap reading SUPER KID signs his own autograph for Snead.

Snead recognizes the talent.

"I've worked for years to get the hitch out of this swing of mine," Snead says, "and along comes this kid. I think I'll toss my clubs in a lake someplace."

Chapter 3

Heartwell Golf Course
Long Beach, California
May 29, 1982

S ix-and-a-half-year-old Tiger is playing in his weekly Saturday juniors tournament at Heartwell Golf Course.

Tiger, a rising first grader, enjoys school, but it's a separate part of his life. "When I'm around other kids, I don't like to talk about golf," he says. "I just like to keep it to myself."

He's a good student—so good that he qualifies for an advanced class, but Tiger refuses. "He does not want to," Tida says, "because all of his golfing partners are so much older than he is and the kids in the advanced class would be older too. He is really excited about being with his own age group."

But not on the golf course.

Competing against teenagers is the "peak of his week," as Earl puts it, though sixteen-year-old Kelley Manos is quick with the reality check. "Do you realize this little s— is tied with us?" There's zero animosity in the observation, only amazement, "like, 'Wow, cool, the little guy did it.'"

On this Saturday, Tiger's teeing up on the 12th, connecting "a nice little two-and-a-half-wood" with his Top Flite 7 golf ball. *The ball carries the bunker, it rolls into the hole. Everybody in my group celebrates but me. I can't see that high. So, one of the guys picks me up, shows me there's no ball on the green. I'm excited—I run to the green, pick the ball out of the hole and I'm celebrating.*

"You idiot," shout the other kids. "Your golf bag's up on the tee!" He's completely forgotten about his clubs.

Tida saves the golf ball and displays it in a commemorative HOLE IN ONE plaque. *Jet* magazine's November 15, 1982, issue pictures Tiger holding a fairway wood and wearing a visor and sunglasses to shield his eyes from the California sun.

Ebony magazine declares, A GOLFING CHAMPION AT SIX: TINY TIGER WOODS HAS DONE IT ALL, INCLUDING A HOLE-IN-ONE. Though Earl envisions a grander award—an entry in the *Guinness Book of World Records*—he tells *Ebony* that golf "is still a game and he is still a child."

Tida and Tiger have a Saturday routine. Driving her Plymouth Duster to Heartwell, she usually drops him off with his clubs and seventy-five cents—enough for him to buy a hot dog and place a pay-phone call for a ride home.

On other Saturdays, they travel to tournaments around Southern California. Tida uses the time to coach Tiger: "When you are ahead, don't take it easy," she tells her son. "After the finish, then be a sportsman."

Her ruthless philosophy doesn't end there. "In sport," she says, "you have to go for the throat. Because if all friendly, they come back and beat your ass. So you kill them. Take their heart."

Tiger names the family dog Boom-Boom after Fred "Boom Boom" Couples, a golfer famous for his ability to drive the ball with distance and accuracy.

Boom-Boom goes everywhere with Tiger. When the boy plays make-shift greens at a local park near Heartwell Golf Course, the dog acts as a canine marker, finding every golf ball Tiger hits and lying down next to it.

Boom-Boom is also a good listener. Tiger struggles with stuttering—he's taking a class to help—and he practices by talking to the dog for hours and hours. "He would sit there and listen before falling asleep," Tiger says of his faithful friend.

When he's not practicing with Boom-Boom, Tiger sneaks onto the Navy Golf Course, which he's technically not allowed to play until age ten. As he's gotten older—and better—some members start to complain and demand that the rule be enforced.

Hence the subterfuge.

I hop in the creek, this ditch, and walk on the south side of the ditch, because the clubhouse is up above, so no one can see me. My dad gets a golf cart, and I walk down past one, past two, and I lie under the bridge on three, and try and be in total disguise, so I can blend into the environment. I put rocks and stuff around me. I hide my golf bag underneath the rocks, totally trying to blend into the environment.

"You there?" Earl asks.

Tiger is always in place.

"Yup. Coming up."

On December 30, 1985, there is a special event: "My father took me to Navy Course for my 10th birthday," Tiger says, excited to be "finally old enough." There would be no more hiding in the bushes to play the course in secret.

Chapter 4

Junior World Golf Championship
Torrey Pines Golf Course
La Jolla, California
July 15, 1986

Adrenaline is coursing through Tiger's four-foot-nine, eighty-one-pound frame. The ten-year-old is sweating so profusely that his thick glasses start to slip. He's so nearsighted that he could be considered legally blind without them, but he's still too young for contact lenses.

"They call him Tiger?" asked ten-year-old golfer Chris Riley in 1984, when the players were both Junior World Golf Championship first-timers. Since 1968, the San Diego County Junior Golf Association has hosted an international field of players from more than eighty countries. Then eight-year-old Tiger won the three-round tournament over Riley, who said, "He had the Coke-bottle thick glasses, but he could flat-out play."

It's now Tiger's third summer in the boys-ten-and-under category. He won again in 1985, and by 1986, he's collected dozens upon dozens of trophies. But after the first round of the Junior World tournament, Tiger throws his clubs to the ground in frustration. It's an unusual outburst, though "lately," his mom says, "he has shown a bit of temper when he didn't make par."

Since he was very young, Tida has stressed to Tiger that he is not to throw tantrums on the golf course, as tennis players John McEnroe and Jimmy Connors do on TV. "I don't want you to ruin my reputation as a parent," Tida tells him, adding, "I will spank you in a minute if you act like that."

"We're working on it," Earl says of his son's impatience. "He's just like any other golfer. He doesn't like to do badly." Still, Tiger tends to bang his clubs around when he hits a bad shot. "I don't want to, Daddy, it just happens," he insists. "I'm trying very hard."

"I know you're trying, just keep trying," Earl says in encouragement, though he's convinced that learning to "play angry" actually helps Tiger, allowing him the space to "take responsibility for his actions."

At the clubhouse—the landmark 1817 adobe home called Casa de Carrillo—father and son have a coaching session.

"It didn't go well today," Tiger says. "I couldn't get anything to go right."

"Well, it's no big deal," Earl replies. "You'll go out and get them tomorrow."

Tiger also grouses about using only his sand wedge and putter. "I have to putt a lot better," he says. "I couldn't putt. I couldn't hit the greens."

He asks his dad if they can go play another course later that day. "I need to use my woods," the ten-year-old says.

Tiger doesn't win the 1986 Junior World title. It's time to find a new coach, especially with Rudy Duran leaving Heartwell to run his own golf course.

John Anselmo, the head pro at Meadowlark Golf Course in nearby Huntington Beach, is Earl's top choice. "I have this new kid named Tiger Woods," Anselmo tells his son, Dan, a fellow pro and coach. "He's a tour player in a little boy's body. He just needs to grow into it."

In and around the Woods family home, Tiger designs a practice course.

"Too long," Earl says of Tiger's backyard setup, "and hit the neighbor's house. Too short and...hit the roof."

Indoors, Tiger decides that the living room coffee table is the perfect height for clearing lob wedges. The ball must stop rolling before it hits the fireplace.

"I chip over that big chair and make the ball stop before it hits the bricks," Tiger explains. The stakes are high—"If I miss, my mother will get after me"—but "it's good training for finesse and getting the right feel for delicate shots."

In 1987, *Golf Digest* launches its first-ever Armchair Architect contest in golf course design. Eleven-year-old Tiger is too young to enter, but he's determined to participate.

Working at the same bedroom desk where he plays Nintendo and does his homework, Tiger decides that an "outlandish and creative" design "would end up winning." Using colored pencils, he draws a 610-yard, par-5 hole featuring a sand trap in the center of the green.

It's an all-or-nothing hole, dependent on a huge element of luck. The U-shaped fairway has two doglegs that reward either three precise shots or one high shot over the top. A player lacking accuracy or distance will land a ball in the bog.

Earl enters the contest on Tiger's behalf.

He doesn't win. When the results come out, Tiger studies the top entry: "a blank hole, tee markers, a green in the distance, and that's it."

I wish I had known that, he thinks. *I would have done that.*

On the course, he's becoming used to the rush of winning. The year of the Armchair Architect contest, Tiger enters—and wins—thirty-three junior golf tournaments. *Thirty-three.*

"There's no feeling I've found that matches the feeling that I've beaten everybody," says the eleven-year-old. "Second place is first loser."

Chapter 5

A letter arrives, addressed to thirteen-year-old Eldrick "Tiger" Woods.

"Dear 'Tiger'!" Stanford University golf coach Wally Goodwin writes. "Here at Stanford I am finding that it is never too early to get word out to you exceptional young men concerning what it will take a few years down the road in terms of application to Stanford."

Goodwin is looking for "Winners!" and goes on to advise the seventh grader that while "athletes get a bit of a break," gaining entrance to Stanford "takes SAT scores of 1200 or so" and a 3.6 GPA.

Nothing could have pleased Tiger's parents more. The rules of the Woods house are:

1. Education before golf.
2. Homework before practice.
3. No back talk.
4. Respect your parents.
5. Respect your elders.

As Tiger later tells the *Los Angeles Times,* "School comes first, golf second. How much practice I do in golf is determined by how soon I finish my homework. You can't accomplish anything without an education. I definitely plan to finish college before thinking of turning professional."

Tiger's strongly self-motivated. The two questions Earl boasts of *never* having to ask are:

Did you practice? And *Did you do your homework?*

The junior high student and three-time Junior World winner (1984, 1985, 1988) replies with what Wally Goodwin calls "a perfect letter," assuring the coach that his current GPA is 3.86, "and I plan to keep it there or higher when I enter high school."

Furthermore, he says, "My goal is to win the Junior World in July for the fourth time and to become the first player to win each age bracket. Ultimately I would like to be a PGA professional. Next February I plan to go to Thailand to play in the Thai Open as an amateur."

Carl Vanderbosch, Tiger's history teacher at Orangeview Junior High, can vouch for the academics. When preparing his lesson plans for the incoming seventh graders and seeing "the name Tiger on the class roster," he "expects a rambunctious kid." Instead, he finds that the new student has "an amazing attention span" and a well-developed "sense of self."

During a lesson on Asian history and religion, Tiger "raises his hand to volunteer that he comes from a Buddhist background. Just the way he carries himself," Vanderbosch says, gives the impression that his student "takes life as I imagine a Buddhist might."

Buddhism has always been part of Tiger's upbringing: Tida is a devout Buddhist who's raised her son in the faith. She grew up north of Bangkok, not far from the famous bridge over the River Kwai, and made Earl accompany her to the Temple of the Reclining Buddha on their first date, which happened to fall on a holy day.

Not exactly Earl's idea of a fun time, but he was no match for his future wife's determination. "What could I do?" he says in faux exasperation. "I took her to the damn church."

Tida also ensures that her son is connected to his Thai heritage and family—her mother, Chardcharvee, lived with them for a while when Tiger was young, and Tida brought him to visit Thailand in 1984, at age eight, where he met his grandfather, Vit. Tida's father, whom she describes as "built like my son, tall and slim," gave Tiger a mother-of-pearl Buddha statue that the boy still treasures.

"Tiger, you pray to Buddha yet?" Tida will ask in the same breath as inquiring after his schoolwork. Every good or bad result requires a visit to the monks at the nearby Buddhist temple, and on special occasions such as his birthday, Tiger presents the monks with gifts of rice, sugar, and salt.

"I like Buddhism because it's a whole way of being and living," Tiger says. "It's based on discipline and respect and personal responsibility.

"I believe in Buddhism. Not every aspect, but most of it. So I take bits and pieces."

He has a small but tight group of friends, including neighbor Mike Gout and junior high pal Bryon Bell. While maintaining a nearly straight-A average, he's also a student of golf. In his bedroom, decorated with books, motivational sayings, and Jack Nicklaus posters, Tiger reads about the great golf courses. *The St Andrews Opens,* by Bobby Burnet, is one well-worn text.

When he's fourteen, *Golf Digest* ranks him "America's third-best junior amateur."

The pressure is on.

But his competitive spirit is strong—so strong that his dad works to keep it in check. "It's a constant fight for me to get him to go out and just have fun playing a round of golf," Earl says.

The thrill of the win, Tiger says, is "hard to describe. It feels like a lion is tearing at my heart."

Chapter 6

Southern California
Summer 1988

Tiger, Earl boasted to *Ebony* in 1982, "is one of the first Black golfers with natural skills whose parents have the means to get pro instructions that even exceed those afforded Jack Nicklaus in his formative years. We are willing to pay the price."

That was when Tiger was six—when Tida stayed home with him and Earl worked as a contract administrator and materials manager at McDonnell Douglas. In 1988, Tida goes back to work and Earl retires, replacing his wife as Tiger's companion at national junior tournaments.

Year-round tournament play is expensive. Costs associated with Tiger's junior tour schedule, including travel, tournament fees, and equipment, run to almost $70,000 annually (nearly $155,000 today). The schedule—fly in on the morning of a tournament, stumble out sleepless for the opening round, then check into a Motel 6—is wearying.

"Pop, do you think we could get to the site early enough so I could get in a practice round?" Tiger asks.

"From this day forward, you will have just as good of a chance as any of these country club kids, and if I have to go broke, that's what we're going to do," Earl vows. And from then on, "we went a day in advance, he stayed with his peers at the Marriott and the Hiltons, and he kicked butt and took names."

Earl and Tida provide unconditional support. "We didn't want Tiger to grow up with an inferiority complex," Tida says. "So even if we have to take out second mortgage or home equity loan, we let him have it."

"Oh, I get everything paid for by sponsors," Earl jokes. "There are three companies: Earl, D., and Woods," the *D* referencing his middle name, Dennison. "I have about five very floating credit cards and two mortgages on the house."

Tiger's health and development have also been placed in the care of professionals, including Captain Jay Brunza, PhD, a navy doctor who has doubled as Tiger's sports psychologist and occasionally, at major tournaments, as his caddie.

"Would you help me give Tiger the kind of advantage that a lot of country-club kids get?" Earl asks Brunza. "Would you work with him?"

They settle on a plan. Brunza will drive up from San Diego to Cypress on weekends, and Tiger will do his golf homework on the weekdays in between.

Using breathing, hypnosis, and visualization exercises he developed for the seriously ill children he treated at Bethesda Naval Hospital, Brunza teaches Tiger how to visualize shots by accessing "a level of real focus technique." Imagining a picture around the hole, he putts to that image rather than to the cup.

Coach John Anselmo, who honed his teaching eye while watching fellow navy man Sam Snead play near the end of World War II, and who has seen a lot of players over the course of his nearly seven decades, marvels that "with Tiger, anything is possible. I kid his dad that Tiger is not his, but that he comes from another world. I just hope I live long enough to see what's going to happen. It's going to be amazing."

* * *

Wally Goodwin at Stanford University isn't the only coach with an eye on Tiger.

Don Crosby, the golf coach at Western High School, in Anaheim, California, keeps noticing a junior high kid—a "little guy, maybe five feet tall in golf spikes"—hitting balls on the driving range where he takes the team to practice. *That's Tiger Woods.*

The entire team is impressed—*Look how good he is. Look how much he practices*—and Crosby can barely believe his luck when one of his high school golfers reports, "Coach, Tiger Woods lives in my neighborhood. He lives right around the corner from me."

"He might just as well have told me that Johnny Unitas, Mickey Mantle, and Michael Jordan were going to play for Western High," says Crosby. *This is a coach's dream.*

Except that Western High School is continually redistricting. Crosby rushes into the principal's office and points at Teakwood Street on the map.

"This little square over here, that's in Cypress, and that's where the future best golfer in the world lives," he tells the baffled principal. "So, if they start messing with our boundaries, you can give away anything but hold onto that little square."

They do, and in the fall of 1990, Tiger enrolls as a freshman at Western High School.

On the first day of practice, a hardworking senior approaches Crosby. "I guess I'm not No. 1 anymore," the senior says.

"You're right. But you'll be a heck of a No. 2," the coach assures him.

Crosby's had experience with other young sports stars—and their overbearing parents—so he cautiously contacts Earl Woods to ask how involved he and Tida intend to be in Tiger's high school golf career.

"Once the high school season starts," Earl tells him, "you won't see me."

* * *

The press keeps calling.

"I'd like to do something on Tiger," *Golf Digest* reporter Jaime Diaz tells Earl.

"Find a place where we can play," Earl says, "and we'll do it."

Earl and Tiger meet Diaz at Coto de Caza Golf & Racquet Club, the first private thirty-six-hole country club in Orange County. But fourteen-year-old Tiger seems rattled, missing short putts on the first two holes.

"Hey, Tiger," Earl says. "It's just a normal day."

With that reassurance, Tiger recovers, and Diaz starts "to see the joy the two of them took in golf and each other. Tremendous joy."

"Earl is the coolest guy I know," Tiger tells Diaz. "He doesn't live through me, which is what some parents do. He might watch me play, but I don't think about him on the golf course. I just think about me. It's all me."

Father and son tease each other. Earl intentionally jingles the change in his pocket just as Tiger lines up a shot. "You can't get to me, Pop," warns Tiger with a grin.

It hasn't always been this easy between them. Last year, Earl decided that it was time to draw on his own military training as a Green Beret, including prisoner-of-war interrogation techniques, for instruction in golf psychology.

"This isn't a very nice world sometimes," explains Earl. "It's to prepare him, not to use as an offensive tactic. I'm not trying to create a little monster."

If Tiger broke stance or reacted, Earl would taunt, "Are you posing or are you going to play? Why don't you play the game and stop being the little pretty boy."

"We had two rules," explains Earl. "He couldn't say anything, and the second rule was the first rule is the only rule we had."

Earl spent a month or so shouting, cursing, standing in Tiger's way, being intentionally disruptive and demeaning. "I pulled every dirty trick under the sun," he says.

He pressured Tiger to get mad, lose his temper. "I know you want to slam down that club, but don't you dare do it. Don't you dare!" Earl warned. Tiger "got so mad he would be grinding his teeth." Earl would ease up just long enough to allow his son to regain some composure, then start again.

"He would push me to the breaking point, then back off, push me, then back off. It was wild," Tiger says. He understands where it comes from. "My dad was a Green Beret and a tough dog. He had to endure a lot. He taught me the mental tactics. He passed on his toughness to me."

Earl is pleased with the results of his psychological warfare. "You could just see the boy toughen up," he says. "By the end of the month, he was pulling that stuff on me."

By then, Tiger's response is just a smile. *That's it; he has it now,* Earl thinks.

"Son, the training's over," he tells him. "You'll never play anyone who's mentally stronger than you are."

Earl holds on to one tradition. When he wants to get his son's attention on the golf course, he doesn't call him Tiger or even Eldrick but a different name entirely.

Sam.

"That was one of our codes, too," Earl says. "Sam, so he'd know it was me talking."

"Why aren't you calling me Tiger today?" Tiger sometimes asks.

Earl answers, "You just look more like a Sam today."

To the press, Tiger is looking more and more like a rising star.

In November of 1990, a television crew from *Trans World Sport* arrives at the Woods home to profile the promising young athlete.

On camera, Earl shares his vision of Tiger's future. "The world is ready. It is absolutely ready for a nonwhite golfer to be successful. The next booming area in the world for golf is Asia. Tiger is already Asian. He is Thai. Uh, in the United States, Tiger is Black...So he can't lose unless he doesn't win, and I don't anticipate him not winning."

The world might be ready, but fourteen-year-old Tiger describes the entrenched attitudes of those whom Earl calls "country-club kids."

"Not every day, but, uh, every time I go to a major country club, I always feel it. I can always sense it. Um, people always staring at you," Tiger says. "I call it The Look. It makes you uncomfortable, like someone is saying something without saying it." It's especially noticeable "when I go to Texas or Florida, you always feel it, 'cause, uh, they're saying, 'Why are you here? You're not supposed to be here.' And, uh, that's probably because that's where all the slavery was. So, uh, oh well."

It's an uncomfortable position for a kid who identifies as more Asian than Black. His father is half Black, a quarter Native American, and a quarter Chinese. His mother is half Thai, a quarter white, and a quarter Chinese. When he's filling out forms that only allow for one ethnicity, "I always fill in 'Asian,'" Tiger says.

"All the media try to put black in him," Tida says. "In United States, one little part black is *all black*. Nobody want to listen to me. I been trying to explain to people, but they don't understand. To say he is 100 percent black is to deny his heritage. To deny his grandmother and grandfather. To deny *me*!"

Earl and Tida were subjected to hostility as the first nonwhites in their neighborhood in Cypress in 1973. Their house was pelted with limes; a rock once shattered their kitchen window. It was a hard adjustment for Tida. "There's no color in Thailand," Tida says of her home country, "not like U.S."

But she also sees the positives of her son's mixed heritage. "Tiger has Thai, African, Chinese, American Indian and European blood," she says. "He can hold everyone together. He is the Universal Child."

Earl's view is more jaded.

"The boy has about two drops of black blood in him," he says. "But like I told him, in this country there are only two colors. White and non-white. And he ain't white."

Chapter 7

Grandpa Charlie

Earl Woods is more familiar than most with the realities of being a Black athlete in America, particularly in a traditionally white sport.

Twenty-year-old Earl played catcher on the Kansas State College baseball team, earning varsity letters in 1952 and 1953, making him not only K-State's first Black baseball player but also the first-ever Black player in the entirety of what was then the Big Seven conference.

"My teammates treated me all right, it wasn't their fault," Earl recalls, "but I wasn't afforded the same privileges as they were. For instance, I would not stay in the same hotels. We would go to the University of Oklahoma and the team stayed in Norman, where the University is, and I had to stay in Oklahoma City, an entirely different town. I had to get in a car in my uniform after the game and drive to Oklahoma City. There were no hotels that would take Blacks in Norman, Oklahoma."

He was offered a contract with the Kansas City Monarchs to play in the Negro Leagues, but in 1953 the new college graduate instead joined the military, desegregated five years before by President Harry Truman's Executive Order 9981. "The theory was that the army was integrated...Just like our society was integrated," Earl says drily.

Of his first posting—as an officer at Fort Benning, in Columbus,

Georgia—he remembers, "Four of us were walking down the street, two black, two white, just window shopping, enjoying ourselves," he says, "and all of a sudden the police came up and threw us against the wall, handcuffed us, put us in the wagon and drove us to jail. We were fined for disturbing the peace—$32 and five cents," equivalent to around $365 today. The charge? "Blacks and whites weren't supposed to mix in public, that was our crime."

Earl stayed in the military for twenty years. After he and Tida married, he posted to Fort Hamilton, in Brooklyn, New York, where in his early forties he discovered a late-blooming passion for golf, devouring books on the subject and playing round after round at the Dyker Beach Golf Course, in the shadow of the Verrazzano Bridge.

With the zeal of the convert to a new religion—golf—Earl began eagerly catching up on the groundbreaking success of Charlie Sifford, who in 1961 became the first Black golfer allowed to join the PGA. On January 12, 1969, forty-six-year-old Sifford had a momentous win at the Los Angeles Open at Rancho Park, the popular municipal course out Pico Boulevard past the 20th Century Fox movie lot. The city declared February 3, 1969, Charlie Sifford Day.

That night, Sifford spoke to a joyful crowd gathered in Los Angeles's Black Fox nightclub: "It's so wonderful to think that a black man can take a golf club and become so famous."

Four days before the January 12 tournament, Pulitzer Prize–winning *Los Angeles Times* columnist Jim Murray devoted a column to Sifford's achievements.

"Prior to Charlie, pro golfers had the effrontery to have a 'Caucasians Only' clause in their bylaws. It was the recreational arm of the Ku Klux Klan.

"Charlie birdied, not talked, his way through social prejudice. He broke barriers by breaking par. His weapon was a 9-iron, not a microphone. Charlie stands as a social pioneer not because he could play politics, but because he could play golf."

Sifford learned the game as a North Carolina country-club caddie, served in a segregated US Army, and survived World War II combat in Okinawa.

In 1947, Jackie Robinson integrated professional sports by joining the Brooklyn Dodgers. Sifford asked the star hitter and fielder how he could do for the Professional Golfers' Association of America what Robinson had done for Major League Baseball.

"I went to Jackie and told him what I wanted to do," Sifford said. "He asked me if I was a quitter. I told him I wasn't a quitter and he told me to go ahead and take the challenge."

Though the five-foot-eight, 185-pound Sifford built a game strong and consistent enough to win six Negro Opens, it wasn't until 1961, when he was thirty-eight, that Sifford (with an assist from the attorney general of California) finally earned a PGA Tour membership card. His Los Angeles Open win earned him $20,000 ($166,000 today) in prize money, national celebrity, and a mailbox filled with letters from Black kids who shared his dream. In 1975, Sifford also won the PGA Seniors' Championship.

"I got one real thought about this," Sifford says. "The Lord gave me some courage to stay in there when it got close. I don't know whether I proved that the black man can play golf, but I proved that Charlie Sifford can."

As Sifford tells *Sports Illustrated* not long after he wins the Los Angeles Open, "Golf has been the white man's game forever, man, and the black man's just comin' to it now. Way behind. You know, you can't play the game where they won't let you play, and they didn't let us play nowhere for a long time. It ain't easy catchin' up now. Not without money and without real good golf courses to play on and without goin' to college to play golf there—you know any black golfers in college, man?—and without good instruction when we're kids. But they did give us a chance to play golf now and it's open for us if we really want to do it."

Back in 1961, when Sifford was new to the professional tour, he traveled to North Carolina to play a tournament in his home state. White spectators verbally harassed him throughout the first round, and that evening an anonymous caller warned him against continuing the tournament.

"Whatever you're going to do," Sifford told the threatening caller, "you'd better be ready at 9:30. Because that's when I'm going to be out there on the first tee."

Through all the challenges, Sifford believed in himself, stating to *Sports Illustrated,* "I don't want to be the best Negro golfer in the world, I want to be the best golfer—period."

It's the same response Tiger gives decades later. "I don't want to be the best black golfer ever," he tells everyone. "I want to be the best *golfer* ever."

There's an immediate connection when Sifford and Tiger meet.

"He's like I was, determined to win," says Sifford. "I chose him as my grandson. I treat Tiger that way. That's how I feel about him."

The feeling is mutual. Tiger refers to Sifford as Grandpa Charlie, despite there being only a decade's age difference between Sifford and Earl.

Charlie Sifford is famous on and off the course for puffing cigars and telling golf stories, but at times the talk turns serious. "There is no way in hell he will have to deal with the hassles that I had," says Sifford. "Man, the way has already been paved." Which is not to say it will be an easy road for Tiger. "The thing is, he will still have opposition. And he will be out there all by himself."

Sifford comes out to watch Tiger play a junior tournament in Texas. Tiger eases into the comfort of what Earl calls in his coaching SOP, or standard operating procedure, working the same preshot routine he's had since he was six.

At one green, Tiger stalks a birdie putt. Earl turns his back to Tiger and begins a hushed play-by-play for Sifford: "He takes one practice stroke, he takes another. He looks at the target, he looks at the ball. He takes another look at the target, he looks at the ball."

And when Earl says "impact" at the exact instant Tiger's putter meets the ball, all Sifford can say is, "Goddamn."

PART 2

Amateur

Chapter 8

Western High School
Anaheim, California
Spring 1991

H ow many tournaments have you won?" a reporter asks.
"I have no idea," fifteen-year-old Tiger says. "I quit counting after 11-and-under. I had 110 trophies. I threw them all into the garage."

"By the time he was 14," notes a March *Sports Illustrated* feature on Tiger under the headline GOLF CUB, "he had won five age-group junior world titles, two more than any other golfer has won. With the trophies for those and more than 100 local junior titles, the Woods house contains more hardware than your neighborhood True Value Home Center."

"The game has never seemed hard," says Tiger with a shrug. "I don't know why, but I've always been good."

"Good" is obviously an understatement. Playing around thirty tournaments a year, Tiger keeps winning, including both the California Interscholastic Federation Southern Section and the California Interscholastic Federation/Southern California Golf Association events.

The victories happen in between practicing trick shots and playing games such as golf-cart polo. "We'll go on a deserted course and take turns trying to hit a tree," says Bryon Bell, one of Tiger's best friends. "Or he'll see how many times he can bounce a ball off his club face. Or he'll practice hitting a ball backward. Your basic stuff."

Tiger's latest stats: he's almost six feet tall and less than 140 pounds.

Sipping a soda outside the clubhouse at the Torrey Pines South Course, the first fifteen-year-old to win the fifteen-to-seventeen age bracket and the first player *ever* to win six Junior World titles, is a familiar face to reporters. The Optimist Junior World runner-up—sixteen-year-old Mark Worthington of Redmond, Washington—admits to the television crew, "I did not play good today but I got to play with Tiger. I had never seen him before. I only read about him in *Sports Illustrated*."

On July 24, less than a week after winning the Junior World in San Diego, Tiger is in Orlando, Florida. Last year, he made it as far as the United States Golf Association Junior Amateur Championship semifinals. His new goal is to become the youngest winner in tournament history. His dad and Jay Brunza, who's acting as his caddie this weekend, are here to support him.

Bay Hill Club & Lodge dates to the 1960s—a transformative time in central Florida, when Walt Disney purchased twenty-seven thousand acres of land for the eventual Walt Disney World resort. In 1975, Arnold Palmer bought the property and four years later hosted its first PGA Tour event, the Bay Hill Invitational.

Tiger wins the 1991 stroke-play qualification round with a 36-hole score of 4 under 140, advancing to match play and eventually the eighteen-hole final against sixteen-year-old Brad Zwetschke of Kankakee, Illinois.

The junior amateur teenagers enjoy playing the 7,027-yard course—the world's first to be planted with Tifway Bermuda grass—where otters are known to swim in the lakes and a family of bobcats once lived on the 17th green. During breaks in play, they take every opportunity to go "play in the pool, or be off shooting pool, playing around."

Not Tiger. "Tiger was always practicing or in his room with his father,"

Zwetschke comments. "He took the road less traveled, while we took the road more traveled."

Right down to a sudden-death playoff hole.

"I never dreamed the pressure would be this great," Tiger says. "In the finals, you're going for the No. 1 in the U.S.—the U.S. title. That means something."

Tiger stands at the tee, "a gangly 15-year-old, wearing shorts and a floppy hat that made him look like a half-opened umbrella," according to the *Orlando Sentinel*.

"Jay, this is what it's all about," he says to Brunza, who's taught him how to focus and "think one shot at a time." This time it's the sports psychologist, ironically, who's too nervous to even reply.

"Jay could not even speak," recalls Earl.

Tiger bogeys.

But then Brad Zwetschke misses a four-foot putt and makes double bogey.

At age fifteen and seven months, Tiger wins big. There could one day be an even younger champion, but Tiger will forever be the first Black winner.

"Son, you have done something no black person in the United States has ever done, and you will forever be a part of history," Earl tells Tiger.

The same day Tiger wins at Bay Hill, Arnold Palmer plays the U.S. Senior Open at the Oakland Hills Country Club, in Bloomfield Hills, Michigan. But it's Jack Nicklaus who wins the Monday playoff, with a course record–matching 65. "That might have been the best round I've seen Jack play in fifteen years," marvels the second-place finisher, Chi Chi Rodriguez.

The *New York Times* headlines its August 1 piece FORE! NICKLAUS BEWARE OF TEENAGER and notes that the new Junior Amateur champion has bested Nicklaus's own Junior results from decades earlier: five appearances, one semifinal, zero wins.

Palmer is favorably impressed with Tiger's sportsmanship, noting that he liked "the kid and his father, Earl, right away."

Tiger is impressed by Palmer "handing out some medals to guys that have played in three Juniors." *I'd like to one day play in as many Juniors as that.* His long-term goals are even loftier: "I want to become the Michael Jordan of golf. I'd like to be the best ever."

There's no disputing Tiger's work ethic. "School, golf, sleep. That's my life," he tells the *New York Times* of his recipe for success. "I don't fear burnout, because nothing can replace the joy of winning. Just that joy of beating everyone in the field. Nothing I could do in life is more fun than that."

Sports psychologist Jay Brunza underscores the point to *Sports Illustrated*. "Tiger shouldn't be portrayed as the Robo-Golfer. He doesn't need motivation from anybody else; his is internal. I don't see him burning out, because golf is pure pleasure for him."

Tiger is playing on four hours of sleep.

The fifteen-year-old recently crowned USGA Junior Amateur champion flew into Chattanooga, Tennessee, from Colorado Springs only eight hours before his 8:42 a.m. tee time at the ninety-first U.S. Amateur Championship.

He'd been in Colorado to headline the Canon Cup at the US Air Force Academy's Eisenhower Golf Course. "I wanted him to have total fun at the Canon Cup, which was really about playing as a team with his friends, and he was so excited that his team won," says Earl of the east-versus-west junior tournament.

"It's a bunch of teenagers away from home, of course there's a lot of goofing off," says fellow California golfer Jason Gore, who roomed with Tiger in Colorado Springs. "But Tiger went to bed every night at 7:30. It was like, Dude, what are you doing? I'll never forget the sight of him with the blankets pulled up under his chin, and he's peeking out in those huge glasses."

Tiger may be "just a golf nerd," but he'll need that rest.

The U.S. Amateur field has 312 players and no age restriction, narrowing to sixty-four over two rounds of stroke play on two qualifying courses. Twenty-one-year-old Phil Mickelson is favored to defend his 1990 title.

But a Tennessee face-off between the two Southern California golf prodigies fails to materialize. On August 21, the *Los Angeles Times* reports: WOODS, MICKELSON OFF TO SLOW STARTS.

The next day, Tiger's out. He fails to make the cut, sending him home to Cypress.

Chapter 9

Old Marsh Golf Club
Palm Beach Gardens, Florida
December 31, 1991

On New Year's Eve, Tiger takes a car ride on I-95 north to Palm Beach Gardens and the Old Marsh Golf Club, PGA pro Greg Norman's unofficial headquarters.

Yesterday, he celebrated his sixteenth birthday by winning the 1991 Junior Orange Bowl International Golf Championship, part of the youth sports and arts festival held in conjunction with the Orange Bowl each year in Coral Gables, Florida.

It's a far better outcome than last year's loss. "We had a debriefing," Earl told *Golf Digest* reporter Jaime Diaz. "This is what I learned in Vietnam — you have a debriefing after a battle. He learned that he can't win everything, even though he may want to. Right now it's important for him to enjoy. When he's 17, I fully expect him to win everything. But not now."

IMG agent Hughes Norton and the agency founder, Mark McCormack, are also thinking about Tiger's future — as a prospective client.

International Management Group has been keeping in touch with the Woods family for ten years, and they've recently brokered an arrangement with the USGA that protects Tiger's amateur status while also

50

providing financial support, in the form of hiring Earl Woods as a talent scout. In return for scouting promising junior golfers, IMG will pay Earl $50,000 per year.

There's no question that Tiger is the most promising player of all.

While Tiger is in Florida, where the agency was sponsoring the Junior Orange Bowl, IMG has arranged meetings with the biggest names on the agency roster.

"Greg Norman and Nick Faldo" are the golf heroes Tiger names to *Trans World Sports*. "I like the aggressiveness of Greg Norman, and the consistency of Faldo. I like to apply that to my game."

Norman, a thirty-six-year-old Australia-born PGA star—famously nicknamed the Great White Shark by a reporter covering the 1981 Masters—is one of Hughes Norton's clients. He's a power hitter, best known for a tournament-tying round of 63 at Scotland's Turnberry course on the way to winning the British Open in 1986. He led the PGA in earnings that year and again in 1990.

Though he didn't win any tournaments in 1991, Norman did use some of those high earnings this year when he dropped close to $5 million for a house on Jupiter Island. "Jack Nicklaus called me," Norman says of his friend and rival. "He said I needed to look at it. So I did and I bought it the same day." The property stretches across eight acres, from the Intra-coastal Waterway to the ocean, and reminds Norman of his youth spent snorkeling and swimming with sharks in Queensland, Australia.

Sports Illustrated reporter John Garrity interviewed Norman for the magazine's October 28, 1991, issue, asking, "Is it possible for anyone to dominate professional golf the way Nicklaus did? The way people expected you to?"

"I don't know if it will ever happen again," Norman answered. "Tom Watson was the last one who really dominated golf. Now, you can just finish in the top 20 every week and still make $300,000 or $400,000 a year. But if I were a young kid, my Number One ambition would still be to dominate... That's what people want to see. They don't want to see this plop, plop, chip, putt stuff. They want to see a guy who hits it 300 yards."

It's what Tiger wants, too. "I want to be the next dominant player. I want to go to college, turn pro and tear it up on the tour," he's said. "I want to win more majors than anybody ever has."

Norman and Tiger meet on the Old Marsh driving range. They board a cart to take them around eight holes of what Norman calls "a quiet game of golf" on the course Pete Dye designed within a marshland border.

Despite their twenty-year age difference, the players both stand six feet tall, though the 180-pound Norman outweighs Tiger by forty pounds and, in his ninth year in the PGA, far surpasses the Junior Amateur champion in experience. But Tiger is curious and engaged, taking the opportunity to ask Norman, "Why do you play so aggressively?"

Tiger's instincts instantly catch the veteran golfer's interest.

"His all-around presence with questions and ambience is fabulous," Norman tells *Sports Illustrated* writer Tim Rosaforte. "I'm just impressed by the guy. I like young talent like that . . . the flair, the cool, calm collectedness that he shows."

Norman steps up to the tee on the par-five 2nd hole to demonstrate the driving technique that ranked him second on the PGA Tour in 1990, with an average distance of 282.3 yards.

Except when they reach the fairway, Norman sees that Tiger's drive is longer. "He was four to five yards past me," the Australian exclaims.

Hole after hole, Tiger holds the advantage. "That little s— was driving it by me all day," Norman says with a laugh.

After he plays with Norman, Tiger's next stop is Orlando, where he plays another IMG client—the 1991 British Open champion, Ian Baker-Finch, whose score is only two strokes better than the teenager's.

PGA pro Mark O'Meara—another IMG client—brings Tiger to play eighteen holes at Windermere, an area west of Orlando that Arnold Palmer and a group of investors purchased in 1984 and have been turning into an exclusive residential community, with tennis courts, docks, and a clubhouse, all surrounding a Palmer-designed golf course.

"Have fun," O'Meara counsels the teenager. "There's no rush to get to the Tour."

Tiger *is* making plans for the future. "I've always wanted to play around the world," he says, so he can learn "to handle all different types of conditions." He's enjoying the conditions in Florida, both the weather and staying on Eastern Standard Time. "When you fly [from the] west you always lose time," he observes. "That's tough on your body, especially on a 16-year-old body, and I'm sick of that."

Chapter 10

Nissan Los Angeles Open
Riviera Country Club
Los Angeles, California
February 27, 1992

A-student Tiger is in the high school principal's office. His sophomore-year advanced geometry class conflicts with his tee time at the Nissan Los Angeles Open, so he needs to be excused.

Tiger's the youngest ever to play a PGA Tour event, and the only amateur among 143 pros in the 1992 matchup, but he hasn't qualified for the tournament via the usual channels. He's here at the Nissan by way of a sponsor's exemption.

The tournament director had looked up the Woodses' number in the Orange County phone book and placed a call to Earl.

"Hello, Mr. Woods? This is Greg McLaughlin with the Nissan Los Angeles Open. I'd like to know if your son would consider taking an exemption into our tournament?"

"Sir," replied Earl, "my son would be honored to receive an exemption into the L.A. Open."

Tiger gets permission from the principal, and geometry teacher Glenn Taylor gives his student a take-home lesson plan that's "sort of like what he's doing on the golf course. Except that out there Tiger's doing it all in his head without a compass."

During a practice round, Tiger pauses at the 9th tee and imagines playing to a packed gallery. "Ladies and gentlemen," he says, "already 19 under par for 26 holes—just playing his normal game...the leader... Tiger Woods."

The hopeful fantasy is broken by harsh news from the clubhouse. Tournament chairman, Mark Kuperstock, has received three anonymous phone calls, including a racist complaint about Tiger receiving the sponsor's exemption—and a threat on his life.

Earl takes his son aside to explain what's happened.

Tiger is stunned into silence. After around ten minutes, he says, "Sixteen years old, and I've already had my first death threat."

Security guards escort Tiger to the Riviera Country Club's iconic 1st tee, elevated seventy-five feet above the fairway on a cliff in Pacific Palisades. The gallery *is* packed. Three thousand fans are lined six deep, and television cameras are in position to capture the opening drive of LA's rising star, dressed in a red-white-and-blue-striped polo and a white cap.

GO GET 'UM TIGER reads a sign one fan holds high. "He's the next Nicklaus, maybe better," exclaims another. Tiger hits his ball 280 yards and birdies the 501-yard par 5.

The electronic scoreboard lights up:

T. WOODS −1

"That was neat," Tiger says.

His lead doesn't last. Tiger scores 72 on the par-71 course. Earl walks alongside while listening to light jazz through his headphones to ease the stress of watching Tiger play against pros his son calls "awesome." Tida's there, too, though there's a new puppy named Joey at home she has to keep an eye on.

The following day, Tiger is treated in the fitness trailer for back pain caused by a growth spurt—five inches in two years. He's six foot one now and too tall for his driver.

"The first few days of that week, I was hitting the ball so good, it was scary," Tiger says. "But then all of a sudden, I outgrew my club shaft. It got real whippy on me. I couldn't control the ball as well."

It's an extra challenge to overcome. "I was having a growth spurt... something which I doubt happened to anybody else."

He's constantly eating, trying to keep up with what *Sports Illustrated* calls "his hummingbird metabolism," devouring whole pizzas and frequenting all-you-can-eat buffets in attempts to fill up and bulk up.

Tiger shoots 72–75 in the first two rounds. With a combined score of 147, he's missed the cut but gets "more than a thrill" from fans' shouts, applause, and autograph requests. He signs simply "Tiger."

The PGA media tent is reserved for tour players, so Tiger gives a press conference behind the 18th green, where hundreds of journalists are waiting.

"I think these were the two best days of my life," he tells reporters. "I really do. Even when I hit a bad shot, people clapped."

Fred "Boom Boom" Couples, the 1991 PGA Tour Player of the Year, goes on to win that year's Nissan Los Angeles Open.

Tiger's parting words: "I've got a lot of growing up to do, both physically and mentally, but I'll play these guys again—eventually."

Chapter 11

USGA Junior Amateur Championship
Wollaston Golf Club
Milton, Massachusetts
August 2, 1992

Tiger's been playing competitive golf for half his life, since he was eight years old. Now sixteen, he's crossed the country from the California desert to the tall pines of New England and won more than one hundred junior tournaments.

As the defending champion of the USGA Junior Amateur, where no player has ever won a consecutive title since competition began in 1948, Tiger has a chance to make history at Wollaston Golf Club, a Massachusetts golf course founded in 1895.

On the 16th hole of the final, Tiger pulls even with leader Mark Wilson, an eighteen-year-old golfer from Wisconsin. Then comes the 18th, a par 4, where each player lands a ball in a different bunker.

Tiger fails to make par from there, two-putting for a bogey—but it's still enough to earn him a win, making Tiger the first ever two-time Junior Amateur champion.

"I knew he would come back," Wilson says of Tiger. "He's just that good a player. I knew because of his reputation."

The gallery watches as sixteen-year-old Tiger and sixty-year-old Earl embrace on the green. A tearful Tiger holds the hug for more than a minute as the one thousand spectators clap.

"I'm not one who usually does that," Tiger tells the *New York Times*. "It just all came out. You just cannot believe how much tension I was feeling. It's over, finally."

August 25 brings a fresh challenge: the U.S. Amateur Championship.

Tiger arrives at the Jack Nicklaus–designed Muirfield Village Golf Club, in Dublin, Ohio, determined to improve his results from last year, when he failed to advance to match play.

He makes a strong move in the second qualifying round, scoring a 6-under 66 that comes at a physical cost: back pain.

"My back got tired," Tiger tells the *Los Angeles Times* after he's eliminated from the tournament. "I couldn't fire my body through."

His self-assessment is unsparing. "People say I could go on tour right now…wrong," he says. "My muscle is not adult muscle. I am not finished growing yet." Not only that, he's also growing *quickly.* "I've grown one-half inch in the last three weeks," he tells the *Seattle Times*.

He's also dealing with other variables. "Other players don't have to worry about getting up one day and suddenly hitting the ball 10 yards farther than you hit it the previous day. That's my problem."

Still, Tiger can't stop thinking of a physical edge he noticed in the pro golfers he competed against at the Nissan Los Angeles Open. *These guys have got their swings fine-tuned. I don't. They know exactly how far they hit it. For me, because my body is growing, every day is different.*

A year later, the seventeen-year-old is a rising high school senior who will soon be competing for golf scholarships. He's narrowed his list of top-choice schools to Stanford, University of Nevada–Las Vegas, and Arizona State.

On August 1, 1993, coaches from all three universities are among the record crowd of 4,650 that has turned out for the semifinal and championship matches of the U.S. Junior Amateur at the Waverley Country Club, overlooking the Willamette River in Portland, Oregon.

Tiger's looking to break his own record and win the U.S. Junior Amateur Championship for a never-before-attempted third time.

He's not in peak form, still recovering from the case of mononucleosis he contracted less than a month ago. Ohio's Ryan Armour, who lost to Tiger in last year's quarterfinals, sets his sights on stopping the defending champion from repeating. In the final, they come to 17 with Armour 2 up, and Tiger has to birdie the 432-yard par-four 17th to stay in the match.

Tiger turns to Jay Brunza, his sports psychologist and major-tournament caddie, looking for inspiration.

"Got to be like Nicklaus," Tiger says. "Got to will this in the hole."

He makes the birdie, then birdies again on 18, leveling the match and forcing a playoff back on the 1st hole.

A par 4 on the extra hole brings Tiger to a record-setting third consecutive U.S. Junior Amateur title.

Earl runs out onto the green when it's over, sweeping Tiger into his arms.

"I did it, I did it," says Tiger as Earl repeats, "I'm so proud of you."

"It was the most amazing comeback of my career," says Tiger—dubbed "the best golfer around among those not yet allowed to vote" by *Sports Illustrated*—"I had to play the best two holes of my life under the toughest circumstances, and I did it."

Even as sixteen-year-old Armour struggles with "the biggest heartbreak I've ever experienced," he knows that in Tiger he's encountered greatness. "It was like he was following a script," Armour says. "I don't think many people could have done what Tiger did, professional, amateur, junior amateur, whatever. That's why he's the best."

Chapter 12

L ochinvar Golf Club, in Houston, is the first course Jack Nicklaus designed in Texas. It's also the professional home of Butch Harmon, whose father, Claude Harmon, won the Masters in 1948. The last club pro to win a major divided his time, summering at Winged Foot Golf Club, in Mamaroneck, New York, and wintering at the Thunderbird Country Club, in Rancho Mirage, California.

In 1960, the then sixteen-year-old Harmon carried Arnold Palmer's scorecard on the way to Palmer's winning that year's Palm Springs Desert Golf Classic (the same year Palmer also won his second Masters and his first U.S. Open). Butchie-Boy, as Palmer called him, grows up "getting a master's degree in watching the greatest players in the world."

Harmon builds those experiences into a distinguished career as a golf coach, earlier this summer supporting Greg Norman's British Open victory.

Throughout 1993, a key member of Tiger's team has been absent: swing coach John Anselmo, who's being treated for colon cancer and isn't well enough to continue working with his prize pupil.

Earl Woods arranges for Tiger to spend two days at Lochinvar, where Harmon will film Tiger and give him a full evaluation. Harmon is eleven years younger than Earl, though the two men share a strong competitive drive and are both army veterans who served in Vietnam.

The coach is familiar with Tiger's history in the sport, including "problems he had as a Black kid trying to get on golf courses. He was sometimes wrongly accused of causing problems at golf clubs, but it was never him. Tiger knew how to behave at a golf club and he loved the game."

When Tiger walks onto the Lochinvar range—in sneakers, not cleated golf shoes—Harmon gives him a bucket of balls, then starts asking questions.

"Everybody has a go-to shot on a tight driving hole, like a little fade. What is your go-to shot?"

"I dunno," Tiger answers. "Just kinda aim over there and it just kinda goes over there."

Tiger's game plan is instantly clear to Harmon: "He just hit the ball and found it, hit it and found it and then made the putt."

When he needs to drive the ball to the fairway, Tiger explains, "I just aim down the middle and swing as hard as I can. No matter where it goes, I know I'm not going to be too far from the green. Then I figure out how to get there."

Tiger wants more time with this coach, who's pushing him to examine things he's never considered.

"Can I come back tomorrow?" Tiger asks.

"Sure," Harmon answers.

Harmon agrees to waive his $300-an-hour instructional fee while Tiger's still an amateur, but first the swing coach needs Earl to agree on an important point.

"If I work with your son," Harmon says, "and then he goes home and you dispute what I am saying, it probably wouldn't work."

"I'll make a deal with you," Earl counters. "I won't try to be his golf coach if you don't try and be his dad."

*　*　*

As teacher and student, Butch Harmon and Tiger click.

According to Tiger, Harmon would "sit for hours on end, analyzing, criticizing, trying to boil the smallest thing down even smaller. Just his hard work gives me confidence."

"I can't get him off the phone," Butch Harmon jokes to *Sports Illustrated* of his new student. "He wants to work with me 24 hours a day."

Time will be scarcer than ever during college recruiting season. Throughout Tiger's years as a junior golfer, twenty-five to thirty coaches have routinely turned up to watch him play. The choice is Tiger's—but it's an agonizing one. He's given himself a deadline of mid-October to make his campus visits.

"I want to get it over with," Tiger told reporters covering the U.S. Amateur Championship back in August. "I don't want to deal with the hassle anymore."

University of Nevada–Las Vegas, with its young and up-and-coming golf program, is one of the top contenders. Coach Dwaine Knight books Tiger a room at the Mirage, owned by Steve Wynn, the mogul who created the Las Vegas Strip as well as Shadow Creek Golf Course, a spectacularly engineered course fifteen miles north into the Mojave Desert that opened in 1990 at a cost north of $40 million.

"The scenery is unbelievable," Tiger says of Shadow Creek. "You think you are in North Carolina or something, or Colorado with the mountains and the trees and the waterfalls."

It's no desert mirage when a golf cart pulls up to the 17th tee carrying Elizabeth Taylor. But teenage Tiger doesn't recognize the sixty-one-year-old movie star.

"He had no clue who she was," Coach Knight says with a grin. "His mind was just focused on golf."

"Well, you don't meet people like that when you are a kid," says Tiger in his own defense. He also later learns that the waterfall on the green at that same 17th hole is where Liz Taylor's good friend Michael Jackson, the superstar singer, likes to come to relax.

The UNLV visit, which also includes a reception hosted by the university's president, impresses Tiger.

Tida is worried. Stanford University is the only school she wants for her son. She takes action, calling Wally Goodwin, coach of the Cardinal team.

"Well, you better come down," she tells him.

Goodwin has invested years in recruiting Tiger to Stanford—first spotting him in a 1989 *Sports Illustrated* Faces in the Crowd feature. "I looked at this kid and I thought 'what a smile,'" Goodwin says of first spotting Tiger in the magazine. "There was something different there. So I wrote him a letter." The then seventh grader's reply impressed Goodwin with its "perfect grammar, capitals, spelling, punctuation, everything."

Now, four and a half years later, it's decision time. Goodwin, Earl, Tida, and Tiger sit around a card table in the Woodses' living room in Cypress. There's pizza for dinner, but to Goodwin it doesn't feel much like a party.

"Hey coach, I've got something to show you," Tiger says.

He reaches under his chair and pulls out a UNLV golf hat and puts it on.

"Hey, you little twerp," Goodwin says. "You wouldn't have asked me to come down here if you were going to go to Vegas."

"Relax, coach," Tiger says. He reaches under his chair again and out comes a second hat—Arizona State, Phil Mickelson's alma mater.

Goodwin had also once recruited Mickelson for Stanford, though Mickelson had admitted, "I love it here, Wally. But I don't know that I want to study that hard while I'm playing golf."

The Stanford coach mentally prepares himself for a long trip back to Northern California without a commitment from his top recruit.

"Tiger, if that's as close as you've come to making up your mind I've got to go," Goodwin says.

That's when Tiger stops him and pulls out a third hat — a Cardinal red Stanford cap. He puts it on, saying, "Coach, I'm with you."

There's no denying the pull of Las Vegas glamour ("It was heartbreaking to lose him right at the end," UNLV's Coach Knight says), but after Tiger's campus visit to Palo Alto, he told his parents, "I knew I was home."

On November 10, 1993, he makes it official. In the gymnasium at Western High — with Earl, Tida, and the press among his many witnesses — Tiger signs his letter of intent.

"I always tell Tiger that golf is not a priority," Tida says. "Nobody can take an education away from you, especially a degree at Stanford."

Chapter 13

National Minority Collegiate Golf Championship
Manakiki Golf Course
Willoughby Hills, Ohio
May 15, 1994

There's a spring chill in the Sunday morning air as a small group of junior golfers warms up at the driving range next to the first tee, surrounded by maple trees.

Tomorrow, the Manakiki Golf Course, a Cleveland Metroparks course named after a Native American word for "maple forest," will host the National Minority Collegiate Golf Championship. Today, Tony Grossi, a Cleveland *Plain Dealer* reporter freelancing for *Golfweek*, is here to cover Earl and Tiger Woods's pre-tournament juniors' clinic.

Grossi's attention is drawn to the range, where Earl Woods unfolds an aluminum stool and opens a suitcase-shaped device equipped with a set of speakers and a microphone. Grossi quickly gets the gist of this traveling road show: Earl directs; Tiger demonstrates.

"Tiger can hit three different shots with each club—left-to-right, right-to-left, and knockdown," Earl says into the mike as Tiger works up a sweat showing the kids how it's done. He cleanly executes a complex drill that has him aiming at a flag set 155 yards down the range. He hits that pin using four different clubs—an 8-iron, a 7-iron, a 6-iron, and a 5-iron.

The training session lasts an hour, during which Tiger never breaks concentration or speaks, though he'd previously joked to Grossi that "these players are older than I am."

The golfers present aren't especially starstruck by the three-time U.S. Junior Amateur champion, though at six foot one, the eighteen-year-old last-semester senior towers over the handful of students who ask for autographs. He's still rail-thin, despite trying to gain weight. "I can eat anything I want and not gain a pound," he laments to the *Los Angeles Times*. "I've eaten two steaks and two prime ribs at a meal. Nothing."

Tiger and his dad have run many similar clinics, particularly for minority kids without much exposure to golf. After the U.S. Amateur in August of 1992, Tiger visited Seattle's Fir State Golf Club, established in 1947, forty-five years earlier, by a group of twelve men and two women because the city's other courses wouldn't allow Black players.

"He's cool," said a nine-year-old, one of the thirty or so kids at Fir State who'd been mesmerized by the then sixteen-year-old. Tiger was happy to hear it.

"I tell kids golf is a very difficult sport, more difficult than basketball," he said, knowing that especially among minority kids, basketball is the more popular game. "Maybe I'm the leader of a new generation of black golfers."

Tiger's partnered in these clinics a few times now with forty-five-year-old Jim Thorpe, currently the only Black golfer on the PGA Tour aside from thirty-one-year-old Vijay Singh, from Fiji.

"It's a shame," notes Thorpe. "When I first came on the Tour there were probably eight or 10 black players out here. Now I'm the only one left." Thorpe, who grew up the son of a groundskeeper, understands that the barriers between these kids and the game go beyond interest and skill—there's a lack of equipment and nowhere to play. It's crucial, he feels, "to get kids to understand what the game can do for them."

Tiger, Thorpe says approvingly, "is doing everything right." In addition to having "one of the most beautiful golf swings I've seen," he says, Tiger's "got a great work ethic and as an amateur he's already played a lot of the great courses. And he's got his dad there with him.

"You look at all that, you figure he won't stray too far."

Teenage Tiger still struggles with how much importance to attach to his racial identity. At the clubhouse in Manakiki, he settles in with a candy bar and a drink of water as Earl steps outside for a cigarette and journalist Grossi asks Tiger his thoughts about being a role model, given tomorrow's National Minority Collegiate Golf Championship. Does he feel a responsibility to open the game of golf to African Americans?

"That's a funny question," Tiger says, pointing to his mostly Asian background. "My mom is part Thai and part Chinese, and my father is actually part Chinese. So I'm actually one-fourth black. When I go to Thailand to visit or to play in tournaments, I'm considered a Thai role model, but over here I'm considered a black role model."

Tiger prefers to take a broader view. "All that matters is I [reach] kids the way I can through these clinics and they benefit from them," he says. "I have this talent. I might as well use it to benefit somebody."

With Earl out of earshot, the reporter digs deeper, asking whether Tiger ever feels parental pressure or fears burnout.

Tiger denies both.

"I love this game to death," he says. "It's like a drug I have to have. I take time off sometimes because of the mental strain it puts on you, but when I'm competing, the will to win overcomes the physical and mental breakdowns."

The *Oregonian* reports an unusual development: "Eldrick 'Tiger' Woods conquered all the worlds of junior golf, and then he did a curious thing. He changed his swing."

The new swing is designed to produce accuracy, consistency, and control, the cornerstones of a swing built to repeat, the goal of any great golfer.

"Butchie harped at me to understand how to hit the ball pin-high," Tiger says of his swing coach, Butch Harmon, whom he's only met in person twice. They mainly exchange videotapes and communicate by fax. "That didn't mean flag-high. Pin-high meant whatever you decided was your number, not necessarily where the flag was. If the flag was 164 yards, maybe I'd want to make sure my ball carried 160 yards to keep it short of the hole and leave myself an uphill putt."

It's also a means to achieving a private goal. Jack Nicklaus was nineteen when he won the U.S. Amateur as a junior at Ohio State University. Eighteen-year-old Tiger wants to win that title before he's even registered for his first semester at Stanford.

First stop on that goal is making it to the U.S. Amateur qualifier in Chino Hills, California. Though it's less than an hour away from where the Woodses live in Cypress, Tiger and Earl aren't at home—they're coming from Michigan, where Tiger has just won the Western Amateur.

After missing their plane out of Chicago, they're put on standby for the last possible flight that would allow Tiger to make his tee time.

Earl prays.

The airline gives the two passengers named Woods the last two seats.

"My prayers were answered," Earl says. "Thank God we got on that damn airplane."

Tim Finchem, a former aide to President Jimmy Carter, is in his first summer as PGA Tour commissioner.

It's August 28, 1994, the final day of the World Series of Golf. Finchem presents the trophy to the winner, José María Olazábal, the Spanish national who in April had won his first Masters, then dashes off to investigate an incident: John Daly and the father of another player escalated an etiquette dispute into a wrestling match outside the clubhouse.

The Arkansas pro is famous for being the tour's longest hitter—and for his competitive streak. "I can't let this thirteen-year-old beat me," Daly said of Tiger back in 1989, when the two played an exhibition at Texarkana Country Club. Daly won, but only by two strokes, admitting that Tiger was even "better than I heard."

Now, five years later, Finchem walks into the locker room at the Firestone Country Club to find a group of pros riveted to the television. They're watching the national broadcast of the U.S. Amateur Championship at the Players Stadium Course at TPC Sawgrass, in Ponte Vedra Beach, Florida.

Tiger is in the final, facing off in a thirty-six-hole match against Texas native Trip Kuehne, an all-American golfer for Oklahoma State.

Finchem is astonished. *I've never seen tour players interested in watching any other golf on a day they were finishing a tournament. It is amazing to me that this kid generates that level of focus.*

TPC Sawgrass is a stadium course designed by architect Pete Dye to maximize the fan experience. As the final opens, Kuehne dominates, ending the morning round 4 up. He overhears Tiger conferring with his caddie and sports psychologist, Jay Brunza. "Trip's playing really good. He's killing me. I don't know how I'm going to beat him."

Tiger also telephones his coach, Butch Harmon, who's watching the tournament from California, for advice.

It's Earl who's struck by inspiration. He whispers in Tiger's ear.

"Son," he says, "let the legend grow."

The words intensify Tiger's motivation. Throughout the afternoon round, the wind picks up, blowing through TPC Sawgrass's hundreds of trees, strategically placed to get in players' lines of sight. Kuehne wins the 2nd and the 6th, but the momentum shifts with the wind, and on the 16th, Tiger pulls even.

At home in Cypress, Tida is watching on TV from her bedroom as Tiger reaches the notoriously difficult par-three 17th, with its legendary island green. Tiger's tee shot hits the green—dangerously near the water's edge.

God, don't let that ball go in the water, Tida prays over and over. *Don't let that ball go in the water.* If he bogeys the hole, or worse, the U.S. Amateur title belongs to Kuehne.

Under pressure with his club selection, Tiger had wavered. He'd picked up his 9-iron, then changed his mind. A pitching wedge would be better.

The pin. I'm going directly for the pin.

"You don't see pros trying to hit it right at that pin," Kuehne says.

That is exactly what Tiger does before sinking a fourteen-foot putt to birdie the hole. He then unleashes an adrenaline-fueled fist pump, having erased Kuehne's 6 up lead. He'll go on to par 18 and win 2 up.

At home in California, Tida rolls off her bed and falls to the floor in amazement. "That boy almost gave me a heart attack," she says. "That boy tried to kill me."

On the course, Earl and Tiger, the first Black player to ever win the U.S. Amateur, embrace for several minutes.

Earl says, "This is ungodly in its ramifications."

Chapter 14

Stanford University
Palo Alto, California
September 1994

Tiger arrives on the 8,180-acre Stanford campus, an architectural wonder of sandstone buildings in the straight-line Richardsonian Romanesque style, with the key to his hometown, a parting gift from Cypress—and seventy-five media requests.

"We took a little poll in the office, asking what athlete has entered Stanford with more notoriety," says Steve Raczynski, the university's assistant sports information director. "We had John McEnroe, who advanced to the Wimbledon semifinals the summer before college; [swimmer] Janet Evans, who won Olympic gold medals before coming here; [quarterback] John Elway. None of them was in Tiger's category."

Hughes Norton—the IMG sports agent most likely to represent Tiger when he turns pro—agrees. "He's everything you could want," Norton tells *Sports Illustrated*. "He's a very genuine kid, he's good looking, long off the tee . . . You add it all up, and it's not fair."

"I've started wearing sunglasses a little more," Tiger jokes.

Stanford University has established its own athletic dominance, winning forty NCAA team titles since 1980—more than any other school.

The golf team holds the 1994 NCAA championship, and coach Wally Goodwin is returning four of five starters, led by Notah Begay III, a fifth-year senior, an ambidextrous putter, and a full-blooded Native American.

Begay was twelve and Tiger was nine when they first met on the junior golf circuit, in the early 1980s. "There was talk that this kid Tiger Woods was winning his age group by 10 to 15 shots," Begay says. "He was better than the rest." Recognizing Tiger as a fellow outlier among the typical country-club kids, Begay approached him back then, saying, "You'll never be alone again."

Begay told *Sports Illustrated* in 1991 that "other guys always ask me before the tournaments if Tiger is really as good as people say he is," noting that the then fifteen-year-old "has taken on a celebrity status, and most of the guys are afraid of him."

While Goodwin talks up the strength of the "five relentless guys" on the team (incoming freshman Tiger plus four senior players: Begay and Casey Martin as well as Steve Burdick and Will Yanagisawa), Tiger describes himself as "very mellow," explaining, "I'm not a guy who has a lot of mood swings—peaks and valleys—I'm pretty stable."

Martin describes Tiger's joining their team as being "like Michael Jordan coming in...You know you're looking at absolute greatness." Both Begay and Martin had gambled on Tiger's choosing Stanford when they'd intentionally chosen to redshirt their junior seasons. "We wanted to stack the tables for our fifth year," Martin tells ESPN.

"Hey, we're Stanford kids, we plan for our future," Begay says with a laugh. Like Begay and Martin, Tiger declares a major in economics, following the custom curriculum promised by Stanford's dean, athletic director, and business director—"We'll work with you, we'll create you a major"—to soften his disappointment that Stanford doesn't offer a major in accounting.

He shares room 8 at Stern Hall with an engineering major who, the *San Francisco Chronicle* reports, disassembles Tiger's computer then "puts it back together again, just for kicks." Their coed dorm is the only one on campus that hasn't been renovated. Conveniently, the building isn't even fitted for cable. If Tiger had a TV in his dorm room, he knows, "I would watch all the time and I wouldn't study."

Even the classes Tiger assumes will be easy are anything but no-brainers at Stanford. The high level of discussion gets him thinking, *Whoa! I need a thesaurus to keep up with these guys!* He tells the *Los Angeles Times* that he's "doing fine" in school, though in truth he's had to drop calculus.

If Tiger's smart, coach Wally Goodwin advises, he'll "chop wood" and put in the grunt work. He assigns Tiger "typical freshman duties," instructing him to "get the luggage into the van when we [go] someplace; then get it out of the van and take it to the front desk."

Tiger makes a counteroffer to the team.

"Ok, I get it. I'll do the job. But I have a proposal. If I win a tournament, and beat the entire field, including you guys," Tiger says, "I'm off the hook. I don't have to carry your bags."

It's a bet bound to appeal to his competitive teammates. "You've got yourself a deal," Begay says. "You beat us, and you're off the hook."

On September 18, Tiger wins his first collegiate tournament—the William H. Tucker Invitational—by three strokes. On the Championship Golf Course in Albuquerque, New Mexico, the Cardinal team finishes outside the top three.

Tiger is no longer required to handle the luggage, but the team's newest member is never allowed to forget his freshman status. Whenever Tiger switches his contact lenses for glasses, Notah Begay III calls him Urkel, after Steve Urkel, the ultranerd character Jaleel White played on the hit ABC-TV series *Family Matters*.

"The more you tell me to stop, the more I'll call you that," Begay says.

Despite their good-natured ribbing, the teammates are supportive of one another. Begay, for example, sleeps on an air mattress in the basement of his Sigma Chi fraternity house, donating the room-and-board allowance from his athletic scholarship to transfer student Yanagisawa. Team captain Casey Martin gives Yanagisawa a Bible and invites him to study sessions organized by Athletes in Action.

But the golfers aren't just studious nerds. Martin also "knows how to party," Yanagisawa says, and once "ripped out 'Great Balls of Fire'" on a hotel piano while the team was traveling.

Although Tiger tells his teammate Steve Burdick that all he does other than play golf is "eat and sleep," that's not exactly true. "He does everything normal kids do," Tiger's high school friend Bryon Bell says. "The only difference is, he has to go out on the golf course every once in a while."

As Tiger, who soon pledges Sigma Chi, too, assures the *Los Angeles Times,* "I'll let loose at parties"—though exactly how, he says with a smile, "I can't tell you."

During the fraternity's house parties, Martin takes to sitting on the stairs "overlooking this big mosh pit" and watching Tiger in action. In addition to Urkel, the freshman has earned another nickname: Dynamite. It's a reference to Tiger's dance moves, which Stanford student Jake Poe calls terrible and golf teammate Eri Crum describes as resembling "blowing up a house, or pumping up a bike."

Martin says, "You know a guy that's so dominant, you've got to bring him down a little. You've got to look for his weakness and really expose it. I think we found it: dancing. It's a bad deal."

The good-natured hazing continues when the golf team travels for tournament play. "Some of the guys were a little in awe of Tiger," Begay says with a laugh. "Number one, he was our teammate; and number two, he was a dang freshman. We had to keep him in his place. I kind of went out of my way to remind the guys Tiger was getting no preferential treatment. He was sleeping on the rollaway."

"That's all right," Tiger says. "The rollaway's better than my bed at home."

* * *

"Hi, Mr. Walsh. It's great to meet you. I'm Tiger Woods."

The first-year student has come to the university athletic department, where the football head coach, Bill Walsh, has his office.

Tiger is thrilled to meet "the great Bill Walsh of the 49ers," a 1993 Pro Football Hall of Fame inductee.

"Sit down," Walsh says. Tiger does, explaining that he wants "to know a lot about football." He's come to the right place. Walsh led the San Francisco 49ers to three Super Bowls before returning to Stanford in 1992 for his second stint as head football coach.

The two hit it off immediately, and Walsh tells Tiger, "Come back any time you want and we can talk." An avid though "terrible" golfer, Walsh is intrigued by Tiger's "incredible blend of intellect and athletic ability, combined with zeal and self-confidence."

Walsh's "door open" invitation makes Tiger feel like he has "a father away from home my freshman year," a trusted mentor he can "talk to for two hours about anything."

Later that fall, Walsh gives Tiger an astonishing gift: the coach's personal key to the weight room. The young golfer spends two hours daily lifting weights, stretching, and doing aerobic exercise, putting in even more time than some members of the Stanford football team.

Tiger may be slim, but he's far from weak. He can bench-press 215 pounds — on repeat. According to a report that the weight-room supervisor delivers to coach Wally Goodwin, "Pound for pound, Tiger's one of the strongest athletes on campus."

And a constant draw for the press. "I was averaging 51 requests a day," says the coach. "And those were only the calls on my personal office line." He makes the protective decision to limit Tiger's availability to a single monthly news conference, explaining to *Golf Digest:* "Tiger is absolutely up to his ass in alligators with schoolwork, adapting to living away from home, handling reporters and trying to play golf."

Tiger's parents stay out of it. They don't set up junkets or even come to tournaments or visit campus. They don't want to interfere.

"It is time for him to have his own life now," says Tida.

But the family home remains a shrine to Tiger's achievements, a place where "nearly every wall and nearly every table is crammed with Tiger tracks: Tiger's awards, Tiger's photos, Tiger's trophies, hundreds and hundreds of them, swallowing the space from floor to ceiling, from window to door," notes *Sports Illustrated* reporter Rick Reilly.

The first time he returns to Cypress, Tiger approaches Earl, who's watching television.

"What are you drinking, Pop?" he asks.

"A Coke. Why?"

"Give me that," Tiger says, and instead mixes the two of them drinks.

Father and son take a walk to the park, where they sip and talk.

"I just want to share this first drink with you," Tiger says. "This is the first drink we've ever had, the two of us."

"One of the most beautiful moments of my life," Earl says.

Chapter 15

Jerry Pate National Intercollegiate golf tournament
Shoal Creek Club
Birmingham, Alabama
October 24–25, 1994

Tiger's on the cusp of winning his second collegiate tournament. But he has no desire to discuss the importance of where exactly it's taking place and why there are protesters outside the front gates.

At age fourteen, Tiger admitted to *Golf Digest* that encountering prejudice "makes me want to play even better. That's the way I am. Little things like that motivate me."

Still, he says, "It's tough enough worrying about one shot."

While the rest of the freshmen were settling into the dorms and starting fall classes, Tiger had instead spent nine days in France, competing for the Eisenhower Trophy at Le Golf National. At eighteen, Tiger was the youngest on the four-man team representing the United States in the nineteenth World Amateur Team Championship.

Despite the stunning location, in Versailles, Tiger hadn't strayed far from the golf course—except to take all his meals at the McDonald's closest to the hotel. In 1990, during an exchange between Californian and French junior golf organizations, Tiger quickly decided French food didn't agree with him. "I can't handle all these sauces," he'd said, crinkling his nose.

The French were fascinated by Tiger—*Le Figaro* comparing him to Mozart; the sports journal *L'Équipe* labeling him TIGER LA TERREUR. Allen Doyle, the forty-six-year-old US team leader, decided that because Tiger "already had the crowd, and the young man is not afraid of pressure," he would "bat cleanup" for the American foursome.

Tiger prepared himself with solo sessions on the practice range at the Golf de la Boulie. One early morning, he was joined by journalist Jaime Diaz.

"You want to see something weird? Watch this," Tiger told Diaz before whiplashing a ball fifteen yards farther than the two hundred yards he'd been regularly hitting.

Do it again, Diaz said. Tiger did, easily sending the ball even farther than before.

"I mean, what's wrong with that?" Tiger asked rhetorically.

"Nothing," said Diaz in agreement. "You ever think of going with it?"

But the swing is too unconventional for Tiger. "Nah. Looks too funny," he decided.

He's been diligently working with Butch Harmon, even calling him from Paris to vent about putting issues, until he found his groove. "I'm going to be tough to beat now," he said.

The American team pulled off a win for their first Eisenhower Trophy since 1982, eleven strokes ahead of Great Britain and Ireland.

Back at school in California, Tiger has to cram to get up to speed.

"When I finally got to my room, my roommate said to me, 'Well, I guess it's time for you to unpack a few of these boxes,'" Tiger says. "I've missed some classes, but I've got the notes. People are so smart here, they know what to write down. I also missed some social events, but the night I got back from France, the whole dorm threw me a party."

His favorite part of being at Stanford is feeling like he can get "lost in the crowd"—though it's impossible for Tiger to avoid being singled out when he's on the golf course.

And that spotlight is especially bright on him at Shoal Creek Club.

The club faced intense controversy four years ago. Just a few weeks before Shoal Creek hosted its second PGA Championship, in 1990, the founder, Hall W. Thompson, was questioned by a *Birmingham Post-Herald* reporter about the country club's lack of female, Jewish, and Black members, to which Thompson replied, "That's just not done in Birmingham, Alabama." The club, he said, had "the right to associate or not to associate with whomever we chose," then doubled down on that statement, saying, "We don't discriminate in every other area except the blacks."

Thompson's unwelcome candor exposed the exclusionary practices of private country clubs, especially those in the South, and prompted the PGA Tour to establish an explicitly antiracist policy.

"I find it highly unlikely that you will see any championships held at all-white clubs anymore," David Fay, executive director of the United States Golf Association, told the *New York Times*. "Sports has often been an instrument of social change. This is another example."

In 1990, following the negative publicity, Shoal Creek quickly admitted a token Black member, but little else has changed in the four years since.

So when Tiger Woods—the most accomplished junior golfer in the country, who happens to be both exceptionally talented and Black—is playing Shoal Creek, it's national news.

Tiger's not the only one downplaying the significance.

"For the most part, I think we've put all that behind us and gone forward," says the 1976 U.S. Open winner, Jerry Pate, himself a Shoal Creek charter member. "Tiger's a super player. He's a little erratic at times, but he's got a lot of poise."

Tiger doesn't want the label of "being the great black hope in golf. I'm a golfer who happens to be black," he insists.

Tiger crosses his legs and leans on his putter. Heading into the final hole of the Jerry Pate National Intercollegiate golf tournament, he holds a one-stroke lead over his Stanford Cardinal teammate Will Yanagisawa.

Before the team headed down to Alabama, they'd discussed the implications of playing at Shoal Creek. "I've talked about it a little bit with my teammates," Tiger tells reporters. "We had a few jokes about it."

Senior teammate Notah Begay III—who chooses to honor his own southwestern Native American heritage on tournament days by wearing gold hoop earrings in both ears and dabs of red clay under his eyes—lightheartedly calls the club "Soul Creek." He tells Tiger "what a great slap in the face it would be to those who think that minorities are inferior, if [you] went down and won."

As Tiger now walks to the 18th and clinches the win with a twenty-five-foot two-putt for birdie, Hall Thompson stands by, impressed. A yell comes from a nearby spectator: "Go Tiger Woods!"

Tiger raises his putter in acknowledgment and smiles shyly.

"You're a great player," Thompson says as Tiger walks off the course. "I'm proud of you. You're superb."

Tiger tries his best to sidestep questions about the social significance of the win.

"I just went out and wanted to play well," he says. When a reporter from the Associated Press asks about the impact of winning at a site controversial for being until recently an all-white club, Tiger replies, "The significance to me is our team won, and I also happen to be the individual champion. That's what we came to do. We play to win."

Tiger is quick to deny that racism gives him any special provocation.

"Of course it does," his father, Earl Woods, counters. "It provides drive. It provides inspiration. It provides motivation. It provides toughness."

To coach Wally Goodwin, toughness only goes so far. "My first concern was the safety of my team," Goodwin says. "I knew Birmingham was pretty far south and something could happen." And Tiger is not the only minority Cardinal: "On the very same team is a full-blooded Navajo Indian [Notah Begay III] and a Japanese American [William Yanagisawa] and a Chinese American [Jerry Chang], and here they're picking on Tiger. It was ludicrous."

Chapter 16

The 59th Masters
Augusta National Golf Club
Augusta, Georgia
April 6–9, 1995

Tiger's Stanford roommate takes a message from "a guy named Greg with an Australian accent"—then forgets to mention the missed call until Tiger is packing his bags.

Greg Norman? Why would he be calling?

As the top two players at the 1994 U.S. Amateur, Tiger and Trip Kuehne have both won automatic bids to the 1995 Masters. They check into the Crow's Nest, Augusta National's dorm for amateur golfers. The friendly rivals laugh and play cards at night, taking practice rounds for bragging rights and five-dollar bets. But the Monday and Tuesday practice rounds feel more like auditions for the PGA Tour.

Five-time major championship winner Nick Faldo is surprised when Tiger outdrives him on the 15th hole. "His shoulders are impressively quick; that's where he gets his power. He's young, and he has great elasticity," Faldo tells reporters on April 3. "He's just a very talented kid; let's leave it at that."

On April 4, Tiger plays a round with three pros: Raymond Floyd, Fred Couples, and Greg Norman.

That's why Norman was calling my dorm in Palo Alto—to arrange a tee time, Tiger realizes. The two of them also share a swing coach, Butch Harmon.

Out on the 2nd fairway, Tiger drives his ball farther than all three PGA champions in his foursome. According to *Golf* magazine, "Tiger's already the longest player in the field."

"My god, I had no idea how long he was," says Tiger's golf hero, Jack Nicklaus, as he watches the nineteen-year-old Stanford freshman play.

While he's waiting for the others to catch up, Tiger chats to the gallery. "What a beautiful day," he says. "You know, I could be in a classroom."

An Augusta National marshal overhears and replies, "Yeah, but you would never be getting an education like this."

Today's lesson: "I really found out how good these guys are," Tiger says.

"When he plays with the Couples, the Normans, the Faldos, the Prices," Harmon says, "he marvels at the way they control the ball in the air."

Greg Norman, a spokesman for Maxfli, suggests to Tiger that he switch from Stanford-issued Titleist golf balls to Maxfli.

Tiger scores an even-par 144 in the first two rounds and makes the cut. Earl tells the *Washington Post*, "We had an agreement between the two of us that he'd never play at the Masters until he earned his way in. I just didn't expect it to happen this soon."

He'll be the lone amateur in the weekend's field of forty-seven and only the fourth Black player ever to compete at the Masters. Earl wears a cap that reads DON'T HOLD BACK, but on questions of racial friction at the club, Tiger answers evenly, "I haven't encountered any problems except for the speed of the greens."

Friday morning, however, Earl and Tida discover an ugly reminder of Augusta's past. One of the windows on their rental car has been smashed.

Undeterred, the proud parents will continue walking alongside their son throughout the tournament, all seventy-two holes.

In the locker room, Tiger receives a telegram. "Go out there, good luck, don't get caught up in the hype," the message says. "Just take care of business and have fun."

The words of encouragement are from Tiger's surrogate grandfather, Charlie Sifford, the Black golfer who never had a chance to play the Masters. The first Black player who did—Lee Elder—is here watching, along with Black fans who've turned out in record numbers.

Near the first tee, Earl confides to Elder that he feels like he's "witnessing my son coming into manhood. It's a stage many fathers never get to see."

At 1:03 p.m., the CBS Sports broadcaster announces, "Tiger Woods now driving."

Tiger signs another round of autographs for the largely Black staff at Augusta National, then he and Earl drive off the club grounds to Forest Hills, the public course in Augusta, where caddies and golfers are gathered on Friday night for a free clinic.

San Francisco Chronicle columnist Scott Ostler explains the rarity of the event: "Almost 900 golfers have played in 59 Masters Tournaments, and only one of them has taken the time to give a clinic at that frumpy muni course."

"It's a Black thing," Earl says, referring to the fact that until 1982, all the caddies who worked the Masters were Black. "We are acknowledging that we know who came before Tiger."

Jerry Beard, who caddied Fuzzy Zoeller's 1979 Masters victory, says of his fellow Black caddies, "We have been the forgotten men of the Masters, but maybe Tiger will help us be remembered."

Earl carries a camcorder to document every moment of the week. Even with all eyes on Tiger, the tournament doesn't belong solely to him.

Ben Crenshaw and Davis Love III are playing for Harvey Penick, their beloved coach and a bestselling author who died at age ninety on the eve of Masters Week. "I felt this hand on my shoulder, guiding me along," Crenshaw—who paused his tournament preparations to serve as a pall-bearer at Penick's funeral in Austin, Texas—tells *Sports Illustrated.*

Crenshaw, the 1984 Masters champion, wins a second Green Jacket at 14 under par, with Love one stroke behind at 13 under.

Tiger finishes nineteen strokes back, tying for forty-first place. It's a respectable showing for his first attempt, but Steve Burdick says what the Stanford teammates are thinking: "If that's how Tiger stacks up against Tour players, we're all in trouble."

Still, Tiger is Low Amateur; his reward is a sterling silver cup and a coveted interview inside Butler Cabin, the 1964 landmark house where CBS Sports broadcasts its Masters interviews in front of a stone fireplace.

At Earl and Tida's request, CBS's Jim Nantz and the Augusta National vice chairman, Joe Ford, tape the interview so that Tiger can attend his Monday morning history class. "College is such a great atmosphere and I really love it there," he says.

Back in the Crow's Nest, Tiger looks up at the walls covered with pho-tographs of Masters champions. "I feel like this place is perfect for me. I guess I need to get to know it better." He makes a pledge—"Someday, I'm going to get my picture up there."

He writes a letter to Augusta National:

Please accept my sincere thanks for providing me the opportunity to experience the most wonderful week of my life. It was fantasyland and Disney World wrapped into one. I was treated like a gentleman throughout my stay and I trust I responded in kind.

The Crow's Nest will always remain in my heart and your magnificent golf course will provide a continuing challenge throughout my amateur and professional career.

I've accomplished much here and learned even more. Your tournament will always hold a special spot in my heart as the place where I made my first PGA cut and at a major yet! It is here that I left my youth behind and became a man.

For that I will be eternally in your debt. With warmest regards and deepest appreciation.

Sincerely,
Tiger Woods

The letter is not the only writing Tiger's done this week. His Masters diaries are also published by *Golf World* and *Golfweek* magazines.

Although Tiger isn't paid for the diaries, Stanford is quick to act, suspending him from the team for one day. The NCAA director of legislative services explains the decision: "It's deemed to be a promotion of a commercial publication."

Amateurs are also prohibited from accepting equipment from manufacturers, so Stanford has even more questions about why Tiger replaced his university-issued gear, using Butch Harmon's Cobra irons instead of Mizuno irons and using Greg Norman's Maxflis instead of Titleist balls.

The Maxfli balls are winners for Norman at the 1995 Memorial Tournament, held a few weeks later, in the first week of June. Norman bests his closest opponent by four strokes, but everyone at the Muirfield Village Golf Club, in Dublin, Ohio—the Jack Nicklaus–designed course near his hometown, Columbus—is talking about the amateur who isn't eligible to play in this PGA Tour event.

No one has a better read on the Stanford student's situation than Nicklaus.

In 1961, Nicklaus—then a twenty-one-year-old Ohio State University student and U.S. Amateur champion—asked to be excused from class. His professor complained to the dean, who told him, "Jack, I can't have a student of ours going to Australia, playing golf when you're enrolled here... I want you to drop out of school."

Nicklaus did, though he was later awarded an honorary doctorate from the University of St Andrews, in 1984.

"Tiger has all the right tools to be a successful and dominant golfer," Nicklaus tells *Sports Illustrated* at the Memorial. "He has a college career he wants to finish, but at the same time he'll be receiving invitations to pro events all over the place. It's up to him to determine how much he wants to focus on golf and what his goals are."

Those details are private.

"My goals are my goals," Tiger says. "Money won't make me happy," he says. "If I turned pro, I'd be giving up something I wanted to accomplish. And if I did turn pro, that would only put more pressure on me to play well, because I would have nothing to fall back on. I would rather spend four years here at Stanford and improve myself."

Earl is characteristically blunt. "Tiger doesn't need the NCAA and he doesn't need Stanford. He could leave and be infinitely better off, except that he wants to go to school."

Tiger sits for final exams. He has no plans for vacation. He'll spend the summer playing against the pros.

Chapter 17

The 95th U.S. Open
Shinnecock Hills Golf Club
Southampton, New York
June 15–18, 1995

As U.S. Amateur champion, Tiger's qualified for the United States Golf Association's U.S. Open. It's unusual for an amateur to issue a pre-tournament press release, but the media's drumbeat of personal questions will not be silenced. "Yes I am the product of two great cultures," his statement reads, "one African-American and the other Asian...The bottom line is that I am an American. And proud of it!"

Shinnecock Hills Golf Club, the oldest links course in America, is covered in high, thick grass that makes for especially heavy rough. Most players will be teeing off with a driver. "Hitting my driver," Tiger says, "you don't have much room for error out there" on the long 6,944-yard course. His chosen club is the 1-iron.

The tournament gets underway with a field of 156 golfers. Tiger shoots a 4-over 74 in the first round, and on Friday he runs into trouble with the rough. On the 3rd, he chooses a wedge to free his ball from the dense grass. He swings and feels a twinge in his wrist. It's sprained. He tapes the injury and continues playing—only to again hit into the rough on the 5th. "I couldn't hold on to the club with the normal grip," Tiger says. The injury forces him to withdraw on the 6th.

"I'm kind of bummed out," Tiger says. "I felt like I was playing good enough to make the cut. But that's what happens when you hit the ball in the long grass."

On the Old Course at St Andrews Links, in Fife, Scotland, Arnold Palmer tips his visor. He's standing on the stone Swilcan Bridge, between the 1st and 18th fairways, where adoring crowds cheer the soon-to-be-sixty-six-year-old golfer—the first to earn more than $1 million on the PGA Tour.

Unfortunately, windy conditions on the iconic Old Course keep Palmer, the 1961 and 1962 winner of the prized Claret Jug, from making the cut.

On July 23, 1995, fellow American John Daly triumphs after a four-hole playoff against Italian Costantino Rocca. "To win here at St. Andrews is a lifetime dream for anybody," Daly says. "And mine's come true today."

Not Tiger's. While he makes his second cut at a major championship, he finishes sixty-eighth.

"Butch, how far away am I?" Tiger asks his coach. "When will I be that good?"

"You just have to keep working," Harmon says. "You've got so much to learn."

As Arnold Palmer says at the Celebration of Champions that week, "If you are going to be a champion, you couldn't be a champion without playing in The Open and hopefully winning The Open."

Tiger now practices even harder than ever. *Okay, let's see who can hit it closer to that flag off one foot. Okay, now closing your eyes. Okay, now using a 7-iron.*

He challenges himself on the distance control that eluded him on the parkland course at Augusta National. The widely voiced criticism — *Tiger Woods hits it far, but he's out of control* — stings. He also perfects the range of shots required to win on a links-style course.

Back in Rhode Island, the Newport Country Club, host of the 1995 U.S. Amateur Championship, is another course where windy conditions come into play. Harmon coaches Tiger on the knockdown — or punch — saying, "There are holes on the golf course where you're going to need that shot."

In 1893, Theodore A. Havemeyer, the United States Golf Association's first president and vice president of the American Sugar Refining Company, persuaded America's most influential businessmen and sportsmen to fund a golf club on Rocky Farm, a 140-acre patch of land overlooking the Atlantic Ocean. Two years later, it hosted both the first U.S. Amateur and the first U.S. Open. The *New York Times* praised its Louis XIII–style clubhouse as "supreme for magnificence among golf clubs, not only in America, but the world."

The course — with its St Andrews–inspired design, unirrigated fairways, and firm and fast conditions — is difficult to play, its rolling ground too windswept for tree cover. "Going to Scotland really helped me understand courses like this," Tiger tells the *Baltimore Sun*. "It makes it all 'feel,' and you have to be creative with some shots. I like playing that way."

Butch Harmon and Earl walk the course alongside Tiger as his sports psychologist and caddie, Jay Brunza, gauges the wind blowing in from the ocean, gusting to thirty miles an hour. Regulation play progresses to a thirty-six-hole final between Tiger and George "Buddy" Marucci, a forty-three-year-old Mercedes-Benz dealer from Pennsylvania, making his first advancement past the top sixteen in the amateurs.

By the 36th hole, with the centennial U.S. Amateur championship likely resting on his next shot, Tiger selects an 8-iron.

"I wouldn't be surprised if he knocks it a foot from the hole," ESPN commentator Johnny Miller predicts. He's wrong.

Tiger knocks it eighteen inches from the cup but still has a tap-in birdie. He secures the Havemeyer Trophy and his second U.S. Amateur Championship.

He's only the ninth player in the tournament's one-hundred-year history to manage consecutive wins.

Marucci, the runner-up, calls Tiger's winning shot "spectacular" and "the sign of a true champion." He tells the *Los Angeles Times,* "I can live with losing to Tiger."

Earl fills the trophy with champagne and makes a toast. "To my son, Tiger. One of the greatest golfers in the history of the United States." He also declares, "Before he's through, my son will win fourteen major championships."

"My place in history, I don't really care about that," Tiger says when asked what his victory means for the record books. "Hey, I'm still a kid. I'm only nineteen."

For Tiger and Harmon, the future can wait. They can't stop talking about the miraculous events of *today.* "That shot at 18 — damn! I didn't have it last year, I didn't have it at Augusta," Tiger tells *Sports Illustrated.* Harmon agrees, saying that before, Tiger "probably would have hit nine-iron and rolled it off the green."

"I spent hours and hours on the range," Tiger tells the *Los Angeles Times,* "and it paid off on the 18th hole."

Chapter 18

Stanford University
Palo Alto, California
Fall 1995

The 1995 National Collegiate Athletic Association first-team all-American puts his clubs in the back of his Toyota and drives north from Cypress to Palo Alto for the start of his sophomore year at Stanford.

"School is the most fun you'll ever have," Butch Harmon tells Tiger. His coach is right. Tiger does have a "great time playing golf at Stanford. Just all the practicing, playing, and qualifying" and the "fun being around each other."

The feeling is mutual—up to a point. "It's been a great experience, having Tiger, but it's also been tough and has probably hurt our performance somewhat," Casey Martin says.

In Tiger's first season as a Cardinal, the 1993–94 NCAA team champions failed to repeat, finishing second by a stroke to Trip Kuehne's Cowboys at Oklahoma State in a sudden-death finale. A new ten-month season (in line with the PGA and senior tour calendars) lies ahead.

On October 3, days into the fall academic quarter, Tiger receives an irresistible invitation from the King, Arnold Palmer.

"Cool," Tiger says. "I'll go out to dinner with Arnold Palmer."

Back into the trunk of the Toyota go the clubs for the ninety-minute drive to Napa Valley, where Palmer's playing the PGA Tour Champions Transamerica event at the Silverado Resort and Spa. It's been four years since Palmer awarded Tiger the 1991 USGA Junior Amateur Championship medal.

But the stakes are higher this time. Much higher. Tiger can no longer ignore the most important question looming over him: *What are the pros and cons of turning professional?*

"Tiger's got the game to do it right now," golf analyst and two-time U.S. Open winner Curtis Strange has commented to the *New York Times*. "He should just go ahead and come on out here and get on with his life."

That's what Strange did, after all. He won the NCAA individual title in 1974 while with the Wake Forest University "Deacs," or Deacons — the two-time NCAA champion squad *Golf Digest* calls "the greatest college golf team in history" — then left to turn pro in 1976.

Palmer also left Wake Forest early. It's well known that the two-time NCAA champion (1949, 1950) left school to join the Coast Guard after the tragic death of his best friend, Bud Worsham, in a car accident. Three years later, Palmer returned to golf, becoming a PGA Tour member in 1953.

Tiger wants to hear from the King. At a quiet corner table, the two golfers swap stories about their shared passion.

"There's not a lot of people," Tiger says, who "can change your life" just by talking to you. Palmer is "one of those guys." He sees the evening as educational. "I wanted to learn from him, what he did, so I wouldn't make mistakes."

Yet to the NCAA, that's exactly what Tiger has done — made a mistake. News of the dinner is reported by a Chicago newspaper, prompting Wally Goodwin to ask: "Did you pick up the tab?"

"Arnold ended up picking up the tab," Tiger tells him. "You know, I'm a college student."

Coach Goodwin is concerned that by accepting the gift of a meal, his top player has broken article 16 of the NCAA bylaws: "Awards, Benefits and Expenses for Enrolled Student-Athletes."

He's right to worry. Tiger's deemed temporarily ineligible to play in Stanford's next tournament, the Savane College All-America Golf Classic at the El Paso Country Club. The cottonwood tree–lined course is a Chihuahuan Desert oasis between the Franklin Mountains and the Rio Grande, but Tiger won't be walking its 6,781 yards.

"The kid was trying to learn knowledge from the legend," Tiger's mother, Tida, protests. "Pick his brain."

"I was pretty angry," Tiger says about the situation. "I didn't do anything wrong." He flies to Texas anyway, but there are requirements to meet before the ban can be lifted. "I'm not allowed to play a practice round. And so I had to write a $25 check to Arnold, he had to cash it, he then had to fax the copy that it was cashed to the [NCAA] to lift up my so-called violation."

"You don't send a kid to a tournament when his mind is not clear," protests his mom. "It's not fair." After what happened with the NCAA and the Masters diaries, she says, "it's harassment. He's trying to stay in school and set a good example for younger kids."

For the first time, there's grumbling about whether Tiger ought to remain at Stanford. Says Tida, "I want him to stay for four years, but the way they're treating him is not right."

Tiger's supporters on campus wear T-shirts reading IF IT'S FAIR AND REASONABLE, IT MUST BE AN NCAA VIOLATION, but only one outcome can ease the pain of this setback.

On October 22, the third and final day of tournament play, Tiger leads by a single stroke. University of Tulsa sophomore Fredrik Soderstrom has a chance to win on the dogleg par-four 18th, but he misses a two-and-a-half-foot putt, forcing a playoff.

On the first playoff hole, Tiger doesn't allow his opponent a second chance and makes birdie to win.

Back in San Francisco, Coach Goodwin hosts an auction to raise money for the Robert Hoover East Palo Alto Junior Golf program. Tiger agrees to donate the canceled $25 check he wrote to Arnold Palmer. The winning bid is $5,000.

Home for the holidays, Tiger accompanies Tida to a Buddhist temple in Los Angeles. She asks a monk to predict what the year 1996 holds for her son.

"The Buddha said that in the beginning of the year, he be just like a fish," the holy man says, "but later on in the year he be like a dragon."

Chapter 19

NCAA championship
Honors Course
Ootelwah, Tennessee
May 29–June 1, 1996

O f the thirteen tournaments Tiger plays as a Stanford sophomore, he wins nine.

"It was eye-opening from so many different perspectives," says Joel Kribel, a freshman on the Stanford golf team. "He made people who'd been No. 1 look like they didn't stand a chance. If he was playing halfway decent, it was kind of soul-crushing for a lot of guys to know, *I could play my best and get lapped by this guy.*"

With last year's redshirted senior players now graduated, Tiger's best friend on the team is upperclassman Jerry Chang, a fellow Californian he already knew from the junior circuit and who took over as this year's team captain. The two are often roommates on the road.

At the 1996 NCAA championship, on the Honors Course, in Ootelwah, Tennessee, the players struggle with the tall, thick grass lining the fairways. Chang plops two balls in the water on the 16th. "I jokingly blame Tiger for bringing these big crowds to college golf and all the nerves that go with playing in front of crowds," Chang says.

Tiger and Chang usually decompress back at the hotel by watching TV or doing homework, but the night before the final round, the team gets together to celebrate the season. "Tiger really enjoyed that team aspect," Kribel says. After scoring 69-67-69 in the first three rounds, Tiger has high hopes for the June 1 final, but "he didn't take any lead for granted," says Chang.

The next day, the twenty-year-old shoots four times his age. It's a shock for everyone—especially Tiger. "It doesn't feel like I shot 80," he tells reporters. "I'm exhausted right now. People will never know how much it took out of me. I had to dig really deep, give all I had."

Tiger had gone into the final round with a nine-hot lead, so he still wins the NCAA men's individual trophy by four strokes over the University of Arizona's Rory Sabbatini. The Stanford team—national champions in 1994, months before Tiger joined—places fourth.

There's always next year, Tiger tells fellow sophomore teammate Eri Crum. He's not planning to leave Stanford early. "Unless," he says, hedging, "something happens at the British Open."

Tiger next attends the Memorial Tournament, at Muirfield Village Golf Club, not as a player but an honoree. On June 2, he accepts the Jack Nicklaus Award, given to the college player of the year. He shakes Nicklaus's hand and assures the pro that he'll graduate with his Stanford class of 1998.

The Golden Bear will be watching closely as the latest "Bear apparent" competes in the upcoming U.S. Open and British Open.

On June 13, Tiger takes an unusual first-round lead in the U.S. Open, at Oakland Hills Country Club, in Bloomfield Hills, Michigan. But in the end, the amateur buckles under professional-grade pressure, concluding the round with three bogeys, a double bogey, and a quadruple. He shoots 294 (76–69–77–72) and finishes eighty-second.

After the tournament, Tiger appears on *The Tonight Show*. The host, Jay Leno, shows his audience a picture of baby Tiger posing with a golf club.

"You don't see many pros in diapers," Leno says.

Tiger's ready with a comeback. "I should have had one on at the Open."

In England for the British Open from July 18 to July 21, twenty-year-old Tiger samples the local cuisine — McDonald's. Between his hotel and Royal Lytham & St Annes Golf Club are two outlets of the American chain restaurant. The burgers taste like home cooking.

"There's a difference between here and the States, but not much," Tiger says. "I order a super-size fries and get about as many as I get in a large in the States. The food isn't as greasy, either, and I love the grease. Just about wherever I go, if there's a McDonald's, I'll find it."

Two years ago, Tim Southwell, a reporter from the UK, came to interview Tiger in Cypress for the inaugural edition of a magazine called *Loaded* and found the young superstar enjoying a cheeseburger for breakfast. "No minders, no entourage, no dramas. Just Woods and his cheeseburger," says Southwell.

"Wow," Tiger said, wiping his hands before greeting the reporter. "You really made it all the way over here just to see me?"

"Well, you are going to be the next great golfer, right?" Southwell said.

"Sure," replied Tiger. "And not the best black golfer either. The best, ever. Period."

His confident sound bite doesn't account for the 174 pot bunkers strategically positioned across the Lytham course, described by a leading British golf writer as "a Beast." On Thursday, July 18, Tiger has a rough start.

Jack Nicklaus pulls Tiger aside, saying, "I don't ever want to see you shoot 75 in the first round of a tournament."

Tiger takes the impromptu lecture as a sign that Nicklaus "cares about me that much. I came to understand that to win a major, or any golf tournament, you can't win it on the first day, but you can lose it on the first day. And I lost it on the first day. When you're not playing well, you still need to get it in the clubhouse around even par. I learned it the hard way."

On Friday, he ups his game, scoring a 5-under 66.

Nicklaus turns in an identical round.

Tiger ultimately finishes twenty-second, his best-ever showing in a professional event so far. It also wins him the Silver Medal for Low Amateur.

The good feelings fade quickly when two weeks later, he takes a first-round loss to the 1994 U.S. Junior champion, Terry Noe, at the Western Amateur in Benton Harbor, Michigan.

"I'm outta here," Tiger tells reporters looking for a comment.

He's got nothing to say to anyone. Except Earl. He tells his father he's now leaning toward turning pro.

Earl and Tida support his choice—on one condition.

"I want you to finish school because Jack Nicklaus did not finish school," Earl says. "Arnold Palmer did not finish school. Curtis Strange did not finish school."

Tiger promises his parents that a college diploma will happen in the future—the distant future.

Once teenage Tiger started playing his first PGA Tour events on top-tier courses and with top-of-the-line equipment, he said, "Daddy, I can get used to this very easy."

Now he says, "I'm ready, Pop."

Chapter 20

U.S. Amateur Championship
Pumpkin Ridge Golf Club
North Plains, Oregon
August 22–25, 1996

NBC Sports decides to add a day to its television coverage of the U.S. Amateur Championship at the Pumpkin Ridge Golf Club just to showcase Tiger's historic quest to three-peat at the U.S. Amateur.

The ratings-boosting adjustment adds $300 to the cost of Earl and Tiger's nonrefundable plane tickets to Oregon for the tournament.

"I'm never flying coach again," Tiger announces to his father.

From his uncomfortable plane seat, he thinks back on last month and the second round of the British Open, when he improved on his opening 75 to score an impressive 66.

Something really clicked that day, like I had found a whole new style of playing. I finally understood the meaning of playing within myself. Ever since, the game has seemed a lot easier.

The hilly, forested terrain of the Portland, Oregon, area is familiar to Tiger from his win at the 1993 USGA Junior Amateur, at Waverley Country Club in Portland, and the 1994 Pacific Northwest Amateur, at Royal Oaks Country Club in nearby Vancouver, Washington.

Jack Nicklaus won two U.S. Amateur tournaments, in 1959 and 1961. Bobby Jones owns a record five titles, won between 1924 and 1930. Tiger is the 1991, 1992, and 1993 U.S. Junior Amateur champion and the 1994 and 1995 U.S. Amateur champion. What better cap to his amateur career than if he can manage a third consecutive Amateur win and a sixth USGA title?

The pressure is intense. In addition to tournament officials, Tiger faces a trio of judges who hold the key to his success as a professional athlete. IMG's Hughes Norton is in the gallery, along with the Titleist president, Wally Uihlein, and Nike cofounder Phil Knight, who's not quite incognito in the black-and-white-striped shirt worn by tournament volunteers.

Like Tiger, Knight has ties to Stanford. He conceived of Nike in a graduate course at the Stanford business school and wrote it up in a paper titled "Can Japanese Sports Shoes Do to German Sports Shoes What Japanese Cameras Did to German Cameras?"

"Nike is going to pay Tiger big," says Ely Callaway, founder of Callaway Golf Company, who's also in the gallery.

Knight has invested three years into tracking Tiger's career, meeting with Earl and Tiger every time they're in the Portland area, where Nike is headquartered. "I hope we sign him," Knight says, adding with a laugh, "If not, I hope he goes to medical school."

With the precision of a surgeon, Tiger recalibrates his team. He replaces sports psychologist Jay Brunza, who's consistently caddied for him in major competitions—match-play record: 36–3—with Bryon Bell, his best friend from Cypress. Bell is stronger on club selection. "I trust Tiger's judgment about what he needs to win," Brunza says in agreement.

Tiger wins his first round against a player from Colorado State. Then Tiger, Brunza, and Bell catch an evening showing of America's number one movie, *Tin Cup,* starring Kevin Costner as a washed-up golf pro— and featuring Phil Mickelson in a cameo as a PGA Tour golfer. Near the theater is Portland's Waverley Country Club, where in 1993 Tiger won his third U.S. Junior Amateur. The three members of Team Tiger walk to the 18th, where Tiger splashed out a forty-foot bunker shot, setting up a birdie for the win.

The spontaneous pilgrimage, Brunza says, is "a positive reverie, a reminiscence that will always be there." The air-conditioning feels good after another day out on the course in temperatures over ninety degrees.

Despite the persistent heat, progress through the quarterfinals and semifinals is smooth. In the thirty-six-hole final, Tiger faces Steve Scott, a University of Florida rising sophomore. Just after seven in the morning on August 25, fifteen thousand spectators converge on the course.

Scott watches as crowds build along both sides of the first fairway.

"All these people," Tida says proudly from the gallery. "They are all here to see my Tiger." This is the first Amateur she's attended in person. It could be the most important match he's ever played.

Caddie Bryon Bell hands him the driver. The clubhead cover, shaped like a plush tiger head and embroidered with the Thai words *Rak jak Mea* (Love from Mom), is a gift from Tida.

"The sound of Tiger's ball coming off the club," Scott says, is "just as crisp a sound as you could ever hear."

Tiger is listening to only one person. Himself. *I've been here before. I have thirty-six holes. I have to make a move early.*

Scott shoots 68 in the morning round. The Florida Gator is 5 up. The stress Tiger's feeling shows in his posture. Butch Harmon spots the worrisome shift, so he and Jay Brunza work with Tiger during the lunch break.

In the afternoon round, Scott holes out from an impossible lie on the 10th hole. His celebratory fist pump lights Tiger's competitive fire. By the time they reach the 16th, Tiger is only 2 down, but he's just missed a four-footer on 15.

"That's when I thought I'd win the match," Scott says. "He was looking frustrated. I thought that would rattle him a little bit, but it didn't."

Yet neither player is prepared for what happens on the 16th. Scott is putting for par and Tiger for birdie. Their balls are on the same line.

"As you do on any Saturday afternoon," Scott says, "I ask my playing partner to move the ball mark over, so he does." Tiger picks up his ball marker, as requested.

Scott pars the hole. Tiger is about to resume play without replacing his marker. The sportsmanlike Scott speaks up, saving Tiger from a rules violation.

Tiger comes back to force a playoff, making the birdie putt on 16 and another on 17.

"Lightning will not strike twice," Earl says of Scott's chances.

The largest television audience in U.S. Amateur history is watching with rapt attention.

Tiger finally closes Scott out on the second playoff hole.

He has solidified his place in history as the first player to win three consecutive U.S. Amateurs.

"It is the most fascinating golf event I've ever seen," Harmon says.

When asked if he's decided what's next for him, Tiger says, "I don't know about that. But I do know this. I'm going to celebrate like hell tonight."

But the festivities are quiet. Tiger and Bryon Bell spend the evening playing cards in the Woodses' rental house.

At the nearby Hillsboro Airport, a corporate jet is waiting.

PART 3
Professional

Chapter 21

Greater Milwaukee Open
Brown Deer Park Golf Course
Milwaukee, Wisconsin
August 28, 1996

Tiger Woods is about to make history—again.
Here at the twenty-ninth annual Greater Milwaukee Open, at the Brown Deer Park Golf Course, Tiger will be playing on a sponsor's exemption—just as he did in his first PGA event, the 1992 Los Angeles Open—but with one huge difference.

He's turning pro. Today.

"We've got a world changer here" is the assessment inside Nike. The company's top executives are among the few insiders aware of Tiger's secret decision, one he's wrestled with for months.

Sports journalists Jaime Diaz and John Strege have been covering Tiger throughout his amateur career. Earl gives them the scoop, but not permission to break the story.

Not yet.

"You can't write it until I let you write it," he tells them.

The call to Wally Goodwin in Palo Alto was a tough one.

In an interview with the *Los Angeles Times* published just yesterday, the Stanford coach had sidestepped rumors. "I never second-guess Tiger. He's very smart and very thorough in his thinking. And his dad is very businesslike. They have it all worked out," Goodwin tells reporters, while acknowledging that Tiger turning professional is undeniably on the horizon. "When he does it, it's because he wants to play against the pros on that level."

Bets are being hedged. As an amateur player, Tiger can't use a professional caddie, but he'll need one right away if he goes pro at the Milwaukee Open. He reaches out to forty-eight-year-old Mike "Fluff" Cowan, who's been caddying since before Tiger even picked up a club in the Teakwood Street garage. Cowan, who sports an oversize Wilford Brimley–esque mustache and "who just might be the only 2-handicap Deadhead in the country," according to the *Baltimore Sun,* usually caddies for Peter Jacobsen, but Jacobsen's been out with back injuries.

"I'm turning pro this week, and I plan on playing the next seven events," Tiger tells Cowan. "How many of those can you work for me?"

Cowan considers his empty dance card. "Well, I expect just about all of them," he replies.

He's conflicted about leaving Jacobsen, whom he's been caddying for since 1978. But Jacobsen—who says his first impression of Cowan was that "he looked like a cross between Grizzly Adams and Jerry Garcia"— gives his blessing. "You have a chance to work for a kid who could be one of the great players," Jacobsen tells his longtime caddie. Jacobsen's wife, Jan, even threatens to fire Cowan if he *doesn't* take it. "The only thing I was mad about," Jacobsen later jokes, "was that Tiger didn't ask me to caddie for him."

On August 27, the rumor mill churns even faster when a few reporters learn that Tiger, a native Californian, has officially declared himself a resident of Florida.

Becoming a legal resident of the zero-income-tax state is taken as proof that he's preparing to sign on to a pair of very lucrative endorsement deals: "Without ever winning a dollar in a pro tournament, Woods has been elevated to the marketing status on par with Nicklaus, Palmer, and Norman," notes CNN.

Now the money is about to come flooding in.

"People close to the situation," reports the *New York Times*, "have confirmed that Nike will pay Woods $40 million over five years to wear its shoes and that Titleist will pay him $3 million over three years to use its balls and clubs."

In his nightly newscast, NBC's Tom Brokaw projects that in Tiger's first year on the PGA Tour, he'll earn — including winnings and endorsements — $7 million. "Not bad," Brokaw says, "for a young man who is dropping out of Stanford just to play golf."

When the news leaks, Tiger has no choice but to issue a confirmation that "as of now, I am a professional golfer," but he holds all questions until a press conference on Wednesday, August 28, at 2:30 p.m.

The Woods family dresses for the occasion in the Nike athletic gear sent to Tiger's hotel room. "I got all these great clothes delivered Wednesday, yes," Tiger says, "but the best thing was they came in these great [Nike] bags. They're unbelievable bags. They have all these pockets and stuff. Just the best."

The $40 million Nike payday far surpasses Greg Norman's reported $2.5-million-per-year Reebok spokesmanship, which IMG's Hughes Norton — Norman's then agent — called "the largest in the industry in a long time."

As expected, Tiger also signs with IMG and Norton, a huge win for the agent who's kept in touch with the prodigy for fifteen years and who's still smarting from Norman's defection to start his own management company at the start of 1994. "There has been a restructuring of the relationship between IMG and Greg but it's no big deal," Norton said at the time, downplaying the move. "Everything changes in life."

The changes today are remarkable. Norton is quick to explain the speed at which Tiger's deals came together. "I'm a voracious reader, and I had read a lot about Tiger," he says. "I'd like to tell you it was brilliance on my part, that I knew he'd win six consecutive USGA championships. The fact is, I was just doing my homework."

Nike cofounder Phil Knight knows the power of branding. He has a single Nike swoosh tattooed on his left ankle. There are ten swooshes on the outfit Earl's chosen. Tida wears ten—though she refuses to toss out her old Reebok sneakers, saying of Nike, "They pay Tiger, they don't pay me."

Tiger is wearing a green Nike shirt, a black Nike cap, and black Nike golf shoes (eleven swooshes) when he goes to the Brown Deer Park clubhouse and is delighted to find more goodies in his club locker: three dozen Titleist Tour Balata golf balls and four golf gloves. "He was like a 10-year-old dropped into the middle of Toys 'R' Us," says his swing coach, Butch Harmon.

His custom Titleist irons won't be ready in time for this morning's GMO pro-am (where, for the last time, he'll be playing as an amateur), but the customized staff bag is ready to go. Tiger and Fluff Cowan, his new caddie, methodically transfer his clubs—taking special care with the driver and its plush tiger-shaped head cover—from the lightweight Ping bag Tiger used at last week's Amateur into a new professional-grade black-and-white Titleist bag stitched with the name TIGER WOODS.

Tiger's pro-am tee time is moved up to accommodate the timing of his press announcement. Just after he tees off in Milwaukee, a call comes through to golf reporter Jeff Babineau at the *Orlando Sentinel* sports desk. It's an excited colleague on the other end of the line, talking so fast Babineau can barely keep up.

"Hear about Tiger?" his fellow reporter asks. "Well, you probably don't know this. When Tiger just teed off, he was announced 'from Orlando, Florida.'"

Sentinel reporters chase down the lead to 9724 Green Island Cove, a golf villa in Isleworth Golf & Country Club, ten miles west of Orlando. The IMG head, Mark McCormack, also owns a property there. The agency will hold the deed to the villa until it can be properly transferred to Tiger.

Back in Milwaukee, the community golf club scrambles to prepare space for all the reporters and film crews arriving to cover the news conference. Officials lease a media tent from a local restaurant and assemble a platform in front of a beer ad.

At 2:30 p.m. on Wednesday, August 28, 1996, Tiger takes the stage.

Earl sits on one of two striped armchairs that flank the podium, facing the press. Tiger grasps his father's hand, then takes a deep breath and greets the room. "I guess, hello world, huh?"

The line strikes the seasoned media professionals as clever, charming.

Reading from a prepared statement, Tiger thanks Earl and Tida for being good parents "who have raised me well." He explains how some "very special people, my parents," helped him through the "frustrating and painful process" of deciding to relinquish his amateur status.

"Instantly," ESPN's Jimmy Roberts says, "Tiger Woods is one of the biggest names in professional golf."

Chapter 22

Greater Milwaukee Open
Brown Deer Park Golf Course
Milwaukee, Wisconsin
August 29 –September 1, 1996

After his first day of play at the Greater Milwaukee Open, Tiger comes off the course and into the TV studio, where he'll sit with player-analyst Curtis Strange for an exclusive interview, broadcast on ABC Sports.

"There couldn't have been a better time for a player like him to come along," Strange says of Tiger. "Golf has never been more popular, and this is a guy who is one of the few who can really push product."

Strange speaks from experience. Before winning consecutive U.S. Opens in 1988 and 1989, he signed a footwear contract with Nike. That was in 1985, not long after the Spanish golfer Seve Ballesteros became Nike's first athlete-endorser.

"We didn't invent it," Knight says of the marketing concept, "but we ratcheted it up several notches." Tiger could be Nike's "Air apparent" to Michael Jordan. "The world has not seen anything like what he's going to do for the sport," Knight tells *Golf Digest* in an interview on newsstands the next day. "It's almost like art. I wasn't alive to see Claude Monet paint, but I am alive to see Tiger play, and that's pretty great."

Not to Nike shareholders. News of the mega–endorsement deal drives the stock price down 5 percent. Tiger can't play with Nike balls or clubs because the company doesn't produce them.

Tiger's Titleist bag gets airtime as a set prop, his plush tiger-head driver cover standing out among the clubs in his brand-new signature carrier.

PGA champion Strange is more than twice Tiger's age and is now a competitor as well as an on-air golf analyst with ABC Sports. He's been doing both for the last year or so: although ABC has asked him to join its broadcast team full-time, Strange defers, saying, "I turned it down simply because I just wasn't ready — I was still playing."

Today's interview with Tiger marks a first for them both — Tiger's first as a professional and Strange's first ever sit-down as an interviewer.

With his own personalized golf bag visible behind him, Strange asks Tiger, "What would be a successful week here at Milwaukee?"

"Two things," Tiger answers. "To play four solid rounds. I'm off to a good start today." He adds, "And a victory would be awfully nice, too."

Strange is caught off guard by Tiger's self-confidence. "A victory," he repeats, his face involuntarily displaying a mixture of surprise and tension. He looks up to the ceiling for a moment.

"To me, that comes off as, uh, a little cocky or brash," he says, almost in defense of his fellow PGA pros. How does Tiger think approaching his first pro tournament with an "I can win" attitude comes across to "the other guys on tour that have been out here for years and years and years"?

"I understand that," Tiger calmly and carefully responds, but as far as he's concerned, "I've always figured, why go to a tournament if you're not going there to try and win? There's really no point of even going. That's the attitude I've had my entire life. And that's the attitude I'll always have."

He gives a quick laugh. "As I would explain to my dad, second sucks. And third's even worse."

"But on tour, that's not too bad," Strange reminds him.

"It's not too bad," Tiger agrees. "But I want to win. Um, that's just my nature."

"You'll learn," Strange says, following his stern prediction with a big grin and a laugh. "I'm kidding ya. Sorry, I just had to say that."

Tiger laughs, too. It's time to stop talking and play golf.

In the first two rounds, Tiger scores 67–69 — identical to his results at Pumpkin Ridge last week. The difference lies in the skill of his opponents. "These guys can go really low," Tiger observes after a third-round 73 puts him fifteen strokes behind Jesper Parnevik, who's leading the field with a 19-under 194. Like Tiger, the thirty-one-year-old Swedish golfer is seeking his first PGA victory.

Tiger draws an 8:28 a.m. tee time for the fourth and final round, on September 2, 1996. Out on the course, caddie Mike "Fluff" Cowan has experience to spare, but even the veteran caddie, who's worked the tour since 1976, is unprepared for the size of the early morning crowd there to see Tiger's greatness in action.

Though it's apparent that his scores won't put him atop the leaderboard, Tiger still has something up his sleeve. To Cowan, he says, "I guess since I can't make anything on the greens I might as well hole something from off them."

On the 14th, Tiger hits a 6-iron...and makes a hole in one.

"I tried to punch a 6-iron under the wind," Tiger tells the *Milwaukee Journal Sentinel*. "The ball hit on the green and kicked left, and I said, 'That should be close.'"

"It was wild," he says. "I thought it might be short, but when it hit and bounced and people started jumping up and down up by the green, I started getting excited."

The ace is Tiger's first since the one he hit at age sixteen on the Navy Course in Long Beach, California. He celebrates by lobbing the ball into a gallery that erupts in cheers from tee to green. The Nekoosa, Wisconsin, man who catches the lucky souvenir also gets Tiger to autograph it.

Despite his stated desire to win, Tiger finishes the tournament twelve back from the lead, tying for a sixtieth-place finish worth $2,544. But he's still thrilled to see the proof printed in the sports page. "That's my money," he says. "I earned this!"

It's all part of his plan to avoid the six-round PGA Tour Q-School—the PGA Tour Qualifying Tournament—by scoring well enough to play on the 1997 tour. Over the course of the next six weeks, Tiger will compete under sponsors' exemptions in six PGA tournaments. He'll need a couple of first- or second-place results—or several in the top ten—to earn the approximately $150,000 in prize money needed to finish in the top 125 on the 1996 PGA money list.

"I'm prepared for whatever happens," he tells the *New York Times.* "I'm out here playing for a living now. I'm not an amateur anymore. This is my job."

Chapter 23

Nike world headquarters
Beaverton, Oregon
September 1996

The "Hello world" tagline launches as an exclusive three-page advertising spread in the *Wall Street Journal* the day after Tiger's initial press announcement.

When Tiger used those same words to greet reporters assembled in the Brown Deer Park hospitality room, Larry Dorman of the *New York Times* found the phrasing "almost sweet, a sort of spontaneous, unaffected way to begin," a last vestige of Tiger's amateur status.

It's quickly evident that "Hello world" was a ready-and-waiting Nike campaign.

"So much for the naivete," Dorman writes. "This is pro ball now, the real world, and welcome to it."

TV spots featuring Tiger start rolling out almost immediately on the CBS telecast of the Greater Milwaukee Open as well as on ABC's *Monday Night Football*, Fox, and ESPN. The ads have been preproduced by Nike's Portland-based ad agency, Wieden+Kennedy, known for its edgy, attention-grabbing style. "Nike has always tended to go out on a limb to take advantage of the moment," says Rod Tallman, director of marketing for Nike Golf.

The ads are scripted in the first person and voiced by an actor who delivers a list of Tiger's astonishing accomplishments, building to the reveal: "There are still courses in the U.S. I am not allowed to play because of the color of my skin."

Creative director Jim Riswold fields so many calls from reporters about the spots that changing his phone number starts to seem like a good idea.

On September 17, James K. Glassman of the *Washington Post* opens his column with "You don't have to like golf to love Tiger Woods." However, he states, Nike's "dishonest ad campaign" is a problem.

"I called Nike to get a list of the courses he's not allowed to play," Glassman writes. "Finally, James Small, the company's public relations director in Beaverton, Oregon, called me back."

Small tells Glassman that he's "absolutely right": "Tiger Woods can play on any course he wants" but that "the goal of the ad was to raise awareness that golf is not an inclusive sport."

According to a Nike spokesman, "the impetus for this text came as much from Woods as from Nike." Another Nike staffer observes, "Tiger approved it, but he had a thousand things going on that week."

Of the "Hello world" ad, Tiger says, "That was the truth and that was based on my own experiences."

But his life, as represented by those few lines of ad copy, has already changed. He is now the chairman of a newly formed Tiger Woods, Inc., corporation. Earl is president. "In a way," Tiger tells *Sports Illustrated,* "I've gone from being a college sophomore to a mini-CEO."

The newly crowned "Fresh Prince of golf" is tired. The young man known to the world by one name — Tiger — is *dog* tired.

"I know one thing," Tiger, the "champion sleeper," says, his eyes drooping. "When I get my Tour card, I'll never play five weeks in a row again."

Since winning the U.S. Amateur and professionally debuting at the Milwaukee Open, Tiger's crisscrossed the continent in a chartered jet, finishing eleventh at the RBC Canadian Open, outside Toronto, during the remnants of Hurricane Fran and topping the leaderboard at the Quad Cities Open, in Coal Valley, Illinois, until he ran into trouble with a quadruple-bogey 8 in the final round and slipped to tie for fifth.

A disappointment for sure, but still amazing to come so close to winning a mere three tournaments into his professional career. He's upset, but he's able to shrug off the loss at dinner that night with his best friend, Bryon Bell, and his dad as well as his IMG agent, Hughes Norton, and his swing coach, Butch Harmon. "Let's face it, I fell on my ass," he says, but "by dessert we were laughing about how bad I blew it."

Tiger reframes the loss as "part of a learning process," saying, "In golf, you lose more than you win."

Now it's on to upstate New York for his fourth PGA Tour event in three weeks—the B.C. Open, in Binghamton, where he checks in to a tenth-floor suite at the Binghamton Regency.

"This is my house," Tiger jokes. "Do you like my house? It's got a lot of rooms. It's got maids. It's got elevators. The only problem is I have to move into another one like it every week."

Practice rounds are canceled because of ongoing rain. "The weather has been a blessing," Tiger admits, since it gives him a chance to finally catch up on sleep—and look through the boxes of clothes Nike has sent over. The color-blocked shirts he likes might become part of the Swoosh 18 line that Nike's designing for him.

The B.C. Open tournament at En-Joie Golf Club precedes the first week of the fall quarter at Stanford, where classes start on September 25. Tiger may not be heading back this semester, but to the Haskins Commission, he's still a Cardinal. Since 1971, the Haskins Award—known as the Heisman of golf—has been awarded annually to outstanding male collegiate golfers, and Tiger's made a clean sweep of the vote for 1996.

He adds the Haskins Award ceremony to his calendar and confirms the event with the commission.

The rain lets up enough on Wednesday for Tiger to play in the pro-am and sign endless autographs. No need to order hotel room service when there's a McDonald's nearby. He eats takeout—a Quarter Pounder with Cheese, fries, and a strawberry shake—and watches the Atlanta Braves play the Houston Astros. By nine thirty, he's in bed for the night. Tee time tomorrow is 9:00 a.m.

"No," he says when golf reporter Jaime Diaz asks about his nerves. "Why should I be nervous? That's for game time. I'm going to sleep like a log."

In Thursday's opening round, Tiger's paired with tour pro John Maginnes. On the par-five 3rd, they're looking at their second shots. Maginnes has about 240 yards to the green. He's thinking he might barely get there with a 3-wood. Tiger drove his tee shot into the woods; it kicked out, but he's thirty yards back of Maginnes, 270 to the green. Tiger chooses an iron for his second shot, and Maginnes, thinking Tiger is going to lay up, is stunned by the result. "I'm standing ten feet away from the hardest golf swing I've ever seen in my life, the loudest contact to a balata golf ball I've ever heard," he says. "And this ball took off and looked like a laser."

Maginnes turns to Tiger's caddie, Mike "Fluff" Cowan. "Fluff, what the F was that?"

"That's our 2-iron we carried about 275," Cowan says.

Fans—young and old, Black and white—line the course, hoping for autographs.

The novelty of it is still exciting to Tiger. "That's been the best part," he says. "The crowds have been super. Most of them are kids. Me being one year from being a teenager, maybe they feel they can relate to me. I think that's great."

In Milwaukee, teenage fans had screamed for Tiger so persistently that he'd had to go to a window and wave to quiet them down. "It was like he was the pope!" Tida says with a laugh.

Some female fans are especially interested in the twenty-year-old.

"Tiger, I love you!" one teenage girl shouts.

That gets Tiger's attention.

"Oh, my god, he looked at you!" the girl's friend gasps.

Not everyone is lucky enough to get into En-Joie Golf Club. Those outside the gates hold up signs that say I NEED TICKETS.

Tournament play is cut short at fifty-four holes by a hard and soaking rain. Fred Funk, winner of two events on the 1995 PGA Tour, takes the B.C. Open title in a one-hole playoff. Tiger ties for third and earns $58,000. His largest prize yet advances him to a total of $140,194 and number 128 on the money list. The top 125—plus exempt status and his full-time PGA Tour card—is just three spots away. Winning one of the few remaining PGA events this year will also get him there.

Watching tournament replays on the Golf Channel, Tiger likes what he sees. "Hey, my shoulders are bigger," he points out. "I'm not such a skinny little kid anymore."

Out on the road, he hits local gyms to keep up his weight workouts, doing incline presses with sixty-five-pound barbells, squatting 250 pounds, and ending every session with five hundred crunches to strengthen the lower back muscles that power his swing. The routines have packed on some muscle weight—he's up to 158 pounds now.

"I'm stronger than I look," he jokes, but the relentless perfectionist is prone to self-criticism. "Tiger! You're terrible," he says to his image on-screen, then checks in with Harmon for advice on club and wrist position.

There's always room for improvement, but it won't mean anything, he says, "if I don't keep my focus. I just have to keep going."

Chapter 24

Buick Challenge
Callaway Gardens Resort
Pine Mountain, Georgia
September 24, 1996

Tiger's chartered plane next heads to Orlando, Florida. It's a quick stop, long enough for him to trade in his California driver's license for a Florida one but not long enough to test-drive a Lexus SC 400 coupe — the new car he's eyeing because it has a trunk "big enough to hold my golf clubs."

Tiger will need those clubs to compete in the Buick Challenge, at Callaway Gardens Resort, in Pine Mountain, Georgia, the last week of September.

He arrives on Tuesday, September 24, and plays nine practice holes with Peter Jacobsen, the pro Fluff Cowan was previously on the bag for, and thirty-two-year-old Davis Love III, a three-time NCAA all-American for the University of North Carolina at Chapel Hill and a ten-year tour veteran who also works with swing coach Butch Harmon. Tiger tells Love, "It would be cool to go head-to-head down the stretch someday."

"Good luck, I hope you get the chance," Love says.

He knows it's just a matter of time. Tiger's only been on the tour for a few weeks, but Love believes it when Harmon tells him, "Davis, when Tiger learns to control his distances, nobody is going to beat him."

Tiger's purpose in Georgia is twofold: in addition to playing in the Buick Challenge, he's there to receive the Haskins Award, given to the year's outstanding collegiate golfer in memory of Georgia Golf Hall of Fame (by way of Hoylake, England) junior golf instructor Fred Haskins.

Typically, the award is presented on the winner's campus at the half-time of a home football game, but given Tiger's media draw, the Haskins Commission is going all-out with a white-tablecloth dinner.

At least, that's the plan.

But the fatigue that's been building in Tiger for weeks, months, maybe even years, finally catches up with him.

He makes a last-minute decision to pull out of both events.

Attendees at Wednesday's pro-am, including *Orlando Sentinel* golf reporter Jeff Babineau, are en route to Callaway Gardens when the van driver gets a call on her walkie-talkie. "That was my husband," she tells Babineau. "He's taking Tiger . . . to the airport."

Hughes Norton of IMG releases a statement on Tiger's behalf. "There was no other choice," Norton says of Tiger's withdrawal. "He was wiped out. He's out of gas . . . I'm amazed that it took this long. I thought he might hit the wall before now."

"He looked beat," Cowan, who caddied Tiger's practice match on Tuesday, says in agreement. "He was just kind of putting one foot ahead of the other, but I didn't think it wasn't anything a good night's sleep couldn't cure."

Despite Tiger's evident exhaustion, the move is terrible PR. Ticket presales were double those for previous Buick Challenge tournaments, and with its honoree gone, the Haskins dinner is canceled. "More than 200 dignitaries had traveled to Callaway Gardens at the tournament's expense," notes sports reporter Tim Rosaforte. "A video was produced. Including flowers, decorations and the special meals, it cost Buick $30,000 to put the event on." It's also a costly move for Tiger, one that zeroes out his winnings for the week and drops him to number 131 on the tour money list.

Reaction by fellow tour players is swift. Davis Love III attributes the misstep to naivete. "He's a rookie and rookies make rookie mistakes."

Stewart Cink, winner of the 1995 Haskins Award and new to the tour himself, is less forgiving. "To some degree I think it offends all the players who have won that award," Cink says.

Curtis Strange says, "This tournament was one of seven to help Tiger when he needed help to get his card, and how quickly he forgot. But I bet the Buick people won't forget."

Paul "Zinger" Azinger, who tied with Tiger a few weeks ago at the Milwaukee Open, says, "Everybody really likes Tiger out here. He's an incredibly likeable kid" and puts the blame on Norton for not being "a better counselor and advisor to Tiger Woods. He's only 20, man."

Even Arnold Palmer weighs in. "Tiger should have played," he tells the *Los Angeles Times*. "He should have gone to the dinner. The lesson is you don't make commitments you can't fulfill, unless you're on your deathbed, and I don't believe he was on his deathbed." But "the important thing," Palmer continues, "is how he handles it from here. I like Tiger very much. I am saying publicly exactly what I would say to him personally."

Larry Guest of the *Orlando Sentinel* addresses Tiger directly in a column dissecting the twenty-year-old player's decision process:

> The next time a sticky situation arises — and there will be more of them, for sure — address it head-on. NEVER, NEVER, NEVER again leave your IMG rep Hughes Norton and a cold, impersonal prepared statement to plead your case, as happened this week ... Your own pleasing smile and natural charm will be far more effective in defusing volatile situations and disarming critics.
>
> Face the music. Be accessible. Openly apologize if the case warrants. This is definitely one of those cases.

"Cop a plea that you're young and learning," Guest advises. "The world will give you the benefit of the doubt and drape an arm around your shoulder."

Tiger is stung by the criticism.

"I thought those people were my friends," he says, surprised by the media reports of comments from fellow players. "Those guys actually had been very nice to me," he notes, saying they've "told me that that's not exactly what they said, so it's just one of those things."

Back in Orlando, Tiger goes fishing with his new Isleworth neighbor Mark O'Meara.

"The media's been hard on me," Tiger complains.

The veteran player is sympathetic but realistic. "The media made you what you are," O'Meara tells him.

"I miss college," Tiger admits to *Sports Illustrated*. "I miss sitting around drinking beer and talking half the night... My mother was right when she said that turning pro would take away my youth. But golfwise, there was nothing left for me in college."

He still has some fences to mend with college golf, though.

Tiger writes to every member of the Haskins Commission as well as to everyone who'd planned to attend the canceled event. In each of the two hundred letters, he sincerely apologizes for his actions.

"I know what I did was wrong," Tiger says to *Boston Globe* reporter Joe Concannon. "I should've withdrawn from the tournament, but gone to the banquet."

He makes a promise to the would-be attendees: if the award banquet is rescheduled, he'll happily, and definitely, attend.

Chapter 25

Las Vegas Invitational
Las Vegas, Nevada
October 2–6, 1996

Earl Woods makes a prediction: Tiger's first PGA Tour win, he tells friends, will happen in Vegas.

In a role reversal, Tiger's mom, Tida, makes the trip from California to watch her son play in person, while Earl stays home in Cypress to watch on TV.

Twenty-year-old Tiger is still too young to legally gamble in a casino, but the invitational has the feel of a giant roulette wheel. The five-round, ninety-hole Las Vegas Invitational tournament, now known as the Shriners Hospitals for Children Open, will be played on three local courses: the Las Vegas Hilton Country Club, the Desert Inn, and TPC Summerlin.

This year, Las Vegas has seen singer Wayne Newton's twenty-five thousandth Vegas concert and magician duo Siegfried & Roy's fifteen thousandth performance. ABC's *20/20* marked the occasion with a special segment, "Siegfried & Roy: The Magic Returns," in which Roy Horn was interviewed about taming the act's large cats—cheetahs and lions and tigers.

Said Horn, "It feels wonderful, I cannot even tell you the feeling of having a full-grown tiger lick your face. But you also have to think that, at the same time, with one swipe of the paw, he can decapitate you. It's that simple. You can take nothing for granted, even if you think you know it all."

Tiger Woods is not taking anything for granted, either. Now that he's turned pro, he says, "everything is different, but my objective is the same — to try to win." Though after his recent missteps in Georgia, he opts out of his usual full-on training. "I didn't play or practice. I just rested," he says. The result: an opening-round 70, 1 under par, at the Las Vegas Hilton Country Club. Solid but not exceptional.

Fred Funk, fresh off his B.C. Open victory, blisters the course with a 62, yet sportswriters don't make much of Funk's early lead. The lack of attention smarts. "Everything has been Tiger, Tiger," Funk says in a testy interview with the Las Vegas Review-Journal. "They kind of forget about everyone else out here."

Funk has a point. The notably strong field includes ten-time PGA Tour winner Davis Love III and Fred Couples, who in March took the Players Championship.

Tiger scores 63 in round 2, rising from a tie for ninety-seventh to a tie for eleventh. Play resumes at the Desert Inn course, and so does the pain from a recurring injury. He strained his groin at the U.S. Amateur in August. "I was hurting all the way in," Tiger admits. "But being the son of a former Green Beret, I know those guys can suck it up. A strain is nothing." He turns in a score of 68 for eighth place on the leaderboard.

When Tiger's fourth-round 67 moves him into a tie for seventh, ticket sales for the fifth and final round soar. The massive turnout at TPC Summerlin — ten thousand more than expected — strains the gallery's rope boundaries as fans chant, "Ti-ger, Ti-ger."

Among the spectators is the University of Nevada–Las Vegas golf team coach, Dwaine Knight, who despite his best efforts to recruit college-bound Tiger lost out to Coach Wally Goodwin and Stanford three years ago.

Coach Knight is watching as Tiger eagles the par-five 3rd, electrifying the crowd.

On the 13th fairway, the cheers give way to uneasy murmurs when Tiger faces an uphill lie. With his 2-iron, he strikes the ball hard and feels an immediate effect in his left leg. He grips the aching muscle, his face etched with pain.

Tiger digs deeper, birdieing 14 to tie for the lead.

"Bring it on home, Mr. Woods," the fans cheer, bellowing, "Get in the hole!" after every shot. They're shouting his name, grabbing at his shirt, asking him to throw a ball their way.

Fluff Cowan tries to talk the unruly fans down, asking, "Can't you see we got a little something going here?"

"There was almost no decorum," *Las Vegas Review-Journal* sports reporter Kevin Iole says. "It was like Tiger was the only person they came to see, and they would run to the next spot after he would hit his shot. That bothered the other players."

Tiger finishes with a 64, giving him a one-shot lead. He signs his card — 8 under for the day; 27 under for the tournament — then heads to the driving range, taking most of the spectators with him.

"I think I had 40 people following me," says Love of his last holes, "and 20 of them I knew."

At the 16th, Love pulls even, then misses birdie tries on 17 and 18. The tournament will be decided in a playoff. It was just last week at Callaway Gardens that Tiger told Love he hoped the two of them would "go head-to-head down the stretch someday."

Here we go, Love marvels. *He got what he wanted.*

On the first playoff hole, Tiger's second shot lands him eighteen feet from the pin. Love's goes left into a bunker. Tiger's birdie putt leaves him a tap-in for par. The best Love can do from the bunker is bogey.

The crowd goes wild at witnessing the young superstar's first tour win, on only his fifth outing, barely a month after turning pro.

Butch Harmon and Tida Woods rush out to take turns embracing Tiger.

As for Earl, "I will call and talk to him," Tiger says, adding, "if he is there. He is probably out playing golf."

"I hope this win will tell people that he is the real one," Tida tells reporters. "Every time the curtain is up, he's right there. Encore every time."

Tiger, Love says, is "not playing for the money. He never thought, I have to make another one hundred and some thousand dollars to make the top 125. He's trying to win. He thinks about winning and nothing else. I like the way he thinks."

Not that the money is meaningless to Tiger. As Love talks with the assembled reporters, Tiger's in a quieter corner of the media tent with golf writer Tim Dahlberg, who's on deadline for the Associated Press.

Huddled over Dahlberg's computer, the reporter shows his story to Tiger, asking, "Anything you like?"

Tiger points to the place where Dahlberg has noted his winnings—$297,000.

"I like that," he says with a grin.

His victory means a two-year exemption on the tour, and today's earnings have raised his total to $437,195, boosting his ranking on the money list up to number 40.

In a classic Las Vegas photo-op, tournament officials pose Tiger between two showgirls—dancers from Bally's show *Jubilee!*, costumed in spangles—then hand him an oversize check. The win also brings another prize, one that money can't buy—an invitation to the 1997 Masters.

Tiger decides to keep the giant check. He'll have it framed and hang it in his office, where he'll be logging hours to fulfill his $2.2 million contract with Warner Books to write a golf instructional and an autobiography. A generous provision allows him between three and six years to deliver the manuscripts.

And he's still processing today's win. As for Vegas, Tiger has a return date in mind. Next year, he says, "I'll be legal. I can actually do some stuff around here."

Master of ceremonies and local golf writer Jack Sheehan reads his audience. "Ladies and gentlemen," Sheehan says, "how about a round of applause for the richest college dropout in America?"

Tiger is quick to correct him. "I think Bill Gates has me on that."

Are you kidding me? Sheehan thinks, then, *He's right. Gates dropped out of Harvard his freshman year. It was almost like he thought about that beforehand.*

"Tiger, this is your fifth tournament as a professional. Are you surprised the victory came this soon?" Sheehan asks.

"To be honest with you, Jack," the twenty-year-old replies, "I'm surprised it took this long."

Chapter 26

Texas Open
La Cantera Golf Club
San Antonio, Texas
October 10–13, 1996

L adies and gentlemen...direct from Las Vegas...where he won his first professional event last week...the three-time U.S. Amateur champion...from Orlando, Florida...Tiiiiiii-gerrrr Woods!"

The director of the Texas Open at the La Cantera Golf Club, in San Antonio, gives Tiger an introduction bursting with outsize Lone Star State hospitality, insisting to his staff that "Tiger Woods is not just a golfer, he's a celebrity."

"Direct from Vegas? I thought they were going to introduce Elvis," joke the tour pros paired with Tiger, laughing almost too hard to tee off.

Tiger and Earl spend evenings with seventy-four-year-old Charlie Sifford, present as a special guest of the tournament. Today's honor can't erase the systemic racial discrimination Sifford's faced here before, though, when in 1961, despite the PGA's finally officially dropping its "Caucasian only" clause (one of the last American professional sports organizations to do so), Sifford still found himself physically barred from the course by pistol-wielding Texas Rangers.

Often called the Jackie Robinson of golf, Sifford is also often called surly and bitter. But he has good reason to mourn his missed opportunities. "I really would like to know how good I could have been with a fair chance," he says of the hardships he endured. "I'm not angry at anybody, but I never will understand why they didn't want the black man to play golf. Nobody ever loved this game more than me."

"Without Charlie Sifford, there would have been no one to fight the system for the blacks that followed," says Lee Elder, one of the first Black professional golfers to come up on the path Sifford forged, despite stiff opposition. "It took a special person to take the things that he took: the tournaments that barred him, the black cats in his bed, the hotels where he couldn't stay, the country club grills where he couldn't eat."

Tennis legend Arthur Ashe, who faced similar barriers while playing a traditionally white sport, notes that "Sifford ultimately had only his homegrown survival instincts and family to sustain him." But that was before Tiger Woods—whom Sifford lovingly calls Junior—burst onto the scene.

"Tiger is amazing—he makes me feel like all the hard work I did was worth it," says Sifford. "I'm quite sure there's a lot of young black kids who have picked up golf clubs since reading about Tiger."

Tiger's honored to have his cigar-chomping surrogate grandfather on hand for this long-dreamed-of moment: joining the PGA Tour as an official full-time member.

Tiger now possesses the ultimate tour status symbol: a personalized PGA money clip.

This heavy piece of metal—TIGER WOODS, 1996, his reads—is the equivalent of a player's ID, allowing access to parking, dining, and range facilities, including the right to walk onto the first tee at each and every host course. It's "pretty cool," says Fred Couples, "to wear it on my belt."

Also on offer: a wives' badge.

"What am I going to do with that?" Tiger jokes with the PGA rules official. "Think about it," he says. "Most of the women my age are in college."

On tour, he has no time for a girlfriend, let alone a wife. He barely has time to even shop for clothes beyond whatever arrives in the boxes from Nike.

"You can't wear Nike twenty-four hours a day," Butch Harmon says, teasing Tiger as he guides him through making purchases at the mall in San Antonio.

The clerk ringing Tiger up announces that not one but two of his credit cards won't go through. It's not for lack of funds. But this is new territory for the twenty-year-old.

"Well, you activated them, didn't you?" Harmon asks.

"What's that?" Tiger answers.

"That just shows he's a kid," the swing coach realizes. He's got a lot to learn about handling his newfound wealth. Especially since Tiger always seems to be short on cash. "For a rich guy, you sure are poor," jokes his IMG agent, Hughes Norton, who often finds himself handing over the cash in his wallet to Tiger.

"What kind of a damn millionaire are you?" Tida grumbles at her son as she covers his expenses.

La Cantera Golf Club is the hometown course for thirty-eight-year-old Texas pro David Ogrin, who leverages his local knowledge into a final-round lead. Aiming for his first win in fourteen years on tour, Ogrin remains steadily confident, even when he triple-bogeys the 6th.

"I had no idea that he was making a run," says Ogrin, who missed the news that Tiger had tightened the gap. But he's been keeping an eye on the newcomer in general. "Anybody who was paying attention knew" that Tiger was something special. "And I was paying attention."

The win and its $216,000 purse move Ogrin to number 32 on the money list, just two spots above Tiger, who moves to number 34 from number 40 after only six tournaments.

Two weeks ago, Tiger was hoping to make it to the top 125. Now he's only four spots from the top thirty and qualifying for the $3 million TOUR Championship at Southern Hills Country Club, in Tulsa, Oklahoma.

Maybe a little Disney magic will help get him there.

Chapter 27

Walt Disney World/Oldsmobile Classic
Magnolia Course, Disney World
Orlando, Florida
October 17–20, 1996

O h, god," says Peter Jacobsen when asked about Tiger's recent performance. "If this is how he is every week, then it's over. He's the
greatest player in the history of the game."

Tiger isn't feeling like the greatest. He's hunkered down with a nasty
cold and sore throat.

But Michael McPhillips, director of the Walt Disney World/Oldsmobile
Classic, is reaping the success of a monthlong campaign. "The Tiger has
landed," McPhillips crows, riffing on Neil Armstrong's world-changing
announcement of the Apollo 11 lunar landing.

"A good crowd for us is usually in the 15,000 range on Sunday, and
with Tiger, we might draw 20,000, maybe more," McPhillips enthusiastically predicts.

Attendance is triple what it was last year.

"You go, T!" a young fan calls out. "Take care of bizness!"

Despite feeling under the weather, Tiger tosses balls, high-fives kids,
and thanks his supporters.

"Tiger Woods just thanked me," says one teenager. "My year is made, dude!"

As he walks the course, four bodyguards keep pace but don't prevent Tiger from interacting with the fans. "To look out here and see so many kids, I think that's wonderful," he says. "It's really nice seeing more minorities in the gallery. I think that's where the game should go and will go."

Time will tell if that prediction is on point. But there's not long to wait on the one Tiger makes at breakfast before his second day of play.

"Pop," he tells Earl, who's staying with him in the rented house. "Got to shoot 63 today. That's what it will take to get into it."

"So go do it," replies Earl. Later that day, when Tiger gets home, he asks his son, "Whaddya shoot?"

"Sixty-three," Tiger says.

"Oh, my god," says Earl.

The noisy overflow gallery makes the Magnolia course at Disney feel more like the wild kingdom than the Magic Kingdom, especially when Sunday spectators cutting through the underbrush startle a deer—and excite an alligator who chases the real-life Bambi across the 6th green.

The deer won't be caught. Neither will Tiger, even though he woke up today feeling worse than ever, saying, "I can't really hear. I'm so clogged. My throat's not doing good. I've got no energy. I'm dizzy. Other than that, I'm great."

He starts Sunday in a four-way tie for fifth place but spends the back nine trading leads with Payne Stewart, until at the last moment, Tiger ends up winning by a stroke.

When he putts out on the 18th, he's won his second PGA tournament.

Mickey, Minnie, and Tigger join Tiger on the course in celebration. Of the seven pro tournaments Tiger's played this season, he's won two and amassed winnings of nearly $800,000. At number 23 on the money list, he's earned a place at next week's TOUR Championship.

Dressed in the colorful golf knickers he's known for, the runner-up and fellow resident of Isleworth Golf & Country Club, Payne Stewart, tells reporters, "All the accolades need to go to Tiger for the way he's played and conducted himself over the last eight weeks." Not to mention: "He's a wonderful player. He's the shot in arm our tour needed."

Tiger returns the compliment. "Payne's a great guy. He's inviting me over for rib-eye tonight," he tells TV reporters. "Maybe, he said, he'll buy me a beer."

"You're twenty, Tiger," the interviewer reminds him. "You gotta wait until you're twenty-one."

"What people don't know won't hurt," Tiger says with a sly grin.

Tiger and Stewart are just two of many professional athletes who own homes in the exclusive and secure eight-hundred-acre development, where savoring a win is a favorite pastime.

"As in any community, we're always getting together to have a good time," says Los Angeles Lakers star Shaquille O'Neal. Though he has a movie theater in his $3.95-million Mediterranean-style lakefront mansion, it's more fun to go four doors down to catch a film with his buddy Dennis Scott of the Dallas Mavericks — or to challenge Seattle Mariners outfielder Ken Griffey Jr. to a pickup game of one-on-one on Shaq's indoor basketball court, painted in Lakers gold and purple.

"As for Tiger," O'Neal says, "once my tennis elbow [heals], I'll be glad to take him to school on my miniature golf course in my front yard."

Payne Stewart and Wimbledon doubles champion Todd Woodbridge partner in both golf and tennis, each spotting the other strokes or points. "Most people at Isleworth are very successful," Woodbridge says. "It breeds success. You breathe the air of success."

And sometimes a whiff of failure. Life among elite athletes is "always very humbling because you think you're the best here and then you find someone who's better than you."

It seems like that's *Sports Illustrated*'s assessment of Tiger versus the PGA Tour field. "Tiger! In Two Months as a Pro, He Has Transformed an Entire Sport" reads the cover of the October 28, 1996, issue, Tiger's first as the cover subject.

Printed praise matters little to Tiger. It matters only that he measures up to his own exacting standards. So winning the Disney Classic isn't enough.

"It may be surprising to some guys, but it's not surprising to people who know me," Tiger says of how well he's been playing since turning pro. "I was never able to get any feel at tour events as an amateur," he tells reporters. "One week I'd play in a junior event, then next I'd play Greg Norman."

What excites his supporters and worries his opponents, though, is Tiger's assertion that he's nowhere near his A game.

"I really haven't played my best golf yet," he says. "I haven't even had a great putting week yet."

Chapter 28

Callaway Gardens Resort
Columbus, Georgia
November 11, 1996

In a ballroom filled with tables covered in white cloths and set for a steak dinner, Earl and Tiger mingle with guests of the Haskins Commission for the rescheduled Haskins Award ceremony.

A man in a suit approaches Tiger.

"I think you're going to be the next great one," the man says, "but those are mighty big shoes to fill."

"Got big feet," Tiger replies.

He's keeping the mood light. So is Cecil Calhoun, longtime Haskins Commission member and the evening's master of ceremonies. As the moment approaches for Tiger to accept the Haskins Award for outstanding collegiate golfer of 1996, the mood in the room swirls with a mix of curiosity and anticipation that heightens as Earl steps from the head table to the podium. Earl—who as a young army officer was once stationed at Fort Benning, ten miles outside Columbus—knows the area well, and he knows tonight's subject even better.

Tears coursing down his face, his voice breaking with emotion, Earl makes a speech that is at once an apology, a confessional, and a hopeful plea.

> Please forgive me...but sometimes I get very emotional... when I talk about my son...My heart...fills with so... *much...joy...*when I realize...that this young man...is going to be able...to help so many people...He will *transcend* this game...and bring to the world...a humanitarianism... which has never been known before. The world will be a better place to live in...by virtue of his existence...and his presence...I acknowledge only a small part in that...in that I know that I was personally selected by God himself... to nurture this young man...and bring him to the point where he can make his contribution to humanity...This is my treasure...Please accept it...and use it wisely...Thank you.

Earl and Tiger embrace as the room erupts in applause and an outpouring of feeling over a father's tribute. The presence of Fred Haskins—mentor to junior golfers, father of two daughters, and the reason all are gathered here tonight—is deeply sensed.

"That's my father," Tiger says, taking Earl's place at the podium.

It's been six weeks since Tiger left Callaway Gardens in a haze of exhaustion. He explains the moments leading up to that decision. He pauses, making eye contact with as many people in the room as he can. They've been waiting to hear what he has to say.

The room is hushed as Tiger speaks. "I should've attended the dinner [the first time]," he says. "I admit I was wrong, and I'm sorry for any inconvenience I may have caused. But I have learned from that, and I will never make that mistake again. I'm very honored to be part of this select group, and I'll always remember, for both good and bad, this Haskins Award; for what I did and what I learned, for the company I'm now in and I'll always be in. Thank you very much."

Forgiveness reigns.

*   *   *

What hangs heavy over Tiger and Earl, though, is Earl's recent health scare—and how it affected Tiger's play two weeks ago at the TOUR Championship.

Joining the top thirty players on the 1996 money list after his win at the Disney Classic (with earnings of $734,494 and a spot at number 23), Tiger earned the opportunity to vie for a $3 million purse and a $540,000 first prize.

Earl and Tida traveled to Tulsa, Oklahoma, to watch their son compete against the elite field—including Phil Mickelson, who topped the money list with $1,620,999—at the Southern Hills Country Club.

Expectations are sky-high. The *New York Times* noted "a huge rush on tickets to the Tour Championship" during a week when "the kid is on the cover of *Sports Illustrated,* on the front page of *The New York Times,* on the cover of *Golf Digest* and *Golf Magazine.*"

On a bright and sunny Thursday, October 24, Tiger shoots an even-par 70, putting him in eighth place. "He was close to shooting a 66 or so," said caddie Mike "Fluff" Cowan. "Pretty solid, but he could have putted a little better." Looking at the weather, Cowan lamented, "It's supposed to get ugly and nasty here the next three days. Low scores are going to be hard to come by."

Cowan had no idea how right his forecast would be.

Earl had been experiencing the same flulike symptoms that had plagued his son the week before, when Tiger celebrated his "victory at Disney by heading home to Isleworth, taking some Nyquil and heading to bed," according to the *Orlando Sentinel.*

At 2:50 in the morning of October 25, Tiger accompanied his sixty-four-year-old father to Saint Francis Hospital, where ESPN reported that he was treated for chest pains and then transferred to the coronary unit.

It's widely known that Earl underwent quadruple bypass surgery ten years ago. His heavy smoking and drinking were surely a factor, but

Earl's also prone to joking that Tiger's close calls on the golf course have contributed to his heart trouble. During the U.S. Amateur in August, Earl sipped from a tumbler of vodka, stating half seriously: "That boy never does anything easy. He has exercised my heart for the past six years."

Unaware that Tiger had been with his father at the hospital until five in the morning before his 12:49 p.m. tee time on Friday, fans at Southern Hills were puzzled not to see Tiger playing with his usual skill and flair. "You want to follow him one more round and see if he breaks out of this funk?" one fan asked another.

"It's obvious he's not concentrating," Tida noted. She'd made it to the course in time to see her son bogey hole after hole. Earl was doing well enough to request a TV so he could watch from his hospital bed.

Tiger shrugged off his disappointing score of 78. "I didn't want to be out there today, because there are more important things in life than golf," he said as he left the 18th green to return to the hospital. "I love my dad to death. I'm going to see him now . . . Hopefully he's OK."

Earl is released from the hospital after four days. "I've got to shape up now, God's telling me," he says. But his father's brush with mortality has rocked Tiger deeply.

Chapter 29

Australian Open
Australian Golf Club
Sydney, Australia
November 21–24, 1996

The headline in the *Los Angeles Times* reads TIGER FOLLOWS THE CASH TO AUSTRALIA. The newspaper reports that Tiger's contract for the Australian Open includes an appearance fee of $190,000, higher than native Australian Greg Norman's rumored $158,000 appearance fee. The tournament, run jointly by the Australian Golf Union and IMG, will be Tiger's first international event as a pro.

His agent, Hughes Norton, initially refuses to give any details, only telling the Associated Press, "I would say that something positive is going to happen." Later, IMG distributes to journalists covering the Australian Open a glossy sheet filled with praise for Tiger from the world's greatest golfers.

Gary Player, who came from South Africa to win nine major championships and build an unsurpassed international record, frames a generational progression: "The first time I saw Arnold Palmer, I said, 'There's a star.' The first time I saw Jack Nicklaus, I said, 'Superstar.' I feel the same way about Tiger Woods. As long as he maintains his attitude, he's got it. He's a superstar on the horizon."

On Thursday, November 21, a huge gallery turns out to see Tiger play his opening round. Under a cloudy sky, whipped by cold and wind, he shoots a disappointing 79.

Greg Norman shoots 67. The Australian, who's won this tournament four times before, says charitably of Tiger, "At least he got the flavor of Australian courses. We play difficult courses here. He got a shock when he shot 79. Perhaps he will appreciate why Australians play so well when they leave home."

The next day's temperature is the lowest Australia has ever recorded during November, typically the warm late spring season. Tiger comes down with another bad cold but does improve his score to 72.

A fifteen-year-old Australian named Adam Scott is in the field. Scott doesn't make the cut, so instead of playing the final two rounds, he's caddying for a friend — and working crowd control.

Scott is "so nervous" that he's "probably looking at Tiger more than I was looking at a yardage book." He's on the 10th hole when he spots Tiger coming down the 18th, "dragging thousands around" in the packed gallery. "I've got a carry bag over my shoulders," Scott says, as he waves both arms to "clear Tiger's crowd for my buddy to hit a shot up the 10th green."

Tiger shoots 79-72-71-70 and ends the tournament in a four-way tie for fifth place and a score of 292 — twelve back from Greg Norman, who takes the top prize for the fifth time. But like a champ, Tiger does recover from that opening-round 79.

"He should find it easier next time," Norman says, but there is one bright spot. "When the sun finally came out today," Tiger says, "I thought I was back in America."

Back in Orange County, California, Tiger takes a break from golf to spend Christmas Eve with his parents at the house he's bought for them in Tustin. Not that they've gotten rid of the house in Cypress: Earl is convinced that Tiger's childhood home will be considered a historical monument. "I am certain that one day the birthplace of Tiger Woods is going to become widely acknowledged," he states.

Yesterday, the best gift imaginable hit newsstands nationwide: the December 23 issue of *Sports Illustrated,* with a full-bleed illustration of Tiger's face on the cover, announcing him as its Sportsman of the Year. *SI's* new top editor, Bill Colson, introduces the issue: "In case you blinked and missed it, golf is no longer your father's sport . . . and Tiger Woods is *SI's* 1996 Sportsman of the Year.

"At least for now.

"Just kidding."

Sportsman of the Year is a serious achievement. Not only is Tiger the youngest athlete to ever get this honor, he's also the first golfer to earn it since Jack Nicklaus did so in 1978, the year he won the triple career grand slam, having won all golf's majors three times.

To Tiger, it's important to keep the comparisons—and the expectations—in perspective. "People can say all kinds of things about me and Nicklaus and make me into whatever," he says. "But it comes down to one thing: I've still got to hit the shot. Me. Alone. That's what I must never forget."

On December 30, 1996—his twenty-first birthday—it's reported that he legally changes his first name. Eldrick is gone. Now there's only Tiger.

He celebrates in Las Vegas, fulfilling a promise he made when he won the Las Vegas Invitational—returning to the host city now that he "can actually do some stuff around here."

Nike chooses a solo image of Tiger—his face a mask of concentration, his torso coiled midswing—for its vintage-style, four-panel photo-strip-format holiday poster, tinted red and green and captioned "Happy New Year . . . of the Tiger." According to the Chinese zodiac, 1997 will be the year of the ox (the year of the tiger will begin in 1998), but Tiger has his own way of making Nike's prediction come true.

* * *

Now that Tiger's twice made the cover of *Sports Illustrated,* national magazines are intensely competing to be next. Art Cooper, editor of *GQ,* hammers out terms agreeable to IMG, then leaves the logistics to the assistant managing editor, David Granger. "Most of the time when we wanted to put someone on the cover of *GQ,*" Granger says, "especially an athlete — they would give us the world."

Instead, Granger gets around three hours: two hours round-trip between the new house in Tustin and Long Beach, where photographer Michael O'Neill will have another hour with Tiger in his studio.

Forty-three-year-old senior writer and sports columnist Charles P. Pierce gets the *GQ* assignment, in part because of his lifelong association with golf—his father was a high school golf coach at North High in Worcester, Massachusetts. "I play," Pierce says. "Whether I like it is another matter."

Before the January 13 interview, Pierce rereads "The Chosen One," Gary Smith's cover piece for *SI*'s Sportsman of the Year issue, and considers its central premise. "Tiger Woods was raised to believe that his destiny is not only to be the greatest golfer ever but also to change the world," Smith writes in his opener, then asks: "Will the pressures of celebrity grind him down first?"

Pierce begins to form his own thesis, focusing on Earl's boundless goals for his son. *This is a pitch made on behalf of somebody who really is unformed, both as an athlete and as a celebrity,* Pierce thinks.

The seasoned journalist sits in the back seat of the chauffeured limousine *GQ* sends to the Tustin house. Tiger steps inside the car.

Chapter 30

AT&T Pebble Beach National Pro-Am
Pebble Beach Golf Links
Monterey Peninsula, California
January 31, 1997

"Tiger's the hottest player in the game," Mark O'Meara says. "We play a lot of golf together."

At the Mercedes Championships at La Costa Resort and Spa, in Carlsbad, California. Tiger, wearing his already emblematic final-round red shirt, wins the first PGA event of the season in a rain-drenched playoff on January 12, raising his winning percentage to an odds-defying .333.

"Red is one of Mom's colors," Tiger notes, explaining that "every day in Thai tradition is represented by a color, and red is for Sunday." Though less superstitious about it than Tida is, Tiger *has* noticed that he seems to win by more strokes when he wears red on Sundays. "How could I argue with Mom?"

He gives Tida the new Mercedes that comes with first place. The $216,000 in prize money makes him an official PGA Tour millionaire after only nine events. Tiger's smashed the record previously held by Ernie Els, who earned $1 million after twenty-eight events.

Raising a glass of champagne, newly twenty-one-year-old Tiger says,

"The coolest thing about all this is that I'm actually able to participate in a toast without worrying that I'm going to get arrested."

Tiger will "compete in drinking a glass of water," Earl likes to say. He's finally met his match in Mark O'Meara.

It's O'Meara's thoughtful wife, Alicia, who welcomes Tiger to Isleworth, telling her husband, "That poor kid is sitting over there in his house alone. Let's get him over here for dinner." On January 13, 1997—O'Meara's fortieth birthday—his wife, Alicia, surprises him with a dinner party and a new Porsche to be delivered by Valentine's Day.

Despite the nineteen-year age gap, Tiger and O'Meara—whom Tiger calls Marko—bond over turning *any* activity into a competition. O'Meara proves superior at washing and waxing cars, but the younger man excels at ironing. "Every morning," Tiger says, "I've got to iron all my stuff. Got to do it. Even if it's dry-cleaned, I'll iron it just a little bit, all of the little creases."

To keep up, O'Meara buys his own clothes iron, but Tiger quickly invents a new wager. "Fly fishing," he says. "Five bucks a cast, ten bucks a catch."

"I'm going to figure out a way to clip you" at the AT&T Pebble Beach National Pro-Am, O'Meara tells Tiger—assuming the 1997 tournament is playable. Heavy rains washed out the 1996 event entirely. And Pebble Beach's greens, planted with its signature poa annua grass, have been soaked by twenty inches of rain this January.

Clint Eastwood, the onetime mayor of nearby Carmel-by-the-Sea, California, has an idea for a way to clear the standing water on the greens. In his latest film, *Absolute Power,* set to open on February 14, Eastwood's playing the role of a US president. Marine One isn't available, but Eastwood has a helicopter of his own. He climbs on board with musician and amateur pilot John Denver, and they hover the chopper over the greens, spinning its rotor blades in an attempt to dry out the grass.

America's number one public golf course, where sea lions sun themselves on cliffside beaches next to the Pacific Ocean, has certainly been good to O'Meara, a.k.a. the "Prince of Pebble Beach." The tour veteran is a four-time event champion—1985, 1989, 1990, 1992—though he has yet to win a major.

"From Hollywood, California, please welcome Kevin Costner," the announcer says. It's 8:40 a.m., and cameras are clicking in the twelve-deep crush around the first tee.

Partnered with Tiger in the team competition, the 15-handicap golfer and *Tin Cup* movie star is all smiles and photo-ops with the fans cheering his terrific play—including three birdies—on the front nine. He's replacing Earl, whose ongoing health problems prevent him from taking part in the pro-am. "When his father couldn't play, I was happy to fill in," says Costner. The movie star "loves the crowds," but Tiger fights his annoyance with the people jostling for photos.

It's a somewhat less golf-savvy crowd than attends other tournaments. One spectator questions a reporter what "the 'negative 13' next to Woods' name means."

"I want to see Tiger for the golf and Kevin 'cause he's a hunk," says one attendee from San Jose. "That's why I'm here."

A fan in the gallery spots Bill Murray of *Caddyshack* fame.

"Bill, you're looking better than Kevin Costner," she shouts enthusiastically.

Murray pauses on the fairway to consider the compliment, then answers, "You've got a point."

Actor Andy Garcia and partner Paul Stankowski win the team competition, setting a course record with 43 under par. It's "the best golf I've ever played," Garcia says. "Actors sort of get used to mimicry. When you get to play with pros, you fall into it."

Tiger and Costner take fourth place. Tiger hopes to beat that in the pro tournament, joking that he's picked up some new tricks. Such as? "Don't hit the ball in the ocean," he says drily.

O'Meara's tied for second going into the final, three back from the leader, David Duval. Tiger's tied for fifth. "I love Mark to death," Tiger says. "We talked about it back home—'Wouldn't it be great to battle it out down the stretch?'"

He nearly makes it happen. A nervy try for eagle ends in a birdie and a fourth-round 64. But it isn't quite enough.

The Prince of Pebble Beach takes the top spot for a fifth time. Tiger ties for second with Duval. "There must be someone floating high above the Monterey Peninsula who's a huge Mark O'Meara fan," O'Meara says.

On February 22, Earl undergoes a second heart bypass surgery: WOODS'S FATHER BETTER, says the *New York Times* headline above an article noting the care Earl's receiving at UCLA Medical Center.

Complications threaten Earl's recovery. Tiger sits at his father's bedside, watching the electronic signals on the heart monitor. Suddenly, Earl flatlines.

"They said he was gone," Tiger says. "We thought we had lost him."

It's a few terrifying moments before Earl is brought back. "I was in la-la-land there for a while," he says.

After regaining consciousness, Earl describes his near-death experience, his feeling of walking into the light.

To Earl, who was raised Christian, it was a spiritual event.

"All I felt was warmth," he tells Tiger afterward. "Do I go to the warmth or not? I made a conscious decision not to go to the warmth."

There's less warmth to be found in the piece journalist Charles P. Pierce has written for his cover story in the April issue of *GQ*, which blows raspberries at the religious overtones some people — including Earl — see in Tiger's success.

Tiger's nearing his second-round tee time at Arnold Palmer's Bay Hill Invitational at the end of March when he first catches sight of the magazine. He recognizes himself in the gray suit on the cover of the April issue, a photo taken at the photographer's studio in Long Beach. What's completely unfamiliar is the bold headline: THE COMING OF TIGER WOODS, SPORTS' NEXT MESSIAH.

Employing the structure and language of a religious tract, the piece is part ode to Tiger's natural talent. "I believe that he is the most charismatic athlete alive today," Pierce writes. "I believe that his charisma comes as much from the way he plays the game as it does from the way he looks and from what he is supposed to symbolize. I believe that his golf swing—never past parallel—is the most perfect golf swing yet devised."

But Pierce is convinced that where there's faith, there's heresy. He has a bigger score to settle: that Earl's presentation of Tiger as a world savior exists only in his own imagination.

To prove his point, Pierce quotes from unguarded remarks Tiger made during their California limousine ride, the off-color jokes he told without realizing that he was on the record. The punch lines, some of them racial, some of them sexual, skew toward the humor of an inexperienced schoolboy with none of the sophisticated innuendo that might be expected of a multimillionaire product pitchman.

Reaction to the piece is instantaneous and treated as a scandal involving a young athlete whose reputation until then has been mostly pristine.

IMG quickly issues a press release containing Tiger's response.

"It's no secret that I'm twenty-one years old and that I'm naive about the motives of certain ambitious writers," Tiger writes. "The article proves that, and I don't see any reason for anyone to pay $3 to find that out. It's easy to laugh it off as juvenile and petty except for the attacks on my father," he continues. "I don't understand the cheap shots against him."

Nowhere in the statement does Tiger say what he's really thinking. *How could I have been so stupid?*

He'll have his guard up with journalists from now on.

Way up.

Chapter 31

Orlando, Florida
April 3, 1997

Tiger's been doing his homework, spending hours with the Golf Channel's video library to learn the contours and the slopes he'll face at the Masters next week.

He knows that the greens at Augusta National are lightning fast. His plan of attack is to identify the course's natural features that play to his strengths: *My length, that the course has no rough, and that it has virtually no trees that will come into play even if I miss the fairways. Augusta National is effectively wide open for me.*

Tiger fine-tunes his swing, working with a driver made from the pros' material of choice—persimmon. His mental game requires no fine-tuning.

He's in a good, confident place, having won several tournaments leading into the event. "Now all of a sudden here I am prepping for the Masters and I'm already hot," Tiger marvels. "You couldn't have asked for a better start. It was a dream scenario."

On April 3, Arnold Palmer invites Tiger to his course, Bay Hill, to play a friendly game for a friendly wager. On tour, Tiger especially enjoys

"Tuesday shootouts," pre-tournament practice rounds in which players keep things interesting—a birdie is typically worth a crisp $100 bill—but because sixty-seven-year-old Palmer is known to be frugal, he sets the bet at $100 for the entire round.

On the par-three 17th, Tiger takes the round and wins the bet. But Palmer isn't quite ready to pay up. He raises the stakes: double or nothing on the 18th hole.

"The hole borders on unfair," Masters winner Raymond Floyd has said of the 18th at Bay Hill and its diabolical design, featuring three bunkers guarding the hole on the left and a lake border on the right.

Tiger likes his odds. He steps to the tee on the 458-yard par 4 and drives well down the fairway, directing the ball left of center toward the fast, undulating green.

Palmer's drive comes up well short of Tiger's. He knows he has to risk hitting driver again if he wants to reach the green in two, so he pulls out that club and goes for broke.

"Arnold never gives up, does he?" Tiger says to their playing partner, Alastair Johnston, Palmer's business manager at IMG.

Palmer lands his ball in the back bunker, but he's still grinding and outputts Tiger. Both players par the hole, and the wager ends in a push.

"Do you think there can be a perfect game in golf?" a reporter from *Sports Illustrated* asked Arnold Palmer back in 1959.

"If you mean the perfect game within the realm of probability, maybe it will be played," Palmer said. "That would mean hitting 18 perfect tee shots and 18 perfect second shots and landing in the cup in no more than one or two putts. But no one is ever going to birdie 18 holes."

In the absence of a truly "perfect" game, a score of 60 is typically considered as close as you can come in golf.

On April 4, Tiger and Mark O'Meara each drive a cart onto their home course, at Isleworth Golf & Country Club. For today's practice round, they'll flip the course, playing the back nine first. Tiger warms up quickly, makes a string of birdies on 11, 12, 14, 15, 16, and 17—interrupted only by an eagle on 13—then birdies again on 1.

Sixty miles to the east, the space shuttle *Columbia* is on the launchpad at Cape Canaveral. At 2:20 p.m., NASA achieves launch of what's meant to be a sixteen-day science mission.

On the par-five 3rd, Tiger selects a 3-iron.

Just then, he notices the *Columbia* taking off. It's a thrilling sight; he's still new to the area and has never seen a shuttle launch before. "I had been interested in the space program since I was a kid, and I often read about NASA's missions," he notes, so it's "pretty cool" to watch the boosters come off and see the smoke from the contrails. *Here I am, playing golf while seven astronauts have just taken off in a space shuttle*, he marvels. *What an accomplishment.*

Piloting the shuttle is rookie astronaut Susan Still. The engineering achievement appeals to Tiger, the twenty-one-year-old science enthusiast—"I felt both small by comparison to space travel, and in awe of what man could achieve"—but NASA's impressive display doesn't improve his score on the hole. He makes par.

It's a momentary distraction. "I still shot 59," Tiger says. The score is an Isleworth course record. "I designed the course," Arnold Palmer says, "so I certainly knew how good a 13-under-par 59 was on the 7,179-yard layout."

Before there's time for the scorecard to be framed and hung in the clubhouse, Tiger and O'Meara are back out on the course the next day. On April 5, they repeat the previous day's round, once again starting on the back nine. O'Meara watches as Tiger birdies the 10th.

At the 11th, Tiger "gets up to the tee, he's hitting like an 8-iron," O'Meara says. "I haven't even gotten out of my cart, but he hits it and it's going right at it. It one-hops and goes into the hole" for a hole in one.

After two holes, Tiger is already 3 under par. O'Meara's hit his pain point. *This is crazy. You shoot 59, and now you make a hole in one. I'm outta here.* He takes a $100 bill and puts it on the seat of Tiger's golf cart.

"That was a really nice shot," O'Meara tells his friend. "I quit. I'll see you later on the driving range when you get done."

As Tiger says afterward, "It was a helluva two days."

Chapter 32

The 61st Masters
Augusta National Golf Club
Augusta, Georgia
April 5–8, 1997

At a postsurgical checkup with his cardiologist at UCLA, Earl doesn't like what he hears. It's too soon in his recovery to risk a cross-country flight, he's told.

"Screw that," Earl says. "I'm going to watch my son."

Tiger's status as the heavy favorite in the 1997 Masters is the number one topic in sports. "For months," says CBS announcer Jim Nantz, "everybody felt like the coronation was coming at Augusta."

"He's playing really well, but Augusta takes a lot of local knowledge," two-time U.S. Open winner Curtis Strange says, ticking off the various reservations he's heard leveled against Tiger. "It's a veteran's tournament. It's a veteran's golf course. This kid is young. He's really still inexperienced in major championships."

The sports talk radio station near Paul Azinger's home in western Florida jumps into the mix. Thirty-seven-year-old Azinger is the 1993 PGA Championship winner and a recent cancer survivor making his way back onto leaderboards.

"What has Tiger Woods done to be the favorite?" the announcer says. "C'mon, there's a better chance he'll miss the cut."

It's true that Tiger missed the 1996 cut, back when it was his U.S. Amateur title that secured his place at the tournament.

Azinger disagrees with the trash talk. He calls in to the radio show, and though he's sure the local announcer will recognize his voice, makes no attempt to disguise it as he takes the radio host to task.

"You have it wrong," Azinger says. "Not only could Tiger win, but he could win by a lot."

Tiger's only the fourth Black man to ever play in the Masters.

It's not for lack of trying.

"I never will set foot inside that place," Charlie Sifford says of Augusta National Golf Club.

Sifford hasn't forgiven Augusta National for blocking his 1967 and 1969 PGA Tour wins from qualifying for those previous Masters. It wasn't until 1972 that the club changed its rules to ensure that all PGA Tour winners receive an automatic invite.

"He did everything that was required," Sifford's son Charlie junior says of his dad, "and they kept changing the requirements."

It's not until April 10, 1975, that the first Black golfer to ever compete in a Masters tournament walks onto the course for his 11:15 a.m. tee time.

Lee Elder is a forty-year-old US Army vet who's had his PGA Tour card since the 1968 season. His first PGA Tour win, at the 1974 Monsanto Open, qualifies him for the 1975 Masters.

Elder's appearance in Augusta that spring—at a club that would not admit its first Black member for another fifteen years—was the latest step in a long, slow series of advancements for Black golfers.

"I'll never forget the ride down Magnolia Lane," Elder tells *Golf Digest*. "Some of the players had told me how it felt, but I wasn't prepared for it. When we turned down that cobblestone road, I started to shake."

For his opening round that Thursday, Elder dresses from head to toe in green clothing—green shirt, green sweater, green trousers—hoping to add a Masters Green Jacket to the ensemble. "This happens to be one of my favorite colors," he notes. "My wife suggested I wear it rather than wait until Sunday."

Around a hundred Black supporters have turned out to cheer for Elder, including Hall of Fame football player Jim Brown, here to watch his friend and fellow athlete "compete in the best tournament in the world," which Brown says is "not only important to Lee or to black players, it's also important for all qualified people."

Many in the gallery are wearing GOOD LUCK LEE buttons, and the boost helps calm Elder's nerves. So does reflecting on the encouragement he's received from other Black sports mentors—especially heavyweight boxing champ (and self-described "golf junkie") Joe Louis as well as Teddy Rhodes, the dominating champion of the all-Black United Golfers Association in the 1940s and 1950s, considered the first Black professional golfer. Louis acted as Rhodes's patron, and Rhodes in turn hired Elder to be his traveling caddie. "Whatever has happened to me in bigtime golf, and whatever success I attain eventually, I owe to Ted Rhodes," says Elder. "He took me under his wing when I was sixteen years old and completely re-built my golf game and my life."

In 1948, Rhodes unsuccessfully petitioned the PGA to remove its "Caucasian only" clause; he's retired by the time Sifford and others finally manage to get it rescinded, in 1961. Elder is the first Black player to benefit from the new Masters rules.

It's not enough to earn Lee Elder a win in 1975, though. He's cut after the second round.

"See you down the road," he tells reporters, fulfilling his prediction by making it to the Masters five more times between 1975 and 1981, including a top-twenty finish in 1979.

In 1980, Calvin Peete becomes the second Black golfer to qualify, repeating the feat seven more times, scoring as high as eleventh in 1986. Jimmy Lee Thorpe follows in 1982, with six Masters appearances between then and 1988 (his best score also a top-twenty finish, in 1985).

It's been nine years since a Black man played in the Masters.

None has yet cracked the top ten.

Like Tiger in 1995, Peete faced backlash for saying of the Masters, "It's just another tournament"—but there's no denying the specter of race hanging over the club's history. Until the last two decades, Black faces were only visible in staff roles: caddies, waiters, attendants. In 1983, Peete snapped at one nosy reporter, "To ask a black man how he feels about the traditions of the Masters is like asking him how he feels about his forefathers, who were slaves."

Sometimes the bigotry is more overt. Lee Elder was subjected to harassing notes and calls, even death threats, before and during his first Masters appearance. It's similar to what Hank Aaron experienced when he was in the process of breaking Babe Ruth's all-time home-run record in baseball.

"I wasn't heckled, but I received strong letters," says Elder. "I saved every one of them."

Elder and Tiger have that in common. In 1995, after he'd first played Augusta as an amateur, an envelope addressed to Tiger traveled across the country—postmarked in Florida, mailed to Augusta National, then forwarded to Cypress, California, where Tida opened it on her son's behalf, since he was away at Stanford.

The anonymous sender used a typewriter to compose a single nasty sentence:

"Just what we don't need, another nigger in sports."

Tiger has kept this letter for two years. It's been nearly fifty since Jackie

Robinson broke the racial barrier in professional baseball. Tiger could do the same at Augusta National.

I've filed everything away. I've played practice rounds with Nicklaus, Palmer, Floyd, Couples, and Norman, guys who have had a lot of success here. I've been lucky enough to pick their brains.

Just don't screw it up, Tiger tells himself.

Chapter 33

The 61st Masters
Augusta National Golf Club
Augusta, Georgia
April 9, 1997

No golf course places a greater premium on putting than Augusta National and its hyperfast roller-coaster greens.

What's going on here? Tiger asks himself. In three days of practice rounds, a crucial element of his game is off. *All of a sudden I've lost my putting. I just completely lost my feel.*

It's Wednesday, close to midnight, and the house Tiger has rented in town is uncomfortably quiet. Tida and Earl are both staying here—as are Earl's physician and two of Tiger's good friends, his childhood buddy Mike Gout and his former Stanford teammate Jerry Chang, who've been accompanying Tiger to various tournaments, including a February trip to the Asian Honda Classic, in Bangkok, Thailand, which Tiger won by ten strokes.

The camaraderie is something that Tiger—who's missing what would be his junior year in college—has always appreciated about his old friends and teammates. "It felt like we were back in college," Tiger says about having his buddies with him. "We had plenty of heated Ping-Pong games, and we also played video games and shot some hoops out back."

But what he needs tonight is his dad's advice.

From the foyer, Tiger can see a band of light beneath Earl's door. He pulls his putter from his bag, grabs three balls, and climbs the stairs.

Earl is dozing, but he rouses to observe Tiger's putting stance.

"How do you like my stroke, Pop?"

"I don't."

"What's wrong with it?"

"Your hands are too low," directs Earl from the bed. "Lift them up — get that little arch in your hands like you always do."

The first professional golfer to ever earn a "verdant green" (Pantone 342) jacket at Augusta National was Sam Snead in 1949. The color was chosen by legendary golfer Bobby Jones, who personally handed the distinctive wool-and-polyester jacket to Snead.

The jackets, though hardly fashionable or luxurious, are now the most coveted item of clothing in all of professional golf. Last year's champion, Nick Faldo, has won three (1989, 1990, 1996) and is aiming for a fourth.

Tradition dictates that the reigning Masters winner is paired with the reigning U.S. Amateur champion, so even though Tiger's been a professional golfer for more than half a year now, he and Faldo are matched on April 10 in the first round of the 1997 Masters.

"He's good for us 39, 40-year-olds," Faldo told reporters about Tiger last October, before the TOUR Championship. "We have to do some extra pushups and situps to get to feeling like a 20-year-old again."

By April, Faldo's feeling a little less charitable about the media's obsession. "Going in, it was, 'What do you think of Tiger?'" Faldo says. "It was unbelievable. It was so total Tiger it was annoying. He came in with such major attention."

Faldo has held the number one PGA ranking for ninety-seven straight weeks, yet it's the rookie who arrives surrounded by a security force of eight policemen.

It's an exciting matchup for spectators. But on the front nine, neither plays well.

Faldo shoots a 5-over 41. Tiger bogeys four of the first nine holes for 40. "You know, I felt a little out of sync," Tiger tells Butch Harmon.

Mark O'Meara is coming off the 15th when he finds Tiger sitting on a bench.

O'Meara takes a seat next to his friend and asks a serious question. "Really?"

"Yeah, what?" Tiger replies.

"Dude, what's going on, man?" O'Meara says. "You never play like this when you play with me at home. All you need to do is pretend like you're playing against me. You shoot 59, you make birdies, you make holes-in-one. I mean, gimme a break."

Fluff Cowan simply reminds Tiger that it's only the front nine. "There's a long way to go in this golf tournament," the experienced caddie tells him. "Just hang in there, see if we can shoot something under par in the second nine, and we'll be alright."

Harmon sees Tiger's initial struggles as a needed wake-up call. "It was kind of a slap in the face, like, 'Hey, you're this great player, but this course isn't just going to let you take it. You've got to go out and earn this.' "

On the 10th, Tiger quiets his mental state, telling himself to let go of the excess force he'd been exerting on his swing and reminding himself that "you can't think and swing at the same time." *That was no way to play—to really play golf. I needed the freedom that comes with* playing. He tries to recall the sensations in his body from when he shot that perfect game at Isleworth. *Just stick with this for nine holes and see if we can get back to even par. Just get to even par somehow.*

Slowly Tiger raises his level on the back nine, hole by hole, eventually making eagle on the 15th and ending his first round with a 70. He "went out in 40 and back in 30," comments Faldo, who finishes five back of his playing partner with a 75 and realizes the "special day" he's witnessing—"the real beginning of Tigermania," he says. "It was quite something."

Jerry Chang and Earl watch the round from the TV in the rental house, then Chang—who's acting as driver for the week—comes to pick Tiger up at the clubhouse. On the way back to the house with Mike Gout, the three stop at the Arby's drive-through for some beef-and-cheddar sandwiches, then it's back to the "fraternity-type atmosphere" at the house, with games of Ping-Pong and h-o-r-s-e to keep their buddy loose. Tiger is on fire; he wins every game.

On Friday, Tiger pairs with Paul Azinger in the second round.

Let's just see what this guy's all about, Azinger thinks—until he sees Tiger tee off on the second hole. "It was the most dead-straight rocket tee shot I'd ever seen in my life."

On the back nine, Tiger drills his eagle putt on 13 and moves to the top of the leaderboard. As he steps to the 14th, CBS announcer Jim Nantz checks his watch and announces, "Let the record show, a little after 5:30 on this Friday, April the 11th, Tiger takes the lead for the very first time ever at the Masters." *This is going to happen a whole lot,* Nantz suspects. *Mark that point in history.*

Tiger posts a 66 for a two-round score of 136 and a three-shot lead.

"To succeed [on Tour], you have to drive the ball well. You have to make putts, and you have to be the best wedge player," Azinger says. Tiger had "all three. Even if he missed a fairway, he hit it a mile."

Every night, Jerry Chang and Mike Gout pick Tiger up and take him to Arby's, where they order more beef-and-cheddar sandwiches. "The boys were superstitious," Tiger claims. "I didn't argue." The repetition is working.

"The only thing I want is a green jacket in my closet," Tiger tells reporters when asked if he's aiming to break the tournament's 72-hole record. "I told my pop before we started I thought someone would make a run, shoot a 66 at the worst because the greens are soft and you can attack."

On Saturday, April 12, Scottish golfer Colin Montgomerie is Tiger's third Masters playing partner. "The pressure is mounting more and more," Montgomerie says, believing that Tiger's lead will crumble. "I've got more experience, a lot more experience, in major championships than he has."

But Montgomerie's third-round 74 doesn't come close to Tiger's 65, which puts him at 15 under par and nine strokes ahead of the current second-place contender, Costantino Rocca, from Italy.

"I thought I would beat him," Montgomerie says. "I was wrong." The Scotsman is now a believer. "There is no chance that it is humanly possible that Tiger will lose this tournament. No way."

Chapter 34

The 61st Masters
Augusta National Golf Club
Augusta, Georgia
April 13, 1997

In the locker room, Tiger reads a message.

"Play the course," it says. "Don't listen to others. You know when to go for the pins and when not to go."

It's a fax from "Grandpa Charlie" Sifford, the latest in a tradition that began when Tiger first played Augusta National, in 1995.

Sifford's been keeping a close eye on his surrogate grandson from afar, watching the tournament on TV from his home in Humble, Texas.

"I've been a golf fan for close to 74 years," he tells a reporter. "Why would I miss it now, of all times?"

Tiger may be only twenty-one, but on the eve of the biggest moment of his life, he's more resolute than he has ever been. "He was determined," Sifford says. "He wasn't going to let nothin' get in his way."

Neither will Lee Elder. The first Black golfer to play the Masters—in 1975, the year Tiger was born—pushes his rental car to eighty-five miles an hour from the airport in Atlanta to Augusta National, collecting a speeding ticket on the way.

The Georgia State Patrol officer who writes the ticket is unmoved by Elder's tale of history in the making. "He didn't know anything about golf," Elder says. "I couldn't believe it."

But Elder doesn't care about the ticket as long as he makes it in time to watch Tiger.

"Nothing was going to stop me from getting here," Elder says. "I made history here, and I came here today to see more history made. After today, no one will turn their head when a Black man walks to the first tee."

He manages to get there in time to catch Tiger on the practice range and wish him well.

"I tried and Charlie tried and Jim Thorpe tried," Elder reflects. "We were just a little before our time. Now, the time is right for a black man to win a major. The doors are all open."

Forty-year-old Costantino Rocca is an Italian veteran of the European tour who played against Tiger at the U.S. Open at Oakland Hills when Tiger was an amateur. This is the third Masters for both, but the crowds clearly want Tiger to win today. "I don't know if anyone remembered I was on the golf course," says Rocca. "It was good for him, not for me."

As they make the turn onto the back nine, Tiger holds a nine-stroke lead. Still, he maintains focus. "I saw only the hole I was playing and felt only the shots I had in mind."

"Ti-ger, Ti-ger," the spectators call out as he walks up the fairways. But he focuses on no one at all.

"I knew Mom was following every shot, but I didn't see her," Tiger recalls. "She's only about five feet tall, but I doubt I'd have spotted her even if she were taller. I didn't see Phil Knight from Nike or Lee Elder."

He hasn't seen Earl yet, but he knows Jerry Chang made sure to get him there by the 15th hole, and his proud dad is already in the press tent giving interviews.

"This is a culmination of a lot of hard work, years and years of training, dreams," an emotional Earl tells reporters. "It's now turned into reality."

Watching Tiger's inevitable win from home in Texas, Charlie Sifford is emotional, too. "When he was walking up 18, I shed a few tears. I felt like I was a part of him. He did what I wanted to do, but I didn't have a chance; I was too doggone old."

On the 18th, Tiger spots Lee Elder near the green, and standing behind it are both his parents, clapping and smiling. There's no question now that he'll win—but if he can two-putt, he'll also break some records.

I enjoyed the rush of having everything on the line, he reminisces later. *I liked having a putt to win. It was on me. To me, that was fun.*

Tiger wins with a fourth-round 69, twelve ahead of 1992 U.S. Open winner Tom Kite, and an incredible 18 under par for the tournament.

The twenty-one-year-old has made his mark:

- He is the youngest golfer ever to win the Masters.
- His score of 270 breaks the record for lowest 72-hole score ever at the Masters.
- His twelve-shot win is the largest margin of victory in any major championship.
- He is the first Black man ever to win the Masters.

"It means so much," Tiger says. "I'm the first, but I wasn't the pioneer. Charlie Sifford, Lee Elder, Teddy Rhodes, those guys paved the way for me to be here. I thank them. If it wasn't for them, I might not have had the chance to play here."

"For him to acknowledge me, Charlie Sifford and Teddy Rhodes was tremendous," says Elder, whom the new champion stops to embrace on his way to Butler Cabin. "Tiger Woods isn't like any other golfer," Elder adds. "Him winning this major event like this, I think it's just like what Jackie Robinson did."

Chapter 35

Byron Nelson Golf Classic
TPC Four Seasons Resort
Irving, Texas
May 15–18, 1997

W hat's the old saying? Winning never gets old?"
      Tiger grins as he talks to the press while holding the winner's
trophy at the Byron Nelson Golf Classic in Texas. His fifth victory in sixteen tournaments as a pro comes a month after his record-setting win at
the Masters.

The crowds have been so massive—one hundred thousand day
badges and fifty thousand weekly passes—that *Sports Illustrated* casts
around for a new way to label the phenomenon: "What started as Tigermania has evolved into something else. Tigerfrenzy? Tigerhysteria? How
about Tigershock?"

"Wherever Tiger goes in the world, it's like the Beatles have landed,"
says his agent, Hughes Norton.

Tiger's final score of 263, 17 under par, matches the record set by Ernie
Els two years earlier, though it comes as no surprise to the eighty-five-
year-old tournament namesake, Byron Nelson, a record-setting golfer in
the 1940s with fifty-two career victories who once won eleven in a row.

Nelson's had his eye on Tiger for years. "He was the best 15-year-old player I had ever seen," he says. "He was the best at 16 and 17 and so on. He's the best 21-year-old player anyone has ever seen. If he keeps getting better, oh boy. I'm not sure golf has seen anything like him before."

"I keep telling you guys, this is just the start," Tiger's swing coach, Butch Harmon, says to reporters. "It's going to get better, it's going to get better."

Still, there are a few hairline cracks showing. Harmon had been in Houston on Saturday when he spotted something off with Tiger's swing on TV.

"He was backing up on his tee shots and flipping his hands through. He missed a few drives left," Harmon says. He calls Tiger. "I see something in your driver swing. Get me a room in Dallas, and I'll drive there tonight."

Harmon travels the three and a half hours to show him in person.

"Thanks, Butchie. I got it. I appreciate you coming," Tiger tells him after they work things out on the driving range the next morning. He's feeling confident. "Don't worry, I'll win today," he says.

He does.

"But what amazed me," Harmon says, "was, from the first tee that day, he never made the mistake he was making the day before. He committed 100 percent to what we worked on that morning, and he drove the ball beautifully."

What Harmon doesn't know, however, is that a total overhaul is on the horizon.

Tiger Woods sits in a darkened room at the Golf Channel studios, wincing at the images on the TV monitor.

By any objective measure, Tiger's on a historic roll. In June of 1997, shortly after his win in Texas, he takes the number one spot on the Official World Golf Ranking. Not only that, but it's also been a mere 291 days since he became a professional—yet another record-setting achievement, this time for fastest ascent to number one.

And yet: something is bothering him. His swing feels out of sync. Tiger makes the short drive from Isleworth to Orlando to watch the tapes of his Masters win. Far from banishing his concerns, revisiting his most seemingly invincible performance does the opposite.

"I saw some of my swings on videotape and thought, God almighty, I won, but only because I had a great timing week. Anyone can do that. To play consistently from the positions my swing was in was going to be very difficult to do," Tiger explains.

As he studies the video and freezes his swing at various points in its arc, he sees only flaws. At the top of his backswing, the clubface is closed and the shaft crosses the line, meaning that it points well right of the target. Distance control on his short irons is inconsistent, and overall his swing seems too handsy through the ball. Before leaving the room, Tiger makes a list of ten or twelve things that he wants to correct.

You know what? I know I can take it to a new level. Tear it down and build it back up, Tiger thinks.

When he calls his swing coach, Butch Harmon tries to assure Tiger that whatever flaws he thinks he's found are minor. When it comes to golf swings, Harmon knows that the pursuit of perfection is dangerous. He's seen too many golfers get lost on their quests for improvement and never find their way back. *Look at your results,* he urges Tiger. *Let's not go crazy.*

But Tiger is talking about a significantly new and different swing: *Less sidespin, less backspin. More control. Simpler. Tighter. Repeatable. A machine hardwired to make the same move again and again. A swing that won't get stuck.*

He wants a complete overhaul.

He's looking to install a weaker grip.

Modify the takeaway.

Shorten and reshape the overall arc.

Adjust his hand position at the top.

The best golfer in the world wants to build a better golf swing. For an athlete at the very top of his game to revamp his fundamentals is unprecedented and borderline insane. Harmon keeps urging caution, one small adjustment at a time. Tiger keeps pushing back. *We'll do the whole menu now.*

Harmon issues a warning. "It's not going to be easy for you to make this change and still play through it." A new swing is a little like an organ transplant — the body's initial reaction is to reject it. Old positions ingrained by hundreds of thousands of repetitions have to be unlearned the same way.

But Tiger isn't concerned. He's twenty-one. He has all the time in the world. Plus, thanks to having just won the Masters, he's got a ten-year tour exemption.

He's not scared of change, not in the name of improvement.

"When I first changed my game drastically, I won three U.S. Juniors in a row, something no one else had ever done," Tiger points out. Then, when he started working with Butch Harmon, he told him, *I want a new game.* "I knew I needed to improve. We tore down my swing, rebuilt it, and I won three U.S. Amateurs."

The ideas and vision conceived in that darkened Orlando studio are Tiger's and Tiger's alone.

PART 4

Superstar

Chapter 36

Kennedy Center Concert Hall
Washington, DC
November 9, 1998

I f you look at my W [wins] column," Tiger says more than a year after reworking his swing, "it's not that great."

Though he's finished in the top twenty at every major championship over the last year—including third place at the British Open—Tiger claimed his sole tournament victory in Georgia, at the BellSouth Classic, in May of 1998. On the cover of this year's *Sports Illustrated* Masters Preview edition, his picture appeared behind that of a white Bengal tiger alongside the words "After a long dry spell, Tiger says he's hungry for another Masters win." That wish did not come true.

"A lot of expectations were placed upon me," he continues. "My life has changed a lot since I won the Masters...From that point on, it hasn't been the same. It's been hard to adjust to."

Even so, Tiger is number one in the rankings when the 1998 PGA Tour ends, on November 1. A week into the offseason, he and Earl lead off the Nation's Capital Distinguished Speaker Series before a Kennedy Center audience of two thousand—not the typical golf gallery.

IMG's Mark McCormack moderates the discussion, presented by the

Greater Washington Society of Association Executives. No one in the business-savvy crowd is surprised to see the agency head appearing with its lead client—especially so close to the recent shake-up within IMG's golf division.

Tiger has "severed his relationship" with agent Hughes Norton, though he plans to remain with IMG.

A headline in the *Los Angeles Times* last month reads: BEING FIRED IS NORTON'S REWARD FOR MAKING WOODS RICH. The October 16 article highlighted the $120 million in endorsement deals Hughes Norton inked for Tiger since he turned pro, in October of 1996. Tiger "earns more than any other athlete in the world, including Michael Jordan," Norton said, referring to the golf star's income from a range of gold-standard brands, including Nike, Titleist, American Express, Rolex, and Wheaties.

"According to sources," Jaime Diaz of *Sports Illustrated* says, Tiger "felt he had been overcommitted in business deals, and had lost faith in the direction Norton wanted to take him."

Or, as Earl puts it, "The decision came down to a fundamental difference. For Hughes, the dollar is almighty. For Tiger, money is not that important. And Hughes underestimated Tiger's personal growth and his grasp of his own business."

Tiger chooses Mark Steinberg, a member of the Flyin' Illini 1989 Final Four basketball team, as his new agent. Steinberg has come up through IMG's women's golf division, representing Annika Sörenstam of the LPGA.

"We'll do well together" is Tiger's assessment. He tells Steinberg, "Always be true to me and tell me what I need to hear, not what I want to hear."

On one of their first outings together, Steinberg accompanies Tiger to an event in London, where the agent finds himself contending with "thousands of people screaming Tiger's name, trying to touch him or just trying to see him."

Just making their way into the back seat of the car is a physical struggle.

"Welcome to my world," Tiger tells him. "Until you've seen it, you can't possibly understand it."

At the event in Washington, DC, Tiger jokes that no one is looking for his autograph. "I haven't been winning. No one knows who I am." Despite holding the number one world ranking for all but a few weeks since June of 1997, almost a year and a half now, he's only had that one tour win—the BellSouth Classic—in all of 1998.

He's undeterred. "I've got a very long road ahead of me" is the way he describes his attitude. "I know I'm on the right track, but sometimes it takes longer to show than you'd like."

Still, fans and sports reporters lament "the new Woods," who, *Sports Illustrated* says, "produced a listless defense in the 1998 Masters, finishing six shots behind winner Mark O'Meara in an event he won by 12 strokes the year before." With "only one PGA Tour victory since July '97," and despite remaining "the most consistent high finisher and charismatic figure in the game," Tiger caused some "to wonder whether his career would turn out to be a major disappointment."

A string of losses is one reason a player parts ways with his caddie. The 1999 PGA Tour opens with speculation that the relationship between Tiger and Mike "Fluff" Cowan has soured.

Cowan's the rare caddie to achieve his own celebrity, fueled in part by Tiger's earlier declaration: "I think Fluff's the best caddie in the world."

On January 19, 1999, Cowan is in St. Augustine, Florida, wrapping a national TV spot for the Golf Channel. The script has Cowan greeting visitors to the World Golf Hall of Fame with instructional tips.

Tiger has a tip of his own for Cowan: get glasses. Cowan wears a pair to a tournament, saying, "My man thinks I need them."

"Is there friction? Yes," admits Butch Harmon. "They have some issues to work out. But it's nothing more than what goes on with players and caddies all the time."

But it may be more significant than that.

The financial arrangements between players and caddies are closely guarded—a weekly subsidy plus a cut of the player's prize money, up to 10 percent of a championship check.

Two years ago, *Sports Illustrated* quoted Cowan telling Tiger, "I want ten percent on wins," four weeks after they started working together, in October of 1996. "And you are gonna win real soon," the caddie predicted.

A more recent interview Cowan gives to *Golf Digest* discussing his and Tiger's current terms is published in the midst of a season when players are pushing back against the traditional pay scale by firing longtime caddies and replacing them with others willing to work for a higher weekly rate and a lower take of winnings.

One top caddie anonymously tells the *Washington Post,* "A lot of guys are running a little scared, and right now, it's probably best not to see your name in the paper."

When Tiger flies to San Diego to play the Buick Invitational at Torrey Pines in early February, Cowan doesn't make the trip. Instead, Tiger invites his childhood friend Bryon Bell—who's caddied for him before, most notably when Tiger won his third consecutive U.S. Amateur—to carry his bag. Tiger explains to the *New York Times* that he was giving Bell a money-earning opportunity to pay his medical school tuition. And on February 14, Tiger delivers, winning the Buick Invitational and its top prize of $486,000.

Bell notes some changes in his friend. "He hits the ball a lot shorter, especially with his irons, and under more control," Bell tells reporter Jaime Diaz. "But I sensed he had some doubt in his own ability. I've never really had to encourage Tiger, but I felt like I had to this week."

Tiger downplays Bell's concerns but appreciates his pal's support. "I respect Bryon more as a friend than as a caddie," Tiger says. "He knows my game, but more important, he knows me."

Even more significantly, Tiger is tightening his inner circle.

Two other caddies insist on anonymity when they talk to *Golf World* about what they saw and overheard at the Nissan Open in Los Angeles the week after the Buick Invitational: Tiger and Cowan spotted in a heated argument. "And I'll tell you something else," one of the caddies says. "Tiger did his own yardage book at LA, and when that happens it's a bad sign for the caddie." On February 21, Tiger finishes the tournament 12 under par and tied for second.

The Doral-Ryder Open is next on the PGA Tour schedule. Tiger withdraws, looking ahead two weeks to the Bay Hill Invitational. Reporters ask whether Cowan will caddie for him on Arnold Palmer's course in Orlando.

Tiger gives a short answer. "Probably."

Thirty-five-year-old New Zealand caddie Steve Williams arrives in Miami for the Doral-Ryder Open. Williams began his career with Greg Norman in the 1980s but has been caddying for Raymond Floyd for the last ten years.

The hotel phone rings. It's late, around 9:30 p.m., but Williams picks up.

"Tiger Woods here," a familiar voice says.

Williams is sure it's his friend Bob, who has a talent for celebrity impressions. He knows that Tiger Woods isn't even playing in the Doral-Ryder Open. "Look, Bob, I'm tired, give me a ring tomorrow, I've just flown in from New Zealand."

As soon as Williams hangs up, the phone rings again.

Maybe it's not Bob, Williams thinks.

It isn't.

Tiger is amused by Williams's skepticism and considers it a "pretty good start."

"Steve, I'm looking for a caddie. Are you interested?" Tiger asks. It's no secret that Tiger and Cowan are splitting up, but Williams is still surprised at the approach. He's actually been thinking about retiring from caddying next year, had already told Floyd that he'd probably be done in 2000.

That idea is soon jettisoned. He gets off the phone with Tiger with a plan to meet the following day at "dawn-thirty"—a half hour after sunrise—to hit some balls.

"Mike and I are friends, and we will always be friends," Tiger tells the *New York Times* on March 3. On March 8, the split is confirmed.

The following week, Steve Williams steps in to caddie for Tiger at the Bay Hill Invitational. But on this first outing together, Williams is hardly impressed by Tiger's 2-over tie for fifty-sixth or his $5,625 in prize money.

"Mate, I don't know what all the fuss is about—you're overrated," Williams says, trash-talking his new boss when Tiger misses an easy wedge shot on the 13th. "That's probably the worst shot I've seen from a golf professional from that sort of a distance."

Tiger laughs.

"Tiger, he loved that," reflects Williams. "He probably used those sorts of comments as motivation."

Cowan is back on the bag in time to make the 1999 Masters with another pro, Jim Furyk, who's won five events on the PGA Tour.

"I needed somebody, and he's the best available," Furyk says. "I'd have been an idiot not to give Mike a call."

As for Cowan, he's not complaining. "I can tell you it's a lot easier not being around Tiger," he tells the *Washington Post*. "I've yet to have anyone come up to me and say, 'Hey, Fluff, can you get me Jim Furyk's autograph?'"

Chapter 37

Isleworth Golf & Country Club
Windermere, Florida
Spring 1999

W
hat do you do to talk to girls?" Tiger asks Michael Jordan after witnessing how easily Jordan and New York Yankees superstar shortstop Derek Jeter work their way around a nightclub they've been to together, chatting up beautiful women.

Jordan and Jeter are taken aback. *Go tell 'em you're Tiger Woods,* they say.

Being popular with women has been an adjustment for Tiger. Not that he's a complete novice—he had girlfriends in high school and in college—but suddenly he's become the kind of celebrity jock that women flock to: a boldface name and bona fide sex symbol, especially now that he's put on around twenty pounds of muscle, courtesy of his devotion to morning runs and weight lifting.

Tiger's celebrity status extends well beyond the echelons of golf. As he jokes with reporters, "I'm not proud of it, but I lead the Tour in *National Enquirer* covers"—such as the one showing him dancing with a busty blonde, accompanied by the memorable headline TIGER'S WILD NIGHT WITH TOPLESS DANCER.

"What I don't like is that the stuff inside is not true," Tiger complains to ESPN reporter Stuart Scott.

"But being linked to Tyra Banks...there are worse things to be on the cover for," Scott replies.

Truly, Tiger isn't *that* upset about being associated with the supermodel, telling Scott, "I don't even worry about it. I have my girlfriend and I am happy just being with her."

Who is this mystery girlfriend? The public wants to know. Though visibly at Tiger's side, she shies away from the spotlight—which Tiger appreciates enormously.

Her name is Joanna Jagoda, and she's attractive, athletic, tall, and blond—very much Tiger's type. A native of Poland who grew up in California and speaks five languages, Jagoda recently graduated from the University of California at Santa Barbara with a degree in political science and plans to attend Pepperdine law school.

She and Tiger have been together for around a year, introduced by Tiger's friend Bryon Bell, who was dating one of Jagoda's Pi Beta Phi sorority sisters and brought Tiger to a party at UCSB after the 1998 Nissan Open. That was in March. Jagoda's first seen accompanying Tiger at the 1998 Byron Nelson Golf Classic in mid-May and since then has been a mainstay at all his tournaments.

Jagoda is good-looking and well liked by both Tiger's inner circle and his professional colleagues, respected for her ability to be simultaneously polite, discreet, and down-to-earth. Golf Channel pundit Peter Kessler calls Jagoda Tiger's "secret weapon," someone he does everything he can to protect from the intrusive press—"the wolves of the golfing circuit," in the words of a tour source. Tiger welcomes the sense of calm and normalcy Jagoda brings, saying, "I like my life right where it is right now. It's a wonderful balance."

Tiger still lives like a college kid at his place in Florida, a relatively normal yet messy two-bedroom house where his Masters trophy shares space with fast-food wrappers and kitschy paraphernalia, including a giant toy ape. "It's not what everyone has reported, this *mansion*," he says disdainfully. "It's interesting. People know more about my life than I do." He spends his downtime reading books, playing video games, and watching *SportsCenter* or the Discovery Channel. He's also got a souped-up golf cart with a seven-speaker sound system. "Try it," he tells a *Golf Digest* reporter. "Turn it up loud and the seat vibrates."

In addition to his place in Florida, Tiger now has "his bachelor house," a condo in Manhattan Beach, California, that his mother holds at arm's length. The woman who was so attached to her young son that she never once used a babysitter has spent the last several years trying to give him more freedom. If there was an event to attend, "I let my husband go," Tida told *Sports Illustrated* back in 1995. "I stay with Tiger. Tiger more important than a party."

She says now, "Do you want Mom to be around to see the things that you don't want her to see? I understand him. I don't bother him; I leave him alone. But his Rat Pack"—as she refers to Tiger's longtime pals such as Bryon Bell, Jerry Chang, and Notah Begay III—"his Rat Pack goes down and enjoys."

Discretion is the trait Tiger values most in his inner circle. And loyalty—though that can be a one-way street. "Very tough, unemotional, very cold," is the verdict on how Tiger ends relationships, business or otherwise. "Tiger coldly cuts through and moves on."

He's very much like his mother in that way. "When Tiger says no, don't ever go ask him again—that's it," Tida says of her son.

Earl is the emotional one in their family. "In my culture we don't show that. It not proper. You lose face," Tida says, comparing herself to Earl. "He's Green Beret and all," Tida says with a laugh, "but he's more compassionate than I am. Tiger's personality is more like mine than Dad's.

"I am a loner, and so is Tiger," she says. "We don't waste time with people we don't like."

Chapter 38

Byron Nelson Golf Classic
TPC Four Seasons Resort
Irving, Texas
May 13–16, 1999

On a perfect spring day, Tiger plays a nearly perfect game. He shoots a first-round 61—including nine birdies and zero bogeys—his lowest-scoring round in a PGA tournament.

According to the Associated Press, the soft greens and sunny, windless sky make for an "easy scoring day in Texas." Finishing one stroke behind Tiger is Sergio "El Niño" Garcia, a nineteen-year-old Spanish golfer who, inspired by five-time major winner Seve Ballesteros, started playing at age three and is making his pro debut in America.

"It's always fun when you can really get it going like this," Tiger says.

But that good feeling is one that's eluded him for the last two years.

Swing coach Butch Harmon has consistently praised Tiger for working "harder than everyone" and using his "tremendous God-given talent" to make "himself better and better." Still, Tiger's working through the kinks of his swing change. It's been a risky choice, especially for a player as gifted as Tiger. According to player-analyst Curtis Strange, "Nothing works like your God-given swing."

Tiger and Harmon's painstaking overhaul of the mechanics of his backswing, topswing, and downswing may yet prove Strange wrong. What Tiger's sacrificed in driving distance—around ten yards—he's more than gained in precision and ball control.

After signing his first-round scorecard at the Byron Nelson, Tiger places a call to the Butch Harmon School of Golf, at the Rio Secco Golf Club, in Henderson, Nevada.

"Butchie, I got it!" Tiger tells his swing coach. "It's all starting to feel natural to me."

The revelation isn't limited to golf. "I understand how things work now," he told reporters in a wide-ranging interview last month. "I understand a lot more about the [PGA] Tour, about myself. And it's a beautiful thing."

Nike has only one day with Tiger to shoot a commercial at the Orange County National Golf Center and Lodge, in Orlando, Florida. It takes top talent to film top talent. Director Lasse Hallström, whose film credits include *What's Eating Gilbert Grape* and the fall release *The Cider House Rules,* is assisted by director Doug Liman, who directed the 1996 indie hit *Swingers* and the just-released *Go.*

The May weather is seasonally hot. The script is simple: A dozen "everyday golfers" on the driving range hit balls—badly—until Tiger appears, upping their games with his presence. The moment Tiger leaves the range, though, they revert to being hackers. But the logistics of a commercial set are complicated, leaving actors and crew standing in the heat for long stretches.

I'm going to try to entertain them, Tiger thinks during a break in the shooting. He picks up his sand wedge and bounces a golf ball, as if it were a Hacky Sack, against the club's flat surface.

I went over there and just started juggling the ball and doing weird stuff, and they were entertained.

The shoot wraps, but Nike's looking for more content. "Get something of Tiger after he changed into his spring apparel for an interview with the Golf Channel," the Nike Golf general manager says to the Nike advertising director, who's on the set along with executives from Wieden+Kennedy, Nike's longtime ad agency.

After a quick conference, it's decided that Tiger's spontaneous hijinks will be perfect for the second commercial Nike wants. The assistant director, Doug Liman, hoists a camera onto his shoulder as the idea is run by Tiger. He'll need to keep up the bouncing for twenty-eight continuous seconds (plus the two seconds during which the Nike Golf logo appears on-screen). Not only is Tiger up for the challenge, he also has an idea to raise the degree of difficulty: he'll end the shot with a final move, swinging his wedge as if it were a baseball bat and smashing the ball.

Tiger's trick moves dazzle. He switches his club from one hand to the other, moving it behind his back and between his legs, all while keeping the bouncing golf ball aloft. "It's really not as hard as you might think," Tiger says. "Hand-to-eye coordination—same principle."

But he gets annoyed when the ad execs pitch in, counting down the time to Tiger's swing at the airborne ball and calling out, "OK, you got ten seconds left."

He shanks it on the first three takes.

"Don't tell me that," Tiger finally instructs them. "Just tell me when I've got three, four, five seconds. I can switch and end it."

Liman also decides to fan the flames of Tiger's competitive instincts. "I can't believe that of all people you are choking under pressure," the assistant director says.

A $100 bill is laid atop the camera along with a dare. "Tiger, I bet that you can't do it on the next one."

The Wieden+Kennedy creative director, Chuck McBride, gives the cue. The fourth take is live. And it's perfect.

Tiger pockets his $100 prize and walks off the set.

* * *

Chuck McBride sits in a New York City sports bar. It's mid-June, and the TVs are tuned to the NBA finals—New York Knicks versus San Antonio Spurs—when the "Hacky Sack" Nike commercial airs for the first time.

The noisy bar crowd is stunned into silence as they watch Tiger bounce the golf ball against his clubface. It's a feat of pure athleticism. And magic. When he drives the airborne ball two hundred yards, the sports fans cheer.

I guess we did something right here, McBride thinks.

"Obviously it was magical," the Nike Golf general manager says of the unplanned spot.

But is it real? Skeptics say of Nike, "They must have used computer animation or something in that commercial." To disprove the critics, Nike provides *Dateline NBC* with outtakes for a TV special about the making of the instantly famous spot.

Its success, says *Adweek* magazine, lies in reminding people how much they like Tiger: "Here he is as a completely liberated, unfettered talent showing his delightful kind of freaky talent."

June 20, 1999, is the date of the final round of the U.S. Open at Pinehurst. Steve Williams and Tiger arrange to meet an hour before Tiger's tee time. The caddie starts to grow concerned when his usually punctual boss is late. Five minutes pass, then ten, with no sign of Tiger at the resort in Pinehurst, North Carolina.

Finally, Tiger's car pulls into the parking lot. "Sorry I was a bit late," he says, "but I was watching this cartoon and it was a really good one that I hadn't seen before."

The twenty-three-year-old is enthusiastic about cartoons and video games—except when hackers messed with his debut video game, *Tiger Woods 99 PGA Tour Golf.*

The game, which launched in late 1998, is part of Tiger's four-year, $10 million deal with the sports division of software developer Electronic

Arts, touted as "perhaps the most highly prized deal in the history of the interactive sports industry." Of the game, which is available in both PC and PlayStation versions, Tiger had proudly announced, "I've played video and computer games for many years, but this is the first time I've ever been able to say, 'This is my game.'"

Shortly after its release, however, a listener of WFLZ-FM, in Tampa, Florida, called in to the station's morning show to report surprising content in the PlayStation version: When the game was played on a computer, an Easter egg featuring a pirated version of the curse-laden 1995 *South Park* pilot, "The Spirit of Christmas," appeared as a file choice. An engineer was ultimately found responsible for what EA described as "an unfortunate and odd thing" that forced the company to recall the first one hundred thousand copies of the game. But if anything, it goosed interest.

Excitement about Tiger's chances at the U.S. Open have also been goosed. After essentially hitting a Pause button of sorts over the last eighteen months while he's reworked his swing, Tiger has been putting better than ever, in part thanks to a heart-to-heart with Earl about technique that resulted in Tiger's returning, as he tells reporters, "to some of the fundamentals that I used to do as a kid."

"Absolutely [Tiger] can win the U.S. Open," says Mark O'Meara.

But no one's counting out Payne Stewart, who won his first U.S. Open in 1991 and who's recently returned to championship form. "Total flowing swing," NBC's lead golf announcer, Johnny Miller, says admiringly. "That does not look like a guy in his forties. That swing might last awhile."

Caddie Steve Williams focuses on Tiger, stating, "Starting the day two strokes behind Payne Stewart, this was a tournament he had a chance to win."

Early on the back nine, Phil Mickelson (who placed fifty-fifth at the U.S. Open in 1991) is tied with Stewart for the lead at Pinehurst, a course dating to 1895 and known as the Cradle of American Golf. The name seems especially apt today. Mickelson's carrying a beeper to alert him in case his wife, Amy, goes into labor with their first child.

Play continues through a steady drizzle. On 16, Stewart astonishes the crowd when he saves par with a double-breaking twenty-five-foot downhill putt. When Mickelson misses his own par putt, the two are tied for the lead. Both hit the green on the par-three 17th, Mickelson just six feet from the pin, Stewart even closer at four feet.

The gallery erupts in ground-shaking noise the scorer likens to "a small earthquake," so tumultuous that it delays Tiger's reset from bogeying 17 to driving on 18.

Making one final par putt on the 72nd hole would clinch a second U.S. Open championship for Stewart.

He lines up a fifteen-footer but initially can't bring himself to look up and actually watch the ball he's just hit until, he says, "it was about 2 feet away from the hole and breaking right into the center of the cup. I couldn't believe my eyes. I couldn't believe I had accomplished my dream."

Tiger, who ties with Vijay Singh for third (both 281 to Stewart's 279 and Mickelson's 280), notes, "I'm glad he made that putt on 18 because I'll be sleeping a little bit better tonight."

A full-scale celebration is happening on the green. Stewart's caddie, Mike Hicks, leaps into his player's arms. Stewart sheds joyful tears over his win and offers fond wishes to Mickelson, cupping the runner-up's face in both hands and saying, "Good luck with the baby. There's nothing like being a father."

Chapter 39

Medinah Country Club
Chicago, Illinois
June 29, 1999

Chicago Bulls superstar Michael Jordan, a fifty-four-hole-a-day golfer, buys a coveted "perpetual membership" in the exclusive Medinah Country Club. The official start date is August 1, but MJ has a guest with a pressing need to walk the host course of the upcoming eighty-first PGA Championship beforehand.

On June 29, Jordan and Tiger play a private practice round. The *Chicago Tribune* reports: TIGER TO HELP MJ DRILL FOR THE CHICAGO OPEN.

Tiger and Jordan first became friendly via their mutual affiliation with Nike. They'd met back on April 6, 1997, when Tiger watched the Orlando Magic lose to the visiting Chicago Bulls at Amway Arena, Jordan leading his team with thirty-seven points, eight rebounds, and five assists.

"First time I met him. It was great," Tiger said after the game, reminding curious reporters that the two Nike pitchmen might not immediately have time to play a round of golf because "Michael will be pretty busy...and so will I."

Two years on, though, they've had plenty of time to spend together.

"We talk a couple of times a week on the phone. But not a whole lot about golf," Jordan told *Golf Digest*'s Bob Verdi in 1998. Jordan recognizes the kind of pressure that Tiger's under. "Just because he hits the ball nine miles and wins the Masters by 12 strokes, he's supposed to have all the answers. He's supposed to be perfect. Believe me, I know," Jordan says.

"We call each other brothers because Michael is like the big brother. I'm like the little brother," Tiger says. "To be able to go to a person like that who has been through it all—and has come out of it just as clean as can be—that's the person you want to talk to. And on top of that, he's one great guy."

Tiger's in town ahead of the Fourth of July weekend, when he'll compete in the Motorola Western Open at the nearby Cog Hill Golf and Country Club. "Every single time I come here, I get good vibes," he says of Chicago.

He likes Medinah, too. Its 120,000-square-foot clubhouse, capped by a sixty-foot rotunda with a hand-painted mosaic ceiling, is eye-popping, but "Tiger loved the course," caddie Steve Williams says of its 7,401 yards, "because it was so long."

The property's 4,161 trees are in full summer leaf, but work on the course is ongoing. "I'm sure the rough will be higher and the fairways narrower," Tiger says. "I talked to the superintendent, and he said the PGA of America wants the course to play harder than the U.S. Open" (which NBC's Johnny Miller in June rated as "super tough").

During the practice round, which Tiger and Michael Jordan share with the tournament director, Greg McLaughlin, and Western Golf Association member Joel Hirsch, Jordan starts asking Tiger about his popular Nike ad.

"It looked like it was digitally enhanced," Jordan says, needling him.

Tiger shakes his head. "Come here, Michael," he says. On the back of the 18th, he starts bouncing a Titleist on his sand wedge, then with a grin, smashes it two hundred yards.

His playing partners are stunned. "It was the only time Michael was quiet all round," says Hirsch.

Tiger makes it look easy, just as he had in the Nike commercial.

To Titleist, the only trick photography is the Nike Golf logo that fills the screen for the final two seconds of the ad. Nike is in its first year of producing golf equipment—products that will directly compete with the Titleist balls and clubs that Tiger is paid to endorse.

The week of the Motorola Western Open, Titleist files a lawsuit in federal court, asserting that Nike's caused "irreparable harm" by suggesting that Tiger's playing with Nike equipment. "Nike is exercising rights consistent with its agreement with Tiger Woods," the company insists. The ads Tiger filmed at Orange County National Golf Center continue to run.

Medinah Country Club dates to the 1920s, and so does Cog Hill, a premier public course thirty miles southwest of Chicago where the galleries at the Western Open fill with fifty thousand people, including many grandparents and parents with children in tow, all asking the same question: "Where is Tiger Woods?"

Tiger's every move is a source of fascination. "Look, Tiger's going to the garbage can to throw out his apple core," one mother alerts her daughter. "Let's go over there and get a better look."

On July 4, twenty-three-year-old Tiger sets off more than the usual holiday fireworks when he takes the Western's top prize of $450,000. In winning the Western—now affectionately renamed Tiger's Tournament—twice in three years, he becomes the first player since 1934 to win ten pro events before his twenty-fourth birthday. He also regains his number one world ranking, which he'd ceded to rival David Duval back in March. "Being #1 in '98 and not winning wasn't that great," Tiger says. "I prefer winning."

The PGA Championship's Wanamaker Trophy, an iconic sterling silver cup, is named for its donor, Lewis Rodman Wanamaker—who in 1916 helped found the PGA—and designed by Dieges & Clust, the same New York firm famed for creating the Heisman Trophy in 1934.

The Wanamaker Trophy is among the largest in professional sports, standing twenty-eight inches high, twenty-seven inches wide, and weighing twenty-seven pounds, with the name of every winner engraved upon its silver surface.

Tiger wants his name to be next. Steve Williams wants that for him, too. Over the past five months of caddying, Williams has witnessed the PGA's top player compete in ten tournaments and win three, but the 1997 Masters, more than two years ago, remains Tiger's sole major championship win. Butch Harmon encourages him: "If you play your game, you can't be beaten. Now let's go get your second one."

The eighty-first PGA Championship is the first one to be held at Medinah. Spaniard Sergio Garcia, in only his third month as a pro, makes a third-round charge to match Tiger's third-round score of 68, bringing Garcia to 207 after fifty-four holes to Tiger's 205. The final may come down to the two youngest players in the field.

Garcia is a fierce competitor who plays by the three-word motto *Suerte o muerte,* meaning "luck or death." Given Tiger's demonstrated ability for winning when he's ahead going into the fourth round, Garcia has no choice but to go for broke.

The *Chicago Tribune* gives Tiger the edge: CALL THE ENGRAVER reads the Sunday morning headline about the blank space on the Wanamaker Trophy. Tiger's dad, Earl, travels to watch his son play.

On August 15, Tiger birdies the 2nd, opening up a four-stroke lead. On the 7th, another birdie extends his lead over Garcia to five. But when Tiger bogeys the 12th and double-bogeys the 13th, Garcia seizes his chance. The teenage phenom storms back, electrifying the crowd with his charisma and shot making. On the 16th, Garcia banana-slices the ball, curving it strongly from left to right around a tree trunk, sprinting along the arc of his shot to see the ball make a miraculous landing on the green. He then two-putts from sixty feet.

Tiger bogeys the hole. His lead is down to a single shot when, on 17, he hears a call from the gallery: "Hope you don't slice it in the water."

He doesn't, but he does miss the 17th green to the left. He needs to get up and down to save par. He studies the line from both sides, then consults with Williams.

"The line is just inside the hole," the caddie says. "Inside left."

"That's perfect." Tiger sinks the putt, looks up, and gives Williams a wink.

On the 18th, a chant rings out from the grandstand. "SER-GI-O! SER-GI-O!"

"It looks like they love me," says Garcia. "I said when I turned pro I wanted to be the No. 1 golfer in the world. So I knew I would be a rival for Tiger."

Tiger feels it, too. Garcia, he says, "has a tremendous amount of fight. You can see it in the way he plays, just the way he walks around the golf course."

Tiger knows his father is watching from afar as his five-stroke lead over Garcia shrinks to one, coming down to one last must-make putt on 18.

"He knows where I am at all times," Earl says of Tiger as he mentally wills his son, *Trust your stroke.*

Tiger makes the putt, clinching a one-stroke victory and becoming the youngest player to win two majors since Seve Ballesteros did it in 1980. When Earl comes out to embrace him, Tiger gives him a grin: "I heard you, Pop."

Chapter 40

Ryder Cup
The Country Club
Brookline, Massachusetts
September 24–26, 1999

F orget Nicklaus and Palmer," *Sports Illustrated* declares. "Woods, 23, and Garcia, 19, have the star quality of Newman and Redford."

The Ryder Cup is the Oscars of golf, a biennial competition showcasing the best in the sport from America and Europe, playing for priceless prestige and zero prize money. The golden Ryder Cup trophy stands seventeen inches tall—3.5 inches taller than an Oscar statuette.

The host course this year is the Country Club, in Brookline, Massachusetts, founded in 1882 and one of the United States Golf Association's five original clubs. Tiger will be appearing for a second time—the third Black golfer, following Lee Elder (1979) and Calvin Peete (1983, 1985), to play for America.

On September 24, Europe takes the lead in the two-day team competition, building on its 1995 and 1997 Ryder Cup wins with standout performances from seven rookie players. With a roster boasting nine of the world's top fourteen players—including Tiger, Payne Stewart, and

Phil Mickelson—pressure is mounting on the Americans, who continue to trail after the second day of team play.

The US team captain, Ben Crenshaw, is a two-time Masters winner and a Texas native. He calls a Saturday night team meeting and invites a special guest—the Texas governor, George W. Bush, who shares a passion for golf with his father, President George H. W. Bush. The governor reads aloud to the team the moving words of a soldier who served at the siege of the Alamo.

Inspiration strikes. "It shows what a number of Americans have done for this country," Phil Mickelson says. "We might not be soldiers who fight in wars, but this is something of its own and we need to fight as if we are."

To reporters, Crenshaw simply says, "I'm a big believer in fate. I have a good feeling about this. That's all I'm going to tell you." Then he gets up and leaves the media room. He hasn't done a mike drop. But it feels that way.

The individual competition draws thirty thousand spectators onto the Country Club grounds, where the narrow course dimensions hint at its original purpose—a track for horse racing.

Crenshaw sends out his top six players, and Tiger contributes one of the six straight singles wins. The tide is turning.

A pair of columnists from the *Boston Globe*—Bob Ryan and Michael Holley—are reporting from the course. "Oh, this is starting to get interesting," Ryan says. Holley is beginning "to get why the Ryder Cup is such a big deal."

Another Texas native, the 1997 British Open champion, Justin Leonard, steps to the 17th green, facing a forty-five-foot putt. He sinks it.

Though it's too soon to celebrate, Leonard and his teammates seem to collectively lose their minds in one of the most famous moments in Ryder Cup history. A wild mix of team members and fans bursts onto the green, delaying Leonard's singles opponent, two-time Masters winner José María Olazábal, from attempting his own twenty-five-foot birdie putt. Olazábal misses, sealing victory for the American team.

Payne Stewart remains on the course as the boisterous celebration pushes the boundaries of good sportsmanship. "That's enough for today, don't you think?" Stewart asks his opponent, Scottish golfer and European Tour star Colin Montgomerie.

"I'd have to agree," Montgomerie says.

Stewart graciously concedes the hole.

Crenshaw makes a command appearance on the clubhouse balcony. "Don't stop believing," the captain says as American flags wave and champagne corks pop. Tiger's played in all five sessions of the tournament. "This is all for Ben," he tells reporters. Before joining the team for victory festivities, he heads back to his room at the Four Seasons Hotel in Boston to rest up—then oversleeps.

Tiger startles awake, realizing, "I get this person jumping on me and scaring the living crap out of me."

The person is Payne Stewart, who knows his Isleworth neighbor well enough to say, "Get the hell out of bed. Get your ass down to the team room and experience what it's like to be part of a Ryder Cup."

Tiger's grateful for the wake-up call.

"This is awesome," he says.

A month later, Payne Stewart's twin-engine Learjet takes off at 9:19 a.m. on Monday, October 25. It's a routine flight from Orlando, Florida, to Houston, Texas, where Stewart, one of the PGA's top thirty money winners, has qualified to play in the $5 million TOUR Championship at Houston's Champions Golf Club. Stewart is traveling with his two agents at Leader Enterprises, Inc., a course architect from Nicklaus Design, and two pilots.

The trip usually takes less than three hours. But half an hour into the flight, at 9:44 a.m., air traffic control loses contact with the pilots. The air force and Air National Guard try and fail to intercept, though they can see signs of cabin depressurization in the frost covering the Learjet's windows. The jet flies northwest, drastically off course, until at 1:14 p.m. it enters a supersonic spiral into a field in South Dakota. All six people aboard are lost.

Mike Hicks, Stewart's caddie, is already in Houston at Champions Golf Club when his cell phone rings. "Oh, my god," he says again and again while receiving the terrible news. Hicks runs off the course.

Everyone who hears the news is devastated.

"There is an enormous void and emptiness I feel right now" is the way Tiger describes his own feelings.

The flag at Pinehurst, where Stewart won the U.S. Open in June, is lowered to half-staff.

"I questioned, should we play golf this week?" Davis Love III says before deciding to "go ahead and get the grieving process started." Love is feeling Stewart's loss more than most. Just over a decade ago, in 1988, he lost his father, beloved *Golf Digest* instructor Davis Love Jr., in a private-plane accident on Florida's west coast.

It's up to the players whether to take part in the pro-am scheduled for Tuesday, October 26. Most do, including Tiger, who finds himself strangely soothed by the rituals of golf.

"When we got to the course, it was so silent," Tiger says afterward. "It was eerie—nobody was asking for autographs or clamoring for pictures. It was real quiet. Even on the range guys were hitting and nobody was talking."

Rather than cancel the tournament, it's determined that the participants will play twenty-seven holes on Thursday and Saturday, allowing for attendance at Stewart's funeral, on Friday. It's also decided that the TOUR Championship will proceed with twenty-nine players, leaving the thirtieth slot open. The last-place prize money, eighty thousand dollars, will be awarded to the Stewart family in his memory.

At eight forty-five on Thursday morning, the first tee is filled with the sounds of prayer and the hum of a lone bagpipe playing the mourning tune "Going Home."

Stewart was open about the renewed Christian faith he'd experienced as a father. His daughter Chelsea and son Aaron had given Stewart the brightly colored WWJD (What would Jesus do?) bracelet that he was wearing when he died. At First Baptist Orlando, six thousand similar woven cotton bracelets are distributed at the service.

Tiger is among one hundred PGA players in attendance; twenty-nine return to Houston to finish a TOUR Championship tournament marred by grief. Twenty-four golfers also wear old-fashioned golf knickers—like the ones Stewart famously wore—during play. Tiger is one of the few holdouts. "You don't have to wear knickers to honor someone," he tells journalists. "I'm comfortable handling things internally. I don't need to show the pain I feel inside."

He compartmentalizes his emotions to focus on what he does best: winning.

Tiger earns the $900,000 top prize, finishing four strokes ahead of Davis Love III, who praises Tiger's performance unconditionally. "I said the first couple of years he was here that he was not even close to how good he could get. We are starting to see that now. He is clearly head and shoulders above the rest of us."

"You hate to keep blowing his horn," analyst Curtis Strange says, "but every time you turn around, he's doing something no one else can."

The future looks not only bright but also clear. The Lasik surgery Tiger had following the Ryder Cup has corrected his nearsightedness—so severe that without glasses or contacts he'd be considered legally blind—and now he has twenty-fifteen vision. "The first thing he said afterward," recalls journalist Tom Callahan, "was 'The hole looks bigger.'" Not exactly what his opponents wish to hear.

Tiger's traveled the world and made many memories this year, but there's one souvenir he won't be keeping: the Shirt.

During the Ryder Cup, the US team captain, Ben Crenshaw, had had photos of winning American teams printed onto a three-button burgundy polo-style shirt with a beige collar and beige cuffs. The day the 1999 team wore the garment—instantly nicknamed the Shirt—the Americans beat Europe and won the cup.

"It wasn't a beautiful shirt, but I thought it was cool," says teammate Jim Furyk, who's still going strong paired with Tiger's ex-caddie, Mike "Fluff" Cowan. "It had a lot of emotion and time spent on it by Ben."

Tiger has no emotional attachment to the garment, though, telling ESPN, "I threw it in the fireplace over Christmas and burned it. It was sooo ugly. It provided more warmth for the house."

He's ending 1999 on a much cooler note. His winnings this year total $6.6 million. He's named PGA Tour Player of the Year. He's had eight PGA Tour wins, ending the season with four in a row. People are starting to speculate that he could beat the record Byron Nelson set in 1945: eighteen PGA wins, including the eleven in a row.

Eighty-seven-year-old Nelson sends the newly twenty-four-year-old a note: *Tiger, I love watching you play on the TV, it's a lot of fun to watch you. If you do break my record, I'll be the first one to congratulate you. I had the record for 55 years. If you go ahead and break it, Merry Christmas.*

Chapter 41

Buick Invitational
Torrey Pines
San Diego, California
February 10–13, 2000

Tiger has an early tee time at the pro-am ahead of the Buick Invitational. It's 6:42 a.m., and nine television crews have already set up their equipment on the 1st. Then comes the thrum of a news helicopter flying above Torrey Pines.

The cameras are focused on a player on the verge of the unfathomable. Three days ago, Tiger won the AT&T Pebble Beach National Pro-Am by closing a seven-stroke gap in the final seven holes of the tournament. A victory here at the Buick Invitational would extend his streak.

No one knows Torrey Pines better than Phil Mickelson, who grew up playing the course. But both as an amateur and as a pro, Tiger's won events on this course, too, including the 1999 Buick Invitational, when childhood friend Bryon Bell was his caddie. Steve Williams has this week off, because Bell "deserved a chance to defend, too," Tiger says.

But the defense is futile. Mickelson draws on his home-course advantage to best Tiger by four strokes, winning the tournament and breaking Tiger's sizzling streak.

"If I had my ball this week, I'd have won by five," Tiger says over the telephone.

It's Sunday, May 14, and Tiger is on the phone at the TPC Four Seasons Resort, in Irving, Texas. He's finished 10 under par in the Byron Nelson Golf Classic, one stroke behind Phil Mickelson, Davis Love III, and Jesper Parnevik, who won the playoff and the tournament.

Even though the playoff wasn't televised—CBS ended its television coverage once Tiger was out of contention—today's results only underscore Tiger's disappointing fifth-place finish at the Masters in April.

"For some reason, the golfing gods weren't looking down on me this week," Tiger said at Augusta National. He played both tournaments with Titleist 681 "T" Forged irons, Titleist Vokey Design wedges inscribed TIGER, and the Titleist Professional—a ball with a liquid core and wound construction—though at Augusta he hinted he was thinking of making a switch.

He'll next play a European Tour event, defending his 1999 Deutsche Bank–SAP Open title at the Gut Kaden Golf and Land Club, outside Hamburg, Germany. Now Tiger's jump-starting the process with this call to Kel Devlin. Nike Golf's global director of sports marketing is in Portland, Oregon, eating his Sunday dinner.

"Can you meet me in Germany on Tuesday morning?" Tiger asks.

Since January of 1999, Tiger has been testing a Nike Tour Accuracy, a solid-core ball developed by Nike and engineered by Hideyuki "Rock" Ishii, of Bridgestone Golf.

Devlin and Ishii log countless air miles bringing prototypes to Tiger whenever and wherever he has time to test them. One version of the ball is eliminated for failing to deliver the satisfying *click* that Tiger hears when he connects his putter with the Titleist Professional.

Tiger makes a game of driving the balls for speed. And his feel is uncannily accurate. "I hit that one a little low on the face, so that's probably 2,600 RPM," Tiger says during one testing session.

The reading from the launch monitor: 2,570.

"This golf ball didn't come by accident," caddie Steve Williams says. "When Tiger signed with Nike, [the ball] was one of the projects. It didn't happen overnight. It was a couple years of engineering that went into developing the ball and getting it exactly right. And it wasn't going to be put into play until such time that it was exactly how he wanted it."

In early 2000, at Big Canyon Country Club, in Newport Beach, California, Tiger chose his two top prototypes, but he wasn't ready to play them competitively—until now.

After Tiger calls him, Devlin reaches Ishii at Bridgestone's offices in Japan. "I'm dead serious," Devlin says. "We're going to meet Tiger Tuesday morning on the first tee." They have less than forty-eight hours. Ishii packs a suitcase full of balls and boards an afternoon flight.

Before Tiger's plane takes off for Hamburg Airport, he makes another call, this time to the Titleist CEO, Wally Uihlein. They added a clause to Tiger's sponsorship agreement last year giving him a contractual right to play a Nike ball in competition, but he hasn't done so yet. That's about to change, Tiger tells Uihlein.

At nine o'clock on the morning of Tuesday, May 16, Devlin and Ishii arrive on the first tee at Gut Kaden Golf and Land Club.

Turns out, Tiger hasn't let his caddie in on his plans.

"What the f— are you two idiots doing here?" Steve Williams says, scoffing at the idea that Tiger is considering switching balls midseason.

Wind and rain are lashing the course, so Devlin uses an umbrella to protect the boxes of Nike Tour Accuracy balls Ishii is carrying. To Tiger, the testing conditions are perfect. The Titleist Professional he drives off the first tee lands in the rough. He next launches a Nike Tour Accuracy. The ball barely drifts in the whipping wind, landing on the fairway and consistently outperforming the Titleist ball in an array of shots.

"I guess we're switching balls," Williams concedes.

Tiger doesn't repeat at the Deutsche Bank–SAP Open, but Nike Tour Accuracy's performance in tournament play convinces him that the ball is a winner. He places an order with Ishii.

"Tiger asked me to make him a couple hundred of the balls so he could take them home and practice with them so he could get ready for the U.S. Open," Ishii says. "That's when we knew he would play it."

On the 18th green at Muirfield Village Golf Club, the Memorial Tournament is celebrating its twenty-fifth anniversary by honoring its legendary founder, Jack Nicklaus. Fifteen thousand people, including Nicklaus's ninety-year-old mother, Helen, have gathered for a fifty-minute ceremony.

It's an emotional tribute, but music from the Ohio State marching band lifts everyone's spirits. Tiger gives an interview fondly recalling the day Nicklaus — now in his last full season on tour — was leading a clinic and offered to watch the then freshman at Western High hit a few balls.

"You might have a future in this game," Nicklaus told him.

"Here I am," Tiger says today as the tournament's defending champion.

No player has ever repeated as champion at the Memorial, but Tiger has a new weapon in his arsenal: the Nike Tour Accuracy.

Lee Patterson, media director for the PGA Tour, asks Tiger: "Is it safe to say the Nike ball issue, we can put it to rest and you're ok with it?" The question comes after Tiger's 9-under second round.

Tiger laughs, saying, "I would like you guys to put it to rest."

He follows it up with a third-round 65. Tour veteran Harrison Frazar says what every player in the field is thinking: "He hit shots today that I don't know if any other human can hit."

Tiger replies with a note of caution. "If it were over, there would be a trophy."

The next day, Tiger wins it, along with a check for $558,000.

To Williams, the value of the Nike Tour Accuracy is a measurable commodity. He says, "You'd have to say it was worth one or two shots per round, for sure."

Chapter 42

Tiger Woods Foundation Junior Golf Clinic and Exhibition
James E. Stewart Golf Course
Oklahoma City, Oklahoma
May 7, 2000

K ids are on Tiger's mind.

Not his own—he denies reports of a Valentine's Day engagement to his girlfriend, Joanna Jagoda, and in answer to reporter Stuart Scott's question "Do you want little Tigers running around?" he replies, "A yellow Lab. That's fine. A Rottweiler." Today, he's focused on bringing the sport he loves to kids, especially those who might not otherwise try it out.

From the top of the driving range, golf carts motor in formation to the beat of rock music. The thumping bass line pumps up the bleacher seats, filled with twenty-five hundred kids from Oklahoma City youth programs who can't wait to watch Tiger Woods hit some golf balls.

The carts pull up to the practice tee. Under the protective watch of well-muscled bodyguards, Tiger and Earl step out.

At the St. John's Missionary Baptist Church morning service, Earl got emotional while giving a talk to the all-Black congregation on the theme of "share and care," the family motto. Those are the bywords of the Woods family and the basis of the Tiger Woods Foundation, which Tiger,

Earl, and Tida founded in November of 1996, shortly after Tiger turned pro. The charitable organization has a strong educational mission as well as an inspirational component.

The goal, as Tiger describes it, is "to make golf look more like America."

These young Americans are hoping for a demonstration of the awesome juggling skills Tiger showed in last year's instantly famous Nike commercial. Tiger picks up his sand wedge, the same club he used to film the spot.

"I heard a rumor that this thing I did on TV was all computerized," he tells the kids. "It's kind of a vicious rumor."

The kids are mesmerized as Tiger bounces the ball on the face of the club, then moves the club between his legs, keeping the ball in constant contact with the club, all the while effortlessly narrating: "I don't know where that rumor started, whether it was the public or the press, but they obviously hadn't seen me do this before."

No one in the bleachers moves or speaks as Tiger works the club left-handed, right-handed, then bounces the ball overhead and neatly lands it on his wedge.

"Now I didn't put this one in the commercial, because it's the hardest one—it's when you hit the ball off the butt end of the club."

Tiger keeps the ball moving as he gears up for a big finish. "Let's see—it took me four takes to do the Nike spot. Let's see if I can do this out here." He bounces the ball, moves his hands into a baseball grip, and swings the club like a bat.

He drives the ball in midair. It lands far down the range.

Exactly like on TV, the kids marvel.

The top junior golfers at the clinic receive Nike clothing, but all the kids get what they came for—a relatable hero who makes them smile and invites them to dream.

"I'm not too far removed from my teens," Tiger says. "I can say 'Dude,' and that's cool—that's fine."

*   *   *

"You can play a few holes," Butch Harmon says to his nineteen-year-old pupil, Adam Scott. Scott is working with Tiger's swing coach at the Butch Harmon School of Golf, where Tiger's spending three days tuning up for the one hundredth U.S. Open. The Australian first crossed paths with Tiger when Tiger was newly professional and Scott was caddying for a friend at the 1996 Australian Open. Four years later, Scott—who's already won notice for the smooth rhythm of his swing—has also decided to turn pro.

Harmon is confident Tiger's new swing is on track to compete in a major championship. "We didn't really have to fix anything," Harmon says. "We just had to shape some shots, curve the ball a bit differently for some of the holes out there."

But Tiger worries about his putting, assessing his posture as "a little off" and his release as "not quite right." It's a valid concern. The greens at Pebble Beach Golf Links are seeded with rough poa annua grass that makes distance and speed especially difficult to calculate.

Wind is another certain challenge on the California course overlooking the Pacific Ocean. On June 11, the Sunday before the U.S. Open, Harmon sends Tiger and Scott out to play in the stiff desert breeze blowing to thirty miles per hour over the course at Rio Secco Golf Club.

Scott is nervous but holds his own, feeling good to be "1 down through the turn at Rio Secco" until his steady play is suddenly no match for Tiger's. Scott keeps a hole-by-hole tally of his opponent's score—"birdie, birdie, birdie and eagles and stuff"—until Tiger finishes his round at 63, besting Scott by nine strokes.

"Maybe I should reconsider turning pro," a dejected Scott says to Harmon.

NBC's lead analyst, Johnny Miller, approaches Mark O'Meara during his practice round on Wednesday, the day before the tournament.

"So how is the kid playing?" Miller asks.

Miller's interest is not only professional but also personal. In 1973, the then twenty-six-year-old Miller won the U.S. Open championship at Pennsylvania's Oakmont Country Club with a stellar final round of 63, a U.S. Open record which has never been beaten.

Tiger's fans are out in force for the opening round, and they're not going to miss a single shot. The intensity challenges even the two Monterey County sheriffs and an FBI agent walking the course with Tiger. On the 6th green, the surging crowd overturns the handicap golf cart a man is riding in. An ambulance arrives, and the man's wife tells the crew to go on ahead to the emergency room without her.

The tournament's general chairman overhears her apologetic explanation. "As soon as Tiger finishes this round," she tells her husband, "I'll meet you at the hospital."

In the broadcaster's booth, Johnny Miller makes a bold prediction: Tiger's "going to do something this week that people will be talking about one hundred years from now...Tiger is going to break every U.S. Open record in the books. This is going to be the week that he says, 'See you guys.'"

Tiger opens by shooting a 65, a score built on the strength of his putting. For Sergio Garcia—who ends the day ten strokes back on the leaderboard—it's *Message received.* "The way to overcome Tiger is to be perfect, and if not, congratulate him," Garcia says.

Sixty-year-old Jack Nicklaus has played forty-four consecutive U.S. Opens and won four: in 1962, 1967, 1972, and 1980. But it's been twenty years since the last time he won the sterling silver U.S. Open championship trophy. He shoots an opening-round 73, one stroke ahead of this year's Masters runner-up, Ernie Els.

"If I'm walking up the 18th hole on Father's Day, it means I'll have made the cut and played a good tournament," Nicklaus tells the Associated Press. "I'll have been delighted to have played 72 holes, and probably sad that it will probably be my last [U.S. Open]."

Nicklaus's nostalgia is no match for reality. "Every time I look at the television, he's making a putt," says Nicklaus of Tiger.

At foggy, windy Pebble Beach, caddie Steve Williams earns his keep. Weather conditions have delayed Friday's second round, so it's not until Saturday morning that Tiger reaches 18, with its oceanfront view of Stillwater Cove. At approximately 8:00 a.m. Pacific time, he tees off, sending his Nike Tour Accuracy ball "halfway to Hawaii." Having hooked his drive into Stillwater Cove, he unleashes a flood of curse words—on national television.

"Sporting events are not done on taped delay," says NBC producer Tommy Roy, who's scrambling inside the TV truck. And there's a certain decorum assumed of golfers. "With the WWF you're expecting that." The techs can't sound the bleep in time.

What only Williams knows is that Tiger's down to his last golf ball. Following the Friday weather delay, Tiger went to his hotel room to practice putting some of the Nike prototypes—but never returned them to his Titleist staff bag. Earlier this morning, he tossed one of his scuffed balls to a young fan.

Williams is sweating. He has to cover the equipment deficit—and the risk of potentially incurring a penalty—by proposing a cautious strategy to close out the round. What he really wants to do is "go to that kid and ask him for the ball back. But I couldn't do it."

"I'd like for you to hit an iron, just to get it into play," Williams tells Tiger.

Tiger does take an iron for what's now his third shot. Williams, still worried about the ocean on the left, wants Tiger to go up the safer right side of the fairway for his fourth. Tiger is suspicious. "Why do I want to go up the right side?" he asks, instead engineering a shot that he starts out "to left over the ocean to cut it back and it just went long over the back and I got up and down for a bogey."

He begins the third round six shots ahead of Spain's Miguel Ángel Jiménez and Denmark's Thomas Bjørn—one of the many U.S. Open records Tiger has broken today.

"He's playing every shot like his life depends on it," Bjørn says.

To IMG's Mark Steinberg, Tiger's image depends on apologizing to the kids who heard him cursing during the breakfast hour. "It was in the heat of the moment, and unfortunately I let it slip out," Tiger says. "And I regret doing it."

The final round is played on Sunday, June 18. The fierce wind and gloomy fog have cleared, and it's a picture-perfect Father's Day, with sunshine glinting off the Pacific Ocean. Yachts bob in Stillwater Cove. Kayakers hold up signs reading GO TIGER, and the cliffside beach is as crowded as the course galleries with spectators hoping to catch a glimpse.

Tiger holds a ten-stroke lead over his playing partner, Ernie Els. But he's really alone now, against history. Two golf records have stood since the nineteenth century: largest U.S. Open margin of victory (1899) and largest major championship margin of victory (1862 British Open).

Tiger sets himself a "mini-goal"—a bogey-free round—on the theory that "someone would have to shoot something like 60 to catch me."

He pars every hole on the front nine. By the 6th, Els decides "to enjoy the walk" with Tiger because his playing is "just awesome to watch": "the ball flight, and the velocity of the ball coming off the club, I've never seen anything like that."

Tiger turns up the intensity on the back nine, birdieing 10, 12, 13, and 14—and then is faced with a fifteen-foot putt on 16. *Bury it. Don't make a bogey. Do what you set out to do.* He executes, then rewards himself with a celebratory fist pump.

Three holes remain. Out on the 18th fairway, Tiger turns and looks out across the Pacific Ocean as if he's all alone at Pebble Beach.

The peaceful moment ends on the 18th green. Tiger hits his birdie attempt four feet past the hole and struggles to collect himself.

Upon sinking the par putt, Tiger exclaims, "That's what I had in mind." A laugh rises up in the gallery.

"Well, I'm honest," Tiger says. He's kept his competitors honest, too.

Ernie Els and Miguel Ángel Jiménez tie for second place at 3-over 287, fifteen strokes back from Tiger's 12-under 272. "I considered squeezing him in a bear hug, or arm wrestling him, or just tackling him," Els says.

"But that wouldn't work because on top of everything else, Tiger is getting stronger every day, too. I don't know what we're going to do with him."

"If you were building the complete golfer," Mark O'Meara says in the press tent, "you'd build Tiger Woods."

In winning the one hundredth U.S. Open at Pebble Beach in his one hundredth professional start, Tiger breaks or ties ten scoring records set in major championships.

"Records are great, but you don't really pay attention to that," Tiger says. "The only thing I know is that I've got the trophy sitting right next to me."

The U.S. Open trophy, he decides, "wasn't too bad a Father's Day present."

His father, Earl, is noticeably absent from Pebble Beach. "The reason I didn't come up," Earl says from Cypress, where he's watching Tiger on television, "was that I wanted to give him the space to perform and be himself. It's all part of the plan."

For Earl, NBC Golf coverage is almost like spending the day with his son. Live and in replay throughout his four-hour final round, NBC cuts to Tiger 407 times for a total of ninety-three minutes and twenty-three seconds.

On the subject of fathers and sons, bonds shared and lessons learned, Tiger's words are simple, eloquent, and addressed to an audience of one—Earl.

"It's Father's Day. And I can't tell you enough about what my dad meant to my golf, and to me—as a person growing up. All the times that I had questions in life, all the guidance that he's given me, I can't thank him enough. My dad always took me out, and we practiced and played and had a lot of fun competing against each other. Those are the times you look back on and you reminisce and you miss. And to have my dad still alive, while I won this championship, on Father's Day, it's very important to me."

*   *   *

On June 22, ESPN columnist Ray Ratto observes that "Tiger is so dominant he has people writing his future into the history books."

Four days later, *Sports Illustrated*'s June 26 edition hits the stands. To writer John Garrity, a Tiger victory at the British Open, and the career grand slam, is predestined. Only four golfers—Gene Sarazen, Ben Hogan, Jack Nicklaus, and Gary Player—have ever won all four of golf's major championships, collectively known as the career grand slam.

"When he wins the British Open at St. Andrews in July," Garrity writes, "he will become just the fifth player—and the youngest by two years—to win all four majors."

Chapter 43

The 129th British Open
The Old Course, St Andrews Links
St Andrews, Scotland
July 20–23, 2000

The 129th playing of the British Open in a millennial year has been dubbed the Millennial Open at St Andrews. Adding to the inescapable variables of wind and rain, the 112 bunkers have been newly lined with sod. Players will have to dig deep to splash out from the steep, sandy traps.

Among the field will be Jack Nicklaus, who after missing the cut at his final U.S. Open continues his farewell-to-the-PGA tour with his British Open swan song. Nicklaus calls out the press for overhyping Tiger. It hasn't helped that the captain and former secretary of the Royal and Ancient Golf Club of St Andrews walked the final round at Pebble Beach with Tiger and declared, "If Tiger doesn't win at St. Andrews, there should be a stewards' inquiry."

"He has to have challengers for the whole thing to be right," Nicklaus says. "It's a bad story if there aren't any challengers. You guys won't have anything to write about."

Three-time British Open champion (1987, 1990, 1992) and three-time

Masters winner (1989, 1990, 1996) Nick Faldo is up for the test, having given his game and his equipment a complete overhaul. "Maybe it will happen again one more time," says Faldo, who for ten years has held the scoring record on the Old Course: an 18-under 270.

Faldo knows his American competitor is increasingly strong, having built out his six-foot-one frame to a muscular 180 pounds. "Biceps almost like Schwarzenegger's," Faldo says. "I'm really making an effort to get stronger," Jesper Parnevik tells *Sports Illustrated*. "It's all Tiger's fault."

Tiger's answer to *Golf Digest*'s request for a shirtless photo shoot? *No.*

But he's hoping Mark O'Meara will say yes to more fly-fishing lessons. "I try to base my golf schedule around the fly-fishing season," O'Meara says. "When the fishing is good that's where you'll find me, and when it's not so good then I'll play more tournaments."

The pastime's been sweeping the PGA. It was O'Meara who got Davis Love III hooked. "There's never a locker room on tour that doesn't have a fly rod in it," Love says. "Some of the guys will bring rods around with them on their practice rounds to make a few casts."

That the outdoor physical pursuit approximates the rhythms of golf and its demands for precision is a huge part of its appeal. "Fly-fishing is like golf in that you don't get a second chance," Faldo says. "Cast, line, position, drag. One thing wrong, and 'bogey!'—you lose the fish."

Since the early 1990s, O'Meara has traveled to Limerick, Ireland, to play the JP McManus Pro-Am and in 1997 he added an annual fishing trip on the River Liffey. This July, he invites Tiger along to the Limerick Golf Club. Tiger takes the tournament, donating his winnings—£33,000—to McManus's charity, benefiting the children of southwest Ireland.

Tiger and O'Meara travel by helicopter to a luxury golf property outside Dublin called the K Club. O'Meara is the first out on the Liffey and, to Tiger's envy, catches a nine-and-a-half-pound Atlantic salmon. The estate manager marvels at the ease of Tiger's practice casts on land, though observing that "he won't go near the water until he gets it right."

Tiger and O'Meara's friendship has always had an element of rivalry, which continues out on the K Club practice tee. The British Open at St

Andrews is days away, and Tiger's not hitting well. He turns to O'Meara and issues a challenge. "You need to start working on your game."

"Bud, you have to work on *your* game," O'Meara says. "Next week's important to me, but obviously it's a lot more important to you."

"Why's that?" Tiger says.

"Because my name's already on that trophy," O'Meara says. In 1998, he won both the Masters and the British Open.

"Yeah," Tiger says, "but I've got more majors than you do. I've got you by one."

"Bud," O'Meara says, "You're going to go so far past me and a lot of other players, it's not even funny."

Tiger gets serious about his pre-tournament practice sessions. His putting regimen: execute one hundred consecutive six-foot putts using only his right hand. The dedication shows in his first-round score of 5-under 67, anchored by a consistent putting game that delivers eight consecutive pars on the front nine and five birdies on the final ten holes. Ernie Els turns in a 66 for a one-stroke lead. The South African's advantage is fleeting. Tiger executes a bogey-free round 2 that puts him three strokes ahead of American David Toms, who finished tenth on the 1999 tour money list, though he's yet to win a major.

Tiger and Toms are paired together in the third round. Toms pulls within two strokes, only to fall four back.

On the par-five 14th, Tiger and Steve Williams confer over Tiger's second shot. The club selection is a fairway wood with twelve degrees of loft. Tiger drives the ball 270 yards. As the Nike Tour Accuracy soars, Tiger says to Williams, "That the one you're talking about?"

"All players have some preshot routine," Nick Faldo explains. "Tiger has blitzed all that. There's no twitch, no lift of the hat, no wasted energy."

Except for the sneezing. Northeast Scotland is in the height of its summer bloom—and the irritants have Tiger making frequent use of handkerchiefs and eye drops. "I'm allergic to grass, trees, dust, pollen," Tiger says. "It's something I've always had. When I was a kid, it was ten times worse than it is now."

The crowds have also become exponentially more intense. "I have never seen so many people on a golf course," David Toms says. Attendance is approaching two hundred thousand with the final round still to be played.

On Sunday, the Old Course is buzzing with forty-seven thousand people waiting to see where Tiger takes his six-stroke lead. His playing partner, David Duval, makes four birdies on the front nine, cutting Tiger's lead to three, only to falter with his putting. On 17, Duval takes on one of golf's most notorious sand traps—the Road Hole bunker—losing four strokes and any hope of winning in the famous hell hole.

The Claret Jug belongs to Tiger, though he has yet to play 18. Before he can step to the tee, Her Majesty's Officers of Arms lose control of security. The crowd bursts through the rope barriers onto the 18th fairway, pushing along the creek known as Swilken Burn and toward the tee. The course marshals toss rowdy spectators into the water but can't reach the flag before a tattooed streaker dances around it in full view of the cameras.

Tiger plays through. "Somebody out there," Denmark's Thomas Bjørn says, "is playing golf on a different planet."

Or maybe he's just used to it. The last time he was at Carnoustie, in 1999, a blond woman in a black thong bikini ran out to give Tiger a hug and a kiss on the cheek as he was preparing to make a putt on the 18th. "Thank you," he said before missing the putt.

"I wasn't worried," he said afterward, joking that "I knew she wasn't hiding anything. She didn't have a whole lot on, so I guess I assumed it was a pretty benign situation."

"It was the best kiss I ever had. It was worth it," the woman, ID'd as exotic dancer Yvonne Robb, said. "I just love Tiger. I'll have to surprise you all again next year."

So far, there's been no sign of her.

Bjørn and South Africa's Ernie Els have tied for second. As Tiger completes his career grand slam, Els's runner-up finish at three of 2000's majors have him in the running for the "mini slam," or "bridesmaid slam."

Without putting a single ball in a bunker, Tiger shoots 69 for the round and a 19-under 269 for the tournament—besting by one stroke Nick Faldo's 1990 record for a British Open played at St Andrews.

Faldo, who finishes well back at 287, praises Tiger for breaking the conventions of this centuries-old sport. "The guy is simply in a different league," Faldo says. "All credit to him. He's thrown all these old myths out of the window, that you can't physically train for golf, you can't be strong or you are going to lose your touch."

The significance of Tiger's incredible achievement is not lost on anyone—not even his typically stoic mother. "When Tiger win at Masters first time, and the old man sobbing, I was very happy but not break down," Tida says. When he won the U.S. Open, and "all the people on the fairway bowed to him, I think 'That's nice.' But that's all." But now, when Tida sees him "coming up the last hole of the Old Course, which is so much history, and all the people are waving and applauding," the magnitude of the moment hits her. "'That is my son.' I got a damp in my eye. It just come up."

At Royal Air Force Leuchars, a nearby air base, an IMG-chartered jet with a flight plan for Orlando, Florida, is waiting on the tarmac. Its passengers are five minutes away at the Old Course Hotel in St Andrews. Two of them, Tiger's good friend David Duval and Australian golfer Stuart Appleby, tied for eleventh today. Both golfers are asking the same question: "Is Tiger ready?"

The British Open champion emerges from the hotel carrying the Claret Jug and a carry-on bag stickered with one of Tiger's favorite cartoon characters, *South Park*'s Eric Cartman.

"Bye, Mom, I love you," Tiger says to Tida. "I'll call you when I get back."

Chapter 44

The 82nd PGA Championship
Valhalla Golf Club
Louisville, Kentucky
August 17–20, 2000

As defending 1999 PGA champ, Tiger heads to Louisville, Kentucky, where the Wanamaker Trophy will be contested for the eighty-second time.

The Valhalla Golf Club is named for a sacred place in Norse mythology—the great hall where the communion between Viking souls and their gods was celebrated. "It sets up well for anyone who hits the ball high," Tiger says of the course, which Jack Nicklaus opened in 1986. "Obviously, that is the way Nicklaus golf courses are designed. You have got to bring the ball in high."

On Wednesday, August 16, Nicklaus is practicing on the 4th hole when he gets sad news. His ninety-year-old mother, Helen, has succumbed to a two-year-long illness. "Her greatest fear in the last year or so was that she would pass away during one of golf's major events," Nicklaus says. "I know her wish would be for me to stay here and play."

Jim Awtrey, CEO of the PGA of America, also has a wish—that

Nicklaus play Valhalla with Masters champion Vijay Singh and U.S. Open and British Open champion Tiger.

The trio tees off at 9:13 a.m. on Thursday, August 17. "He shot the easiest 66 today," Nicklaus says after the round. "It looked like a 60. Phenomenal control, phenomenal concentration, phenomenal putter."

On Friday, Tiger says to Nicklaus, "It's been an honor playing with you, Jack, I've enjoyed it, now let's just finish off on a correct note."

"You got it, let's go," says Nicklaus. The emerging story on Friday is not that Nicklaus misses the cut but *Who's Bob May?*

Thirty-one-year-old Bob May is a little-known PGA pro who sits just five shots behind Tiger after round 2. Sportswriters scramble to pull together a profile. But Tiger's already up on May's stats.

May, a Southern California golfer seven years Tiger's senior, was named the 1985 American Junior Golf Association Player of the Year (an honor Tiger won in both 1991 and 1992) and at sixteen qualified for the Los Angeles Open at the Riviera Country Club (seven years before sixteen-year-old Tiger played there on a sponsor's exemption).

Back then, Tiger's goal was "to hopefully one day win as many tournaments as [May] did." Though May hasn't fared particularly well in the PGA, he did win the 1999 European Masters last September.

Going into Sunday, Tiger leads May by a single stroke: 203 to 204.

"This guy won't back down," Tiger says to Steve Williams.

He's right. Tiger has an early bogey, and May pulls ahead by two on the 4th. Tiger evens it up by birdieing 7 and 8, but May goes a stroke ahead again on 11, and that's how it stays through 16.

"What have we got, Stevie?" Tiger asks his caddie as they stand in the 17th fairway.

"Ninety yards," Williams says.

Tiger selects his club. "Lob wedge."

He overhits by five yards—to two feet, making the birdie putt and pulling even with May.

On 18, an uphill 542-yard par 5, Tiger and May each reach the green with two good strikes. Having knocked his first putt fifteen feet past, May sinks the second for a birdie, leaving Tiger with a short putt, a six-foot knee-jerker, which he makes. "That's why he's Tiger Woods," May says when the ball drops.

The new three-hole playoff format begins at the 16th. Tiger makes a twenty-foot birdie, but on the 17th drives the ball off the cart path yet miraculously saves par—then pars again on 18, leaving him one stroke clear for the win.

"This was one memorable battle," Tiger says after he hoists the Wana-maker Trophy for the second consecutive year.

After the champagne toasts, Tiger sinks into a stretch limousine. "My calf is killing me," he says of the pain settling into his right leg. "Man, I'm tired. It's been a long day."

Tiger has won three of the four majors this calendar year, the first player to do so since Ben Hogan in 1953. He ends the 2000 season with six wins and eight top-ten finishes, leading the field in money and scoring.

After the PGA Championship, Jack Nicklaus revisits his assessment of Tiger. "I kept saying, 'I can't understand why we don't have anybody else playing that well.' I am more understanding now. He's that much better."

The Masters is eighty-six days away when the questions start. The 2001 PGA season opener, on January 10, is the Mercedes Championship at Hawaii's Kapalua Resort.

"Would you say," a reporter asks, "'I don't care if I win another tournament this year, I'll just win the Masters?'"

"I couldn't live with myself if I said that," Tiger answers. "It wouldn't be me."

With the Masters looming in April, the press closes in on the definition of the grand slam.

Q: There's going to be a debate at Augusta, if you should win, whether that's a Grand Slam or whether it has to be done in calendar year. . . . If you were to win Augusta this year, is that a Grand Slam?

TIGER WOODS: Let me ask you this. Do I hold all four?

Q: Yes.

TIGER WOODS: Then there's the answer.

Q: Does it have to be in a calendar year?

TIGER WOODS: I [would] hold all four at the same time.

Q: First you have to win it. Then will you let us argue it?

TIGER WOODS: You can do whatever you want as soon as I win.

Tiger ties for eighth at the Mercedes and for fifth at the Phoenix Open, then it's on to the PGA's West Coast Swing.

At one point, fans injure Tiger's left knee in their push to get his autograph. "I can't hit balls right now, no way," he tells reporters covering the AT&T Pebble Beach National Pro-Am on February 1, 2001. "I tried to swing. It's not going to happen today."

Tiger plays the pro tournament, finishing at 8 under, eight strokes back from Davis Love III's 16-under 272.

Agent Mark Steinberg describes Tiger's existential niche: "Now, he is world icon status."

He can afford to focus on winning the majors, but he still needs a home. Tiger's outgrown the town house IMG secured for him when he turned pro, in 1996.

In mid-March, he moves into a new house in Isleworth. The location is prime—the south end of the driving range—but the space is barren of furniture.

Tiger improvises, decorating the mantel with his prized possessions. They all have the gleam of precious silver: the U.S. Open trophy, the Claret Jug, and the Wanamaker Trophy he's held for the second consecutive year.

"Put another one up there," Tiger says, "and it would look pretty good."

Chapter 45

Bay Hill Invitational
Bay Hill Club & Lodge
Orlando, Florida
March 15–18, 2001

W hen will Woods win?" the *Los Angeles Times* asks.
Whispers of a slump have become shouts. In an interview leading up to Arnold Palmer's Bay Hill Invitational, Tiger is on the defensive as to why he's competed in eight tournaments and failed to win a single one.

"I've been working on stuff for Augusta since the beginning of the year," he says. "I knew some of the changes they made to the golf course and some of the things we're going to have to...be aware of. So I've been trying to get ready for that."

Phil Mickelson, who since joining the tour, in 1992, has yet to win a major, admits to *Sports Illustrated* that he's "desperate" to win the Masters.

In Orlando on March 18, Mickelson looks on as Tiger celebrates on the 18th green at Bay Hill Club & Lodge, cheering, pumping his fist, and hugging caddie Steve Williams. Runner-up Mickelson is not happy with the way Tiger wins. Tiger gets a lucky break when his drive bounces back in bounds after hitting a spectator, setting up a birdie on the ultimate hole to beat Mickelson by one.

One week later, Tiger wins again in Ponte Vedra Beach, Florida. It's his first victory at the "fifth major," the Players Championship at TPC Sawgrass, while Mickelson ties for thirty-third.

"Some of the writers—and I know who they are—had suggested and said I was in a slump," Tiger says in the post-tournament interview. "Obviously, they don't really understand the game that well.

"It is a game that's very fickle. You can try as hard as you want, and sometimes it just doesn't work out."

Tiger and Earl travel together from Orlando to Augusta, where Tiger and Mark O'Meara are sharing a house. This Masters Week, there will be no time for the daily trips to Arby's for the beef-and-cheddar sandwiches that fueled his 1997 win. Tiger and O'Meara are subsisting on reheated meals prepared in Isleworth by O'Meara's wife, Alicia, to allow for maximum time on the practice range. The media are not invited.

"He was locked down," Earl says.

All the players are intently studying the greens, as if taking a crash course on this legendary course.

After the 1980 Masters, traditional Bermuda grass was abandoned for a new cultivation: bent grass. As four-time Masters champion Arnold Palmer (1958, 1960, 1962, 1964) explains it, "Augusta National's greens already are among the most undulating in the world—that's part of the Masters tradition. Bentgrass greens are lightning fast; when the speed combines with the severe sloping of Augusta's greens, they can get out of hand."

This April, the greens are soft, almost forgiving.

Not so the media glare, which burns bright around a single, inescapable question: Can Tiger win his fourth consecutive major championship?

Mickelson is driven. So is David Duval, who, though he's recovering from a wrist injury, has achieved two top-three finishes in Augusta—tied for second in 1998 behind winner Mark O'Meara and tied for third last year behind winner Vijay Singh.

Celebrating past winners is one of the many Augusta National traditions. Byron Nelson, Masters champion in 1937 and 1942, is this year's honorary starter. Two days from now, on April 5, he'll step to the first tee and hit the ceremonial shot that will open the tournament.

"Do I feel the burden of it? No," Tiger says during an April 3 interview. "Come Sunday night, win or lose, life is going to go on. The sun will come up on Monday."

Mickelson, Duval, and Tiger quickly emerge as the players to beat. Tiger's 70–66 places him two strokes off the lead going into the third round, where he delivers a 68 that puts him atop the leaderboard and paired with Mickelson (67-69-69) in the final round.

On Saturday night, Tiger hits the practice range, surrounded by the tall pines of Augusta National and some nagging thoughts. He's detected a problem with his swing and works it out, hitting ball after ball until darkness sets in.

On the par-five 13th, Mickelson trails Tiger and David Duval by two. The dogleg hole named Azalea is one of the most famous in all of golf, bordered on its south side by sixteen hundred of Augusta National's signature plants. Unfortunately, "Tiger is allergic to everything on the golf course," his father says. "When he gets to Georgia in the spring, that pollen gets to him."

Mickelson is the first to tee off, then he crosses the Nelson Bridge over a tributary of Rae's Creek to the spot where his fade has landed in the middle of the fairway.

Tiger selects a 3-wood. His shot lands thirty yards beyond Mickelson's drive, which puts him in position to birdie the hole and preserve his two-stroke lead.

On the CBS broadcast, commentator Ken Venturi gets animated. "That's huge. That's really big," he says. "You thought Mickelson was big? Hit it right by it."

"Do you always hit your 3-wood that long?" Mickelson asks.

"Further," Tiger says. "Normally further than that."

Of the shot he calls a high sweeper, he "practiced on the range all week just in case I might need it," Tiger says. "I had to pull it out. I had to step up and aim another 15 yards right and hit that big slinger around the corner to give myself a chance."

Duval is playing two groups ahead of the leaders. After birdieing seven of the first ten holes, he pulls even with Tiger. He can't see how Tiger and Mickelson are playing, but he's learned from his previous rounds at Augusta National how easily the crowd noise carries through the pines. He listens and hears... nothing... then thinks, *I'm in it.*

Then comes Redbud, the par-three 16 named for the pink flowering plant commonly known as the Judas tree. The hole, played entirely over water onto a green with three bunkers, proves to be Duval's downfall. He bogeys the hole.

So does Mickelson.

Tiger pars 16 and 17 and takes control.

Augusta National's par-four 18th hole is Holly, an uphill-cresting fairway. Tiger's tee shot soars 330 yards, then it's a seventy-five-yard pitch and a twelve-foot putt for birdie. A fourth-round 68 brings Tiger to 272 and 16 under par to capture the 2001 Masters.

There's a momentary pause before Tiger processes what has happened. "When I didn't have any more shots to play, that's when I started to realize what I had done; I won the tournament, and I started getting a little emotional, and I was trying to pull it together."

Tiger covers his face with his cap. The cameras keep rolling as he struggles to regain composure while Mickelson sinks his own final putt.

Earl and Tida join Tiger on the 18th green. The family embraces in celebration of what Tiger says "probably will go down as one of the top moments in our sport."

Per tradition, the 2000 Masters champion, Vijay Singh, puts the Green Jacket on the new two-time champion Tiger.

David Duval, once again a Masters runner-up, offers some context. "It's very difficult to win any of these major tournaments. To have your game in the right place at the right time, there's an art to that. I don't know what you can compare it to because there's not something to compare it to in modern golf."

In the lead-up to the Masters, there was talk of a Tiger Slam—if he won four consecutive major tournaments outside the scope of a calendar year. The name sticks.

"When I won here in '97, I hadn't been pro a full year yet," Tiger says. "I was a little young, a little naïve and I didn't understand what I'd accomplished. This year, I understand. I've been around the block a few times now, and I have a better appreciation of what it takes to win a major championship. To win four in succession, it's hard to believe."

PART 5
Family Man

Chapter 46

The 130th British Open
Royal Lytham & St Annes Golf Club
Lytham St Annes, England
July 19–22, 2001

I want to get married and do the family thing at some point," Tiger Woods tells *Newsweek*. "I'd like that a lot. But right now my focus is golf. That's where all my energy goes."

The twenty-five-year-old is in no rush to settle down. In early 2001, he quietly split from Joanna Jagoda, his girlfriend of two years.

Heartbreak, some say, drove him into a so-called slump. But as David Duval slyly points out, "He's won four tournaments so far, including the Masters, so it's been a disastrous year, I guess."

Earl Woods similarly dismisses critics' talk. "He wasn't in a slump," he says, defending his son. "He was in spring training."

Amping up to get "tournament tough" is best done as a bachelor. Earl rejects reporters' suggestions that "maybe Tiger needs a Tigress"—and tabloids touting steamy new romances with Miss Universe Lara Dutta and volleyball superstar Gabrielle Reece.

"It is very difficult for a professional golfer to maintain the level he has to if he has a honey-do, a girlfriend on tour" is Earl's opinion. Girlfriends, he says, "can either help you or hurt you. In Tiger's case, he doesn't need any help or any hurt."

Tiger's parents were not fans of his first girlfriend in high school, Dina Gravell. Gravell, a blue-eyed blond cheerleader a grade ahead of Tiger, was charmed by his "sweetness" but had zero interest in golf. "I just didn't think of golf as a sport," Gravell later admits. "I thought of it as a recreational activity for older people."

Tida didn't mind Tiger's teenage romance but disliked Dina's attitude. "He must find a girl that loves golf," Tida told *Sports Illustrated* back in 1993. "If she doesn't know anything about golf, she will go on the course with him and say, 'Where's the ball? What's the ball?' And then she will leave."

Gravell and Tiger dated for nearly four years, but the relationship abruptly ended when Tiger was away at Stanford and sent a cold breakup letter. "He said my parents are very concerned that you're a big distraction for me, and I have to listen to them. We have to break up," Gravell recalls. "I felt I was punched in the stomach."

Earl puts it bluntly. "What I thought was a bad idea was what her family had in mind. They had determined that Tiger was going to make a lot of money. They were meaning to make the relationship a permanent relationship. I could see this, but Tiger couldn't."

Journalist Fred Mitchell, who spent a lot of time with the Woods family in the late '90s while working with Earl on his book *Playing Through*, recalls girls frequently calling the house looking for Tiger. "Gold diggers! Gold diggers!" as Tida refers to them all.

It's an open secret that Tiger's parents are years into their own separation—Tida lives in the Tustin house, purchased in 1996, and Earl lives in Cypress, at Tiger's childhood home. Though they've remained legally married, respectful toward each other and devoted to their son, Earl's cynical about the very institution. "I've told Tiger that marriage is unnecessary in a mobile society like ours," he informed a *New York Times* reporter during the Masters.

Earl doubles down in the June 9, 2001, issue of *TV Guide*. "I don't see Tiger marrying before 30, if then, because he has a lot to accomplish," he declares. "And let's face it, a wife can sometimes be a deterrent to a good game of golf." Dealing with "the finite little problems" that come with marriage, Earl says, "would destroy him."

Jack Nicklaus, who by 2001 has been married for more than forty years to Barbara Nicklaus, a.k.a. "First Lady of Golf," counters Earl's viewpoint in an interview with the Scottish *Daily Record*. "Who's Tiger going to play for? For newspaper clippings? Trophies?" the golf legend asks. "Who's he going to talk to in his hotel room after rounds?"

Right now, it's Tiger's friend group, which still includes close pals from high school and college such as Bryon Bell and Jerry Chang (whom Tiger nicknames B-Bell and Jer-Dog) as well as fellow celebrity athletes, some a decade or more older: basketball legends Michael Jordan and Charles Barkley (a.k.a. M and Chuck); baseball stars Ken Griffey Jr. and Alex Rodriguez (Junior and A-Rod); and of course Mark O'Meara (Marko).

"I have business advisers I rely on for some things and celebrity friends I talk to about other things," Tiger says. "I need both perspectives."

"Even though we played different sports, the level of commitment was there, and you can bond over that. I see him as a brother, handling a lot of the same pressures that I did," Jordan says about Tiger.

"Our younger brother—that's the best way to describe him," Barkley says in agreement, pointing out that "our bond is that we're black, famous and rich, and living in a fishbowl."

Tiger enjoys "the times when I can just hang out with any of my friends and relax and do nothing—which is not often." A group of them traveled to the Bahamas last December to celebrate his twenty-fifth birthday. In addition to golfing and gambling, some of the birthday party went fly-fishing and scuba diving—pastimes Charles Barkley was happy to leave to the others.

Tiger "does that scuba-diving stuff with his white friends," says Barkley, "so we're glad they come along, because Michael ain't getting in no water and neither am I. We don't swim or fish," he says with a laugh. Besides, Tiger's childhood friends are "a good group of young people around him who keep him grounded. We can't do that."

Tiger's the defending British Open champion going into the 2001 Open after winning at St Andrews in 2000 as part of his spectacular grand slam season.

"My swing really has not been as solid as I would like it to be, but it is OK," Tiger tells reporters on July 18, the day before the 130th Open begins at Royal Lytham & St Annes Golf Club, in England. "Hopefully, it will be ready by Thursday."

But a back-to-back victory is not to be. David Duval instead manages his first win at a major, while Tiger struggles his way to twenty-fifth place, nine shots behind.

Still, the tournament week holds one unexpected outcome for Tiger:

He meets a young woman named Elin.

Chapter 47

Bighorn Golf Club
Palm Desert, California
July 30, 2001

"A re you ready for some golf?" Tiger asks in his latest national TV spot.

The line promoting ABC's *Monday Night Golf* is a wink at the famous "Are you ready for some football?" lyric that Hank Williams Jr. has sung since 1989 to introduce the ABC Sports blockbuster *Monday Night Football* broadcast.

In a venue bigger than any football stadium—more than seven thousand yards on the Canyons Course at Bighorn Golf Club, in Palm Desert, California—Tiger will be competing for a $1.2 million first prize. He's well on his way to a fourth consecutive year atop the tour money list, having earned $9,188,321 in the 2000 PGA season and millions more in the 2001 season still underway, not to mention his position as America's top athlete endorser, representing a dozen brands, including American Express, Buick, and Wheaties.

Disney's determined to have Tiger promote its theme parks, but there's a major obstacle: his "iron-clad deal with Nike," which poses "a serious problem," as an anonymous Disney source tells the *Los Angeles Times*.

Even between two behemoth corporations, "there was a concern that the Disney brand name would overshadow the Nike name."

In September of 2000, Nike and IMG concluded eighteen months of negotiations to extend the $40 million, five-year contract Tiger signed in 1996 for a further five-year term, reportedly worth up to $100 million. According to the Portland *Oregonian,* Tiger's new deal to "plug Nike's shoes, clothes, and equipment" includes a cut of Nike Golf's profits and could "make [Woods] the highest paid sports endorser in history."

"Did he get a big raise?" Nike Golf's president, Bob Wood, says. "Yes, he did, and he's worth every penny of it."

Despite the record-setting paycheck, Earl Woods insists that money is not and has never been a driving factor for his son. "He doesn't need someone waving dollar signs in front of his face to get him going," Earl tells the *New York Times.* "Tiger has no comfort zone when it comes to competition. People don't believe me, but he's going to get much better. We've only seen the tip of the iceberg."

Disney settles for a smaller piece of that ice. The entertainment giant secures a deal with Tiger guaranteeing that he will continue to appear in future televised golf exhibitions and in "Battle at" broadcasts.

Nike remains a major player on the Palm Desert set. Nike Golf's business director, David Hagler, is responsible for "scripting" Tiger's clothing for major events, telling Canada's *National Post* that Tiger "pretty much wears the same cap every tournament, it's just a question of which colour he wears. The specific cap and the pants we kind of leave up to him, we're not that stringent. He has good enough taste that he knows what colour cap and pants to wear."

ABC's changed up the competition format. In 1999, Tiger defeated David Duval in the "Showdown at Sherwood," then lost to Sergio Garcia in last year's "Battle at Bighorn." This year, PGA and LPGA stars will face off in mixed doubles: Tiger and Annika Sörenstam versus David Duval and Karrie Webb.

The alternate-shot competition stretches on for so long that the last five holes are played under floodlights. Tiger's unbothered.

"I grew up playing under the lights," he tells reporters. "The tee shots are all right. The second shots are all right." The hard part, he says, is "just seeing what the ball is going to do on the ground." Tiger and Annika Sörenstam clinch a win in extra play well after midnight on the East Coast.

Sörenstam, a thirty-year-old Swedish native who's already qualified for the LPGA Hall of Fame, says, "It was a great day for women's golf, and for Karrie and me to have a chance to play with these guys." Back in April, in the final round of the Kraft Nabisco Championship, Sörenstam had her own Nike moment, making sports—and sportswear—headlines by donning a custom pair of shiny, cherry-red Nike leather golf shoes to defeat Karrie Webb.

Nike's next challenge: meeting Tiger's exacting standards for golf equipment. Kel Devlin, Nike's sports marketing director, worked with Tiger on the development of the Nike Tour Accuracy. Tiger debuted the golf ball, Nike's first, during his record-setting 2000 PGA season. "He makes us work hard because his standards are so high," Devlin says. "But for us, it's fun trying to bring our game up to his level."

Nike Golf's Stan Grissinger describes the extent of Tiger's sensory perception: he'd take four balls, bounce each four times off the edge of his sand wedge, then report to the Nike tech team.

"Here they are, hardest to softest," Tiger would tell them.

"And he was always right," Grissinger says. "We're talking about a compression point or two, something only a machine can detect accurately."

Equipment engineer Tom Stites brings his entire company in-house to Nike. Stites, who designed clubs for eighteen-time major champion Jack Nicklaus and nine-time major champion Ben Hogan, is now tasked with creating clubs for Tiger and David Duval.

"A golf club has to be manufactured just like building a house," Stites recalls Hogan saying. "You've gotta engage the dirt first. And so look at the sole of the golf club, and then build back to the hands from that."

Stites studies the clubs Tiger used throughout his childhood and teenage years, then cuts prototypes from blocks of steel billet. The irons are forged at Endo Manufacturing, in Japan, leaving one hundred to three hundred grams of excess metal to be trimmed away once each club is tooled at Stites's firing ovens, in Fort Worth, Texas.

He, too, notes Tiger's sensitivity to tiny differences. "Around here, we say he's a space alien," Stites remarks. "He has tactile skills we cannot comprehend."

"I like the heavy one," Tiger says when Stites sends him six drivers to test.

"What?" The distinction doesn't immediately register.

Stites's team reweighs each club. "There couldn't have been a difference of more than a gram in any of the drivers," he says of the prototypes. But "sure enough, he'd picked the one that was maybe a half-gram heavier than the rest. That's like if I gave you two stacks of 150 $1 bills, then tore one bill in half and told you to pick the heavier pile."

The meticulous attention to detail pays off in late 2002, when Tiger starts using a Nike driver.

On Monday, March 4, 2002, Tiger is in New York City to promote his new video game with EA Sports, *Tiger Woods PGA Tour 2002*. He plays the game on a PlayStation 2 — as Mark O'Meara.

"I don't play me because it's too weird," Tiger tells the Associated Press. "I usually like playing O'Meara or someone like that, so I can be old and gray."

Tiger's two opponents — each playing as Tiger — are boys being treated for serious illnesses. Tiger loses the game but delights fans when he appears in Times Square at Toys "R" Us and on MTV's *Total Request Live*, wearing a black leather blazer with the tips of his hair frosted a reddish blond.

MTV host Carson Daly is a passionate amateur golfer, but he and Tiger talk more about music than sports. The last concert Tiger attended? Janet Jackson. His favorite band? U2.

Next month, Daly will attend Tiger Jam V, the fifth of Tiger's celebrity golf-entertainment benefit events, which raise money for children's charities. Daly, who was also at Tiger Jam III, calls it "a chance to do the right thing with Tiger. And the golf and the gambling didn't hurt."

Chapter 48

Players Championship
TPC Sawgrass
Ponte Vedra Beach, Florida
March 18–24, 2002

The main attraction at the 2002 Players Championship is not its defending champ.

"Is that her?" a trio of young men ask, gazing at a tall blond woman.

"I think that is her."

"She looks Swedish to me. That's definitively her."

The three guys are on the prowl. "We're not here to see Tiger Woods," they explain. "We're here to see Tiger's girlfriend."

The girlfriend in question is twenty-two-year-old Elin Nordegren, a smart, athletic, blue-eyed blonde from Sweden—a psychology student who enjoys kickboxing and diving and who's done some swimsuit modeling with famed Swedish photographer Bingo Rimér. It's those racy bikini-model photos, recently published in a London tabloid, that have ignited the public's interest.

Who is this woman, and what's the story with her and golf's number one phenom?

Fellow Swede and pro golfer Jesper Parnevik, who introduced the pair at last year's British Open, tells *Golf World*, "They're very compatible and madly in love with each other."

For Tiger, it was apparently love at first sight.

Elin, however, needed some convincing. She's unimpressed when Tiger first asks her out via a third party, a tactic she deems "weird and pathetic." Besides, the then twenty-one-year-old has a boyfriend back in Sweden, "a normal, decent guy, driving a forklift in a warehouse," says *People* writer Steve Helling. And frankly, Tiger "simply wasn't her type."

The gorgeous blonde and her identical twin sister, Josefin, have spent the last year in Jupiter Island, Florida, working as au pairs for Mia and Jesper Parnevik's young children: their daughters—Peg, Penny, and Philippa—and their infant son, Phoenix (named in honor of Parnevik's first PGA Tour win, at the 1998 Phoenix Open).

Elin comes from an intellectual family—her mother, Barbro Holmberg, is a political adviser; her father, Thomas Nordegren, is a radio journalist; her older brother, Axel, works in banking; and her sister, Josefin, plans a career in law. "It is flattering to be called a model, but I hardly think a few shoots in my teenage years make me a model," Elin says. She's taking a gap year from school but plans on going into "psychology with a focus on children who have had a hard time."

"She's very mature for her age" is Parnevik's opinion. "And she's not like many American girls who want Tiger for his money."

"She had her opinions about celebrities and they were not high," adds Elin's friend Sandra Sobieraj Westfall. "And she's very shy, so the idea of joining that world was not appealing to her."

Photographer Bingo Rimér confirms it: "She told me a million times, 'I feel so stressed out about the whole celebrity thing, the media focus.'"

Tiger's smitten, and he continues trying his luck with Elin for months. When Elin ends her long-distance relationship, she finally relents. To her surprise, a night out with Tiger *is* fun. He wins her over with his normalcy, not his money or celebrity. And maybe he is her type after all: when asked what she finds sexy, Elin lists "charisma, humor and self-confidence"—all traits that Tiger has in abundance.

The two start quietly spending more time together. By January of 2002 — while competing at the New Zealand Open on caddie Steve Williams's hometown course, Paraparaumu Beach — Tiger's calling and messaging Elin several times a day.

"Elin is exactly what Tiger needs to get stability in life," Parnevik tells a Scandinavian tabloid. "The personal chemistry really works. They complement each other."

The downside for the Parneviks: they need to hire a new nanny, since Elin quits her job to follow Tiger.

On March 18, Elin's first spotted cheering Tiger on and winking at him from the sidelines at Arnold Palmer's Bay Hill Invitational, his first win of 2002. It is also his record-setting third consecutive win at Bay Hill.

PGA Tour members note that Tiger seems totally infatuated, unable to keep his eyes off Elin.

"It's anybody's guess whether this will last. But the feeling is that Tiger doesn't fall in love easily, and that he is 100 percent committed to Elin," one of Tiger's friends says.

Tiger himself puts it plainly. "Yeah, I'm happy!"

Chapter 49

The 66th Masters
Augusta National Golf Club
Augusta, Georgia
April 11–14, 2002

Past winners of the Masters gather at Augusta National Golf Club for an annual tradition. On Tuesday night of Masters Week, the Champions' Dinner—officially called the Masters Club Dinner—brings the club's Green Jacket winners together to dine on a menu chosen by the current title holder.

As defending champion, Tiger selects sushi and sashimi appetizers, a main course of porterhouse steak and chicken, and for dessert, chocolate cake with ganache filling and vanilla ice cream. The green-inked menu card for April 9, 2002, reads: SERVED IN HONOR OF MR. TIGER WOODS. It's more elevated than the cheeseburgers and fries with milkshakes and strawberry shortcake he chose in 1998, as the twenty-one-year-old 1997 champion.

The following evening, on April 10, Tiger and Elin make their first official public appearance together, at the Golf Writers Association of

America awards dinner, where Tiger receives his fourth consecutive PGA Tour Player of the Year award. The couple looks relaxed and affectionate while at a table with LPGA Rolex Player of the Year Annika Sörenstam, who also shares IMG agent Mark Steinberg with Tiger.

Augusta National chairman Hootie Johnson has something new to debut, too. Johnson has made major changes to the golf course, extending the distance on nine of its eighteen holes in a technique sportswriters call "Tiger-proofing." The 1st now has an additional forty-five yards; the 18th is *sixty* yards longer. Not only have tees been moved back: fifty-year-old trees have also been uprooted and replanted and bunkers reconfigured to maximize course hazards.

"On 18 you've got to drive it up a gnat's ass," Greg Norman complains.

Jack Nicklaus (1965, 1966) and Nick Faldo (1989, 1990) are the only two players to have won back-to-back Masters titles. Tiger's looking to join their ranks, defend his 2001 title, and earn his third Green Jacket in six years.

Through steady rainfall, Elin joins Tida, Tiger's mother, in the gallery to watch as Tiger shoots 70-69-66. Going into the final, he's tied at 11 under with South African golfer Retief Goosen, the 2001 U.S. Open champion and fourth on the Official World Golf Ranking. Second-ranked Phil Mickelson is four back, tied with Ernie Els and Sergio Garcia.

In his ongoing quest for his first major victory, Mickelson has been studying New Age spirituality with Deepak Chopra and reading Stephen Hawking's books on quantum physics. The newfound calm drains away when Mickelson, waiting to play the 8th, hears the crowd roar for Tiger's chip for birdie on the 6th. In his call for CBS Sports, Verne Lundquist captures Mickelson's devastation. *"Hello! If he doesn't get you one way, he'll get you another!"*

"I don't care what any of these guys say about not looking at him or not noticing what he's doing," says Earl Woods. "Tiger intimidates through osmosis. You feel it. It freaks people out."

Six of the world's top seven players chase the lead, but none of them can make a run. Tiger manages to squash them all with a 12-under 276, successfully defending his title and securing his seventh major in six years.

"I was kind of surprised, no doubt about it," Tiger says of repeating his 2001 victory. "But that doesn't deter me from my concentration."

"Do I get the green pants for finishing second?" jokes Goosen, who ends his Masters Sunday three strokes behind Tiger.

Tiger accepts a check for $1,008,000 from Hootie Johnson, along with his third Green Jacket. He's less besotted with the coveted garment these days than he was in 1997, when he cuddled it all night as if it were a teddy bear.

"I mean," Tiger says now, "it's not like you're going to walk around with this thing on, are you?"

The Green Jacket is nowhere in sight by Sunday evening, when Tiger leaves the clubhouse with a cold Budweiser tucked into his right hand, his left arm wrapped around his girlfriend. It's clear that he'd rather be snuggled up with Elin than with an inanimate article of clothing.

The couple is next off to Las Vegas, to the Mandalay Bay Resort and Casino, for Tiger Jam V. The Tiger Woods Foundation's annual celebrity-packed music, golf, and entertainment benefit has raised almost $4 million for charities supporting inner-city children since its inception in 1998.

Tiger Jam V will include a three-hole "better-ball" celebrity skins golf match, a youth leadership clinic, and an evening concert headlined by Train and veteran rocker Don Henley, who tells the *Las Vegas Sun* that he admires people like Tiger, who use their success "to turn around and do something good for the community at large...so I'm happy to help out, particularly when it comes to children."

When Céline Dion headlined Tiger Jam II, she gushed, "He's not only the No. 1 golfer, he's the No. 1 human being."

In addition to Tiger's best celebrity pals, Michael Jordan and Charles Barkley, this year's attendees include MTV host Carson Daly, comic Dennis Miller, producer Quincy Jones, and TV stars Dylan McDermott and Kevin James.

Tiger's still riding the high from his third Masters win. He wins big at the craps table at Mandalay Bay in front of a huge crowd of spectators, celebrating alongside Stanford pal Jerry Chang, and later plays blackjack with Elin perched on his lap.

But even after a late night at the tables, Tiger's up early Saturday morning, hitting the practice range at Rio Secco Golf Club in preparation for today's match, which he'll play against Barkley, McDermott, James, and former pro volleyballer Gabrielle Reece. "I came out at 7 a.m. to hit balls," Reece says, "and there was only one person already here." With Tiger, "it's impossible for him to shift down a gear. For him, it wasn't a ha-ha thing out there at all."

After the match (which Kevin James wins, to Tiger's annoyance) and before the concert comes the leadership and community activism conference in support of the Tiger Woods Foundation's Start Something program. Inspirational speakers include a Las Vegas SWAT team member, a chef, Miss Teen USA, Cirque du Soleil performers, and Earl Woods himself.

Struggling to his feet, Earl speaks to the crowd of kids but pointedly addresses his own son. "As for his golf, you ain't seen nothin' yet," he says. "But his impact on this world can be so much greater. It's a hell of a responsibility, to make that impact. So there's your task, son," he intones as Tiger nods.

Earl is still a persuasive speaker, despite his increasingly poor health—and his stubborn refusal to do anything to improve it. The recently turned seventy-year-old is a prostate cancer survivor who's also had three open-heart surgeries yet continues to smoke Merits, drink liquor, eat fatty foods, and avoid exercise. "His energy drains away so easily that he tends to doze off. He's short of breath. His refusal to change old habits hits his family like a suicide note," *Sports Illustrated* stated two years ago. Nothing's changed since then.

"He said, 'This is the way I want to live my life,'" Tida recounts. She and Tiger have both thrown their hands up in resignation. "But I want to see my son's future. I want to see my grandkids. Dad wants to check out first? Fine with me. But I want to stay longer."

Chapter 50

The 102nd U.S. Open
Black Course, Bethpage State Park
Farmingdale, New York
June 13–16, 2002

The "People's Open" has been seven years in the making. For the first time, the United States Golf Association's national championship will be played at a publicly owned venue: the Black Course at Bethpage State Park, an hour's drive from New York City. The USGA has sponsored a $3 million renovation of the Depression-era public works project for the 102nd U.S. Open.

USGA commissioner David Fay successfully navigated New York's notorious bureaucracy. Course designer Rees Jones (son of famed architect Robert Trent Jones) faced an even tougher challenge: re-create A. W. Tillinghast's original course architecture working from nothing but a 1938 aerial photograph.

Six-time major winner Nick Faldo is astonished at the results. "I'm amazed this has been sitting here 65 years unknown," he says of the Black Course, a.k.a. Bethpage Black. "It's an absolute monster diamond, it's a monster gem." Forty-four-year-old Faldo plays wearing an I ♥ NY hat in support of the city's post-9/11 recovery.

On June 13, the galleries are bursting with forty-two thousand lucky ticket holders. The same capacity crowd is expected for all four days of tournament play. NBC Sports anticipates that the "People's Open" will be the largest golf television broadcast ever.

Rabbi Marc Gellman, a leader in the transformation of Bethpage Black, says, "I have this vision of a working-class guy sitting on a couch watching the U.S. Open and he turns to his son or daughter and says, 'Tiger better watch out because I know that putt, and it breaks to the left,'" Gellman says. "That could not have happened in any other U.S. Open ever."

Rees Jones tells the *Washington Post* that Bethpage Black's 7,214-yard length "sets up very well" for Tiger, however, because the redesign "favors the long hitters, Tiger chief among them."

Tiger's arguably the tour member most familiar with playing municipal courses. "I grew up playing at public facilities," he reminds reporters. "I've slept in cars to get tee times."

Despite now being the heavy favorite, eyeing a second U.S. Open victory for a potential 2002 grand slam, Tiger wins over scrappy fans when he steps out of a portable toilet to applause, then jokes, "Are you guys clapping because I'm potty-trained?"

Still, the crowd is pulling for Phil Mickelson. The final round coincides with his thirty-second birthday. "Let's go Mick-el-son," thousands chant as the birthday boy pulls to within two strokes on the 13th...only to have Tiger birdie the hole and end his rally.

Tiger bests Mickelson by three strokes, winning the tournament and notching his second majors for 2002. The twenty-six-year-old has now played twenty-two majors and won eight of them—a record that outpaces Jack Nicklaus's seven major victories during his first six years on tour. To many, Tiger's continued success is a foregone conclusion. "Who dares to think he won't get the Grand Slam this year?" demands the *New York Times*.

Mickelson concedes, "Having the chance to compete against arguably the greatest player of all time is a special opportunity, and I'm getting closer to breaking through." But Sergio Garcia (who finishes fourth) is more cynical about Tiger's historic run coming to an end, saying, "It's only a matter of time."

Chapter 51

The 131st British Open
Muirfield
Gullane, East Lothian, Scotland
July 18–21, 2002

In early July, Tiger joins Mark O'Meara on his annual trip to Ireland, where they tune up ahead of the 131st British Open.

Scotland's Muirfield hosted its first Open in 1892, and has hosted it thirteen times since. The links course measures 7,034 yards in two loops of nine holes played in opposite directions to minimize favorable winds for any one player. Nick Faldo knows it well, having won the last two times Muirfield hosted the Open, in 1987 and 1992. "You can't have one game plan" to win on a links course, Faldo tells the *New York Times*. "With the winds changing all the time, you have to study the golf course."

The weather this summer's been dry enough to brown the fairways and greens, and the rough is dangerous, with three cuts ranging from short grass to waist-high hay. No one's expecting rain.

On Sunday, July 14, Ernie Els watches a gorgeous sunset over the Muirfield clubhouse and the dunes that line the Firth of Forth estuary. "If that doesn't inspire you, nothing will," Els tells a friend of the spectacular sight.

Els and Tiger both open with 70, then in the second round Els pulls ahead with a 66 to Tiger's 68. Tiger and Mark O'Meara are paired in the third round for a 2:30 p.m. tee time toward the end of the field.

On Friday afternoon, Australian golfer and 1995 PGA Championship winner Steve Elkington stops in at a North Berwick pub overlooking an ancient harbor. "I go into the Auld Hoose and there's an old guy who has a silver jug that they just leave for him. They call him the harbor master, and he has this big, long beard," Elkington says.

The man, who's been reading the currents, issues a stern warning.

"Listen to me," the harbormaster tells Elkington. "The weather is going to be s— at about three p.m. tomorrow."

After finishing an early morning third round, Elkington returns to the Auld Hoose for a rest. "When I came back out, two hours later, I looked out the front door and there was a guy crawling along hands and knees trying to get in the pub, the weather is so bad."

Though unaware of the harbormaster's prophecy, Tiger is barely out on the first hole when apocalyptic weather strikes: "The temperature dropped, rain was coming sideways, blowing. And the gusts were over 40 [mph]."

Almost as abysmal as the weather is Tiger's score. His third-round 81, the highest he's ever shot in a professional round, is no reflection on his performance.

"It was just blowing so hard out there, it was tough to stand up straight at times," Tiger says afterward. "I'm disappointed and frustrated, but I tried all the way around." Still, he's typically pragmatic, calling it "one of those fluke days that you had to throw out. It was just brutal for all of us."

Irish golf prodigy Padraig Harrington shoots a 76, slipping from his spot at the beginning of the day—a five-way tie for the lead—in "the worst weather I've ever played golf in." Two factors, Harrington explains, "were making the wind seem extreme—cold and wet—yet the wet was stopping the ball from rolling off."

It feels miraculous when the weather finally clears, though it would take divine intervention — or a score of 59, one stroke better than what's considered a perfect game — for Tiger to catch Els and ascend to the top of the leaderboard.

"I never gave up the chance of winning until the last three holes," Tiger says, but his fourth-round 65 and 284 total is only enough for him to be in a nine-way tie for twenty-eighth — six strokes back from the winner, Ernie Els. The two-time U.S. Open champion emerges victorious in a four-way playoff for his first British Open win.

So much for a 2002 grand slam repeat.

As Tiger walks off the 18th green, he tips his hat to the Muirfield crowds, his mind already in Florida. "I'm going home to put some shorts and a T-shirt on and walk outside," he says.

It's only a quick stop home before Tiger is back on the road, traveling north to Chaska, Minnesota, for the 2002 PGA Championship, at the Hazeltine National Golf Club. In the second round, he hits into the fairway bunker on 18. With the ball below his feet, he hits a full 3-iron into the middle of the green. Broadcasting from the CBS booth, Jim Nantz declares it "one of the best golf shots I've ever seen."

"Hard left to right wind, and my heels were up against the lip of the bunker. I've never felt contact that solid," Tiger says. "It was the greatest-feeling shot I've ever hit in my entire life. On top of that, I made a 20-footer for birdie, and Ernie Els flipped me off."

Els finishes at 72–71, three strokes back from Tiger's 71–69. The five-way tie for the lead at 138 includes Texan Justin Leonard, 2001 U.S. Open champion Retief Goosen, and Rich Beem, an Arizona golfer ranked seventy-third in the world.

After winning the 1997 British Open at Scotland's Royal Troon Golf Club five years ago, Leonard struggled on tour until he began working with Tiger's swing coach, Butch Harmon. Over the course of the 2000 and 2001 seasons, Harmon has helped Leonard stabilize his base and shorten his swing.

In the fourth round, Beem unexpectedly begins to surge while Tiger makes two consecutive bogeys. Even birdieing the final four holes can't put him ahead of Beem, who ends up winning his first PGA Championship by a single stroke.

The fallout is swift.

Days later, an unhappy Tiger cuts ties with Butch Harmon, his swing coach of a decade.

Just a few weeks earlier, Harmon told reporters, "One of the reasons Tiger and I have had such a long run is mutual respect." To Harmon, that means a hands-off technique. "The teaching of Tiger Woods is totally over with," Harmon notes. "It's now pure maintenance. If he's a little off, I've been with him so long, I can see it instantly."

But Harmon misses the signs that Tiger is fed up.

According to Earl, Tiger's displeased with Harmon's self-referential style in TV interviews, saying, "We hit this 2-iron" and "We won this way."

"We?" Tiger turns to Earl, incredulous.

In the span of a single month, Tiger's gone from grand slam contention to losing two consecutive majors.

Ernie Els marks the changes as having begun back at Tiger's disastrous third round at the British Open on Saturday, July 20. "That Saturday changed a lot of things," Els tells *Sports Illustrated*. "Tiger had been getting all the breaks, with tee times, weather, everything. Since then it's been different."

Chapter 52

TOUR Championship
East Lake Golf Club
Atlanta, Georgia
October 31–November 3, 2002

Phil Mickelson's getting impatient.

It's 12:55 p.m. on Halloween, and Tiger and Mickelson are about to tee off in the TOUR Championship, the season-ending contest among the PGA's top thirty money winners.

The East Lake Golf Club announcer introduces Tiger by naming the five tournaments he's won in 2002. Mickelson, with two wins, interrupts.

"Alright, alright," he says, playing the implied "enough already" for a laugh.

His joke lands big. The packed gallery erupts in laughter. So does Tiger. But the lightness doesn't last.

After the first two rounds, the players are tied at 1 under. In the third, Tiger bogeys 18. Though he finishes the round at 67, he's angry. Outside the scoring trailer, he kicks a fence post.

The next day, Tiger's visibly limping on the course. He's got bigger problems than his run-in with the fence post. His left knee has been bothering him the entire season, to the point where painkillers have become part of his pre-round regimen.

He knows the constant pain is damaging the technique he's spent his career perfecting. "The more the knee hurt, the more I'd have to make alterations in the swing to try to make solid contact," he says. "The more alterations I made, the more distance I lost, because I was actually moving away from the ball a lot, slowing down, trying not to make it hurt."

At the TOUR Championship, Tiger ties for seventh and Mickelson for fifth, well back from the winner, Vijay Singh, and the $900,000 top prize.

An examination of Tiger's left knee shows inflammation. Treatment with ice and anti-inflammatories isn't enough. He needs knee surgery. "I've been playing in pain most of the year and felt it was time to take care of it," Tiger says.

On December 12, he checks into the Healthsouth Surgery Center in Park City, Utah, where Mark O'Meara and his longtime swing coach, Hank Haney, both have ski condos. O'Meara accompanies Tiger and waits for him in recovery.

For one hour, Dr. Thomas Rosenberg operates on and around Tiger's anterior cruciate ligament (ACL) to remove built-up fluid and cysts. It's Tiger's second surgery on the left knee; he had an unrelated surgery in 1994 to excise a benign tumor.

"From what I've been told, the operation went well," Tiger later posts on his website, tigerwoods.com.

The reality is more complicated. Tiger's left ACL, he's informed, is only around 20 percent intact. He says to Haney, "I'm going to have to change my swing."

Tiger says that 2002 has been "a tough, tough year, one I don't want to have to go through again." The pain in his leg was "brutal," and he admits that "a lot of times, I didn't want to go out there and play. I felt nausea in my stomach because the pain was so great. I had it injected numerous times to play."

The beginning of the 2003 PGA season may be uncertain — "Playing my way into shape is going to take a little time" — but there's still a lot to celebrate, including his upcoming twenty-seventh birthday, on December 30, followed two days later by his girlfriend Elin's twenty-third birthday, on New Year's Day.

"I may not touch a club until after Christmas," Tiger says. Instead, he's looking forward to spending some of his holiday visiting Elin's family in her hometown, Vaxholm, a small municipality north of Stockholm, in Sweden.

"I've never seen snow fall in my life," marvels the California native and Florida resident.

Chapter 53

Buick Invitational
Torrey Pines Golf Course
La Jolla, California
February 13–16, 2003

Tiger's two months' recuperation postsurgery is the longest he's gone without playing golf since he first learned to walk.

The question is, Can he walk—and play—now?

"I have absolutely no pain, and that's great," Tiger says as he readies for his season opener, the Buick Invitational. "I'm curious to see whether or not [the knee] will hold up. I haven't been my best for a couple of years now."

Tiger Woods, the number one–ranked player in the world since August of 1999, hasn't been at his best for *years*? The idea is enough to send a chill down the spines of most competitors.

Phil Mickelson, however, takes a few potshots at Tiger, boasting to *Golf* magazine, "Tiger hates that I can fly it past him now. He has a faster swing speed than I do, but he has inferior equipment. Tiger is the only player good enough to overcome the equipment he's stuck with."

Tiger declares Mickelson's comments "foolish" and calls him "kind of a smart aleck. He tried to be funny, and it didn't work." Still, the allegation that anything about his playing or Nike gear is "inferior" is just the grist Tiger needs. He and Nike immediately put out a new TV ad in which Tiger bluntly states, "I am not a Nike athlete. I am a whoever-makes-the-best-equipment-in-the-world athlete."

Tiger comes to Torrey Pines on February 13 with something to prove, both to himself and to the world. Despite the rainy and foggy conditions, he's motivated and a little salty, turning to spectators after a particularly good drive to announce, "Pretty good for inferior equipment, eh?"

There's some tension when Mickelson ends up in the final group alongside the score leader—Tiger. When Mickelson misses a shot on the 6th, a voice from the gallery taunts, "Hey, Phil! Must be the shoes!"

Tiger steps back from the edgy exchange. Focusing on controversy, he says, is "not going to win you a golf tournament." Taking his own advice, Tiger maintains his lead and wins by four strokes.

"Tiger was gracious about it, but I think he used it as fuel," Brad Faxon, who finishes third, says of Mickelson's earlier comments. "As if he needed any more fuel."

Mickelson, who ends up in a three-way tie for fourth, laments his own performance but praises Tiger's rapid return to form. "I like to play a couple of tournaments and work my way into a competitive mind-set," says Mickelson. "He's able to walk in and out of it at will."

Easing back into things is simply not Tiger's MO.

"I've missed competing," Tiger says. "That to me is my rush, going out there and having to hit a golf shot that really matters."

Tiger's "off to his best career start . . . back atop the money chart after just four events, again imbedded in the national sports consciousness and seemingly playing better than ever," gushes the *Orlando Sentinel*.

A decisive win at Arnold Palmer's Bay Hill Invitational on March 23 is notable not only for being Tiger's fourth consecutive victory at that tournament, making him the first golfer in seventy-three years to win any particular tournament four years in a row, but also for the conditions he plays under on Sunday to earn his record-setting eleven-shot victory.

It's not just the pouring rain, enough to turn fairways into lakes. It's also that Tiger spends the entire round visibly doubled over in pain, alternating between puking and putting.

The culprit is a nasty bout of food poisoning that also caused his girlfriend, Elin, to collapse two days earlier at the clubhouse.

After accompanying Elin and paramedics to Sand Lake Hospital, in Orlando, Tiger paused before teeing off for the second round to update reporters on her condition. "With food poisoning and then walking 18 holes yesterday and getting dehydrated, it was hard for her to keep anything down. I told her she should just stay home today, but she's stubborn."

Not as stubborn as her boyfriend, it turns out.

His own symptoms hit on Saturday night. "Bad spaghetti," he tells final-round partners Brad Faxon and Stewart Cink.

Who made it?

"E," Tiger says, meaning Elin herself.

"I don't want to be too graphic about what he said," remarks Cink, but "Tiger told me he'd been up all night with stomach problems."

Tiger gingerly sips a Sierra Mist and pauses periodically to heave into the bushes at the 2nd, into the woods at the 3rd, and into a nearby parking area at the 5th.

Faxon notices Tiger hurry to a porta-potty on the 12th and exit a while later.

"Are you OK? Do you want some Imodium?" Faxon asks.

Tiger gratefully accepts the medication. "Thanks."

He vetoes going to the hospital himself. "The problem is, it's easy to check into a hospital. Getting out is the hard part. I wanted to get an IV drip, get my fluid levels up, but I didn't know if they'd let me out, so I decided not to."

The five-stroke lead he holds coming into the final round is the only reason he's here. "If I wasn't in contention, I wouldn't have gone. There's no way," he says. "Every single tee shot hurt because my abs were obviously sore from last night, and I continued on while I was playing."

Even at such a steep disadvantage, Tiger's lead only increases throughout the day. He hits a 3-wood shot on the 4th that stuns observers. "That three-wood was a beautiful shot," Faxon says. "That iced the cake. As sick as he felt, he was ready to play. I don't think he would've played much better than that if he'd felt great."

Tiger wins with a final-round 68, eleven ahead of the second-place finishers: Faxon, Cink, Kirk Triplett, and Kenny Perry. But his only thought concerns "when I can get out of here and go to the bathroom."

"The night was long, and the day was probably even longer," Tiger says, adding in apology. "That being said, I'm very happy with the way I played."

Chapter 54

Presidents Cup
Links Course, Fancourt Hotel and Country Club Estate
George, Western Cape, South Africa
November 20–23, 2003

It's almost too dark to even see where the balls are going.

The fifth Presidents Cup, with the US team in red versus the Internationals team in blue, has been an intense four days of back-and-forth single-match play. The defending champs, the Americans, are led by captain Jack Nicklaus, fielding a twelve-player team that includes Tiger Woods, Davis Love III, and Phil Mickelson. Gary Player captains the Internationals team, featuring Ernie Els, Vijay Singh, and rookie Adam Scott, among others.

Player and Els are feeling the extra pressure of representing South Africa, their native land. "Ernie was playing on home soil," says Dennis Alpert, the Presidents Cup tournament director. "He's the Big Easy and was like the ambassador of the event." On top of that, Player designed the Fancourt Links Course himself.

There's also a lot of pressure on Tiger to perform. After earning back-to-back Green Jackets at the Masters in 2001 and 2002, this year he tied with five other players for fifteenth place. He's won five tournaments in 2003 and no majors. But he's still the number one–ranked player in the world.

The two teams are well matched. Maybe too well matched—after Sunday's singles session, they're tied 17–17, necessitating a sudden-death playoff. As the sun sets, Tiger is chosen to play for the United States and Els for the Internationals. After the announcement, Alpert says, "Tiger's demeanor completely changed. He went stone cold."

With ten thousand spectators watching and darkness quickly falling, the two set up on the 18th for their first playoff hole. Both par.

Next comes the second playoff hole, on the 1st.

Tiger pars. Ernie drives into the rough, flies his second shot over the green, and now, facing a twelve-foot putt for par, calls over his caddie, Ricci Roberts. "Best you come have a look at this."

"The pressure of reading that putt was massive," Roberts says. "What a relief when Ernie banged it in, dead center."

"It was really fascinating stuff," says Adam Scott. "And incredibly, incredibly nerve-wracking watching them on the sidelines."

It's near-total darkness by the time Tiger and Els arrive at their third playoff hole, the 2nd, a par 3. Tiger knocks it ninety feet from the pin, over a ridge.

"We couldn't even see the hole," Nicklaus says. Miraculously, Tiger manages to two-putt for par. "He just played it perfectly."

"That was one of the most nerve-wracking moments I've ever had in golf," Tiger says, calling it "one of the biggest putts in my life."

Now the heat is on Els, who steadies himself by asking, "It's only a game, isn't it? It's a game you don't want to lose, but it's a game."

The relief is palpable when he manages to also make par.

At this point, the team captains, Nicklaus and Player, step in. They've been on the phone with the PGA commissioner and have reached a decision. As defending champions, the US team could argue that they ought to keep the Cup, but instead they're making it an official tie.

"Competition is about goodwill," says Nicklaus. "In the spirit of the game, my guys have agreed that we will share the Cup."

Tiger is on board. "I think it's the perfect decision."

In the van, he holds up his trembling hands for inspection. *I've never been this nervous in my life,* he says. As they near the clubhouse, Tiger has one request: "Do you guys have cranberry juice here? Can you get me a vodka cranberry?" he asks. "Make it a big one."

Dennis Alpert, the Presidents Cup tournament director, handles the drink order personally. He mixes a pint of the stiff drink and brings the glass to Tiger in the locker room.

"Tiger took the drink and chugged it like it was water," Alpert says, noticing Tiger's hands still shaking.

"Could I get another, to take the edge off?" he asks Alpert, who happily brings Tiger a second cocktail as well as a Miller Genuine Draft. Tiger makes short work of both.

"It was like a musician winding down at the end of a concert," remarks Alpert.

Tiger's emotions are equally high two days later.

He's been making important plans. He's going to propose to Elin.

"After a very short time in our relationship, I knew I was going to marry Elin and she was going to be in my life forever," the twenty-seven-year-old admits. After months of planning, he's finally found the "perfect and romantic setting."

Instead of returning to the States after the Presidents Cup, he and Elin—and a party that includes caddie Steve Williams and his fiancée plus Tiger's longtime pal Jerry Chang and his wife—arrange to spend Thanksgiving week at the Shamwari Private Game Reserve.

Shamwari is owned and founded by Adrian Gardiner, a family friend of Ernie Els. The superluxurious reserve is located on the banks of the Bushmans River between Port Elizabeth and Grahamstown on the South African coast and is home to leopards, elephants, hippos, and antelope.

When fellow PGA player and Masters winner Mike Weir and his wife vacationed there a week earlier, they even saw rhinos and lions.

Tiger's group is exclusively booked in a lodge called Lobengula, and Gardiner ensures that "not one press person got near him during his entire stay—we went the extra mile to protect his privacy."

On Tuesday, November 25, Tiger is looking for even more seclusion.

Shamwari ranger "Lucky" Nhlanhla Khumalo supervises a romantic "bushveld" overnight safari for Tiger and Elin, during which they'll sleep under the stars and cook over an open fire. But at sunset, the couple disappears into the bush.

Khumalo starts to worry as twenty minutes go by. *Have they been eaten by tigers?*

Luckily, the couple reappears safe and sound, along with a new glittering star: Elin "sporting a huge diamond," an impressive antique engagement ring with a circular diamond worth around half a million dollars today. Khumalo later tells *People* magazine, "The diamond was half as big as my finger."

The moment, Tiger admits, "was a thriller. To putt for victory in a major is nothing in comparison," he says. "Even if you say 'Will you marry me?' with the right feeling, the answer could be 'No.'"

Thank goodness, Elin says yes.

The twenty-three-year-old bride-to-be calls her father, Thomas Nordegren, to tell him, "Daddy we are engaged."

He congratulates the couple, then tells the Swedish newspaper *Expressen,* "I'm very happy about this."

Gardiner is also happy and in his enthusiasm posts an ill-advised message, including photos, about the engagement on the Shamwari Private Game Reserve website. "I am pleased that the couple chose Shamwari for a break, and that he chose their sojourn in the wildest area of Shamwari to propose to Elin," Gardiner writes.

The intensely private Tiger is furious. "For a place that supposedly prides itself on privacy, they totally let us down," he says, lashing out on his own website a few days later. The worst of it is the slight to his parents. "I really wanted to talk to them about it before the news got out," he says, "but it was too late."

As Tiger and his new fiancée fly home aboard a private Gulfstream jet, word of their engagement is shared and celebrated across the globe. Many reports focus on what a catch the millionaire number one–ranked golfer is—though Elin's former employers have a slightly different take.

"Tiger is the one who got the catch," Mia Parnevik states. "With the weird lifestyle he leads, he might never have met a nice girl. He's lucky he found Elin."

"I think she's a bit too good for him," Jesper Parnevik says, only half joking.

Chapter 55

Isleworth Golf & Country Club
Windermere, Florida
March 2004

E ver since Elin came into my life," Tiger writes on his website, "things just became a lot better. Someone you can bounce things off, somebody who is a great friend. We do just about everything together," he says of his new fiancée. "She's so much like me. She's very competitive, very feisty, just like I am."

Some people feel that Tiger needs to lean in to that competitive spirit a little more.

Aboard "Tiger Woods Airlines," Tiger's leased Gulfstream, Mark O'Meara is making his case. "Tiger," he says, "you've got to get someone to help you with your game."

They're returning to Florida from Dubai, where O'Meara's just won the European Tour's Dubai Desert Classic, besting Tiger by five strokes.

"OK, who should I get?"

Tiger has been without a coach since August of 2002, when he and Butch Harmon parted ways following the PGA Championship.

A dubious anniversary is fast approaching. This June will mark two years since Tiger's won a major. It's time to stop drifting and take action.

Back when Tiger won the 1996 NCAA individual championship, *Golf Digest* polled top coaches about the then Stanford sophomore's chances as a prospective new pro. Hank Haney boldly—and correctly—predicted that in Tiger's first full year on tour, he'd top the PGA money list.

Haney, who coached the Southern Methodist University men's golf team and established three golf schools in Dallas before taking on O'Meara as a client, never expected Tiger to notice his comment. But he soon learns that Tiger has a way of drawing on key pieces of information when he's pressed to make a decision.

During a 1999 practice round at Isleworth, Haney had been coaching O'Meara but also noted an overly upright position in Tiger's backswing. When Tiger made the adjustment Haney suggested, he won the PGA Championship—and five of the next six majors.

Cruising in the Gulfstream, O'Meara says, "Tiger, I know Hank's my friend and I've been with him for years, but he's the best teacher in the world."

"Yeah, I know," Tiger tells O'Meara. "I'm going to call him tomorrow."

By 6:00 a.m. on Monday, March 15, Haney's on a flight from Dallas to Orlando, then driving through the gates of Isleworth to Tiger's house. *This is going to be a challenge,* Haney tells himself. *This guy is different, and that's part of why he's great. This is going to be an incredible learning experience.* It's impossible to forget that the sixty-eighth Masters tournament begins in less than a month.

Tiger and Haney ride a custom golf cart—with "TW" spinner wheels and a top speed of twenty-eight miles per hour—to the least populated area of the Isleworth range as Tiger spells out his goals. "I want to get more consistent in every phase, so I have the kind of game that at majors will always get me on the back nine on Sundays with a chance," he says. "I don't want to just have a chance on the weeks when I'm hot. I want to have a chance all the time. Always putting yourself in the mix, that's the only way you're going to win a lot of them."

Haney enjoys spending time with Tiger and Elin during his visits to

Isleworth. The engaged couple shares a competitive streak and is evenly matched in Ping-Pong, tennis, and running. Elin delights in every point or match she wins, laughing and shouting, "I'm going to take you down!"

Tiger levels with *Sports Illustrated* in the lead-up to the 2004 Masters that he's having trouble trusting his self-directed swing changes, which have left him with diminished power and precision. "You can hit things on the range," he says, "but when you've got water left, water right, bunkers, the wind is blowing, you've got to hit the ball into a tight spot, yeah, it makes it a little more stressful."

Phil Mickelson has spent the first months of 2004 working with a swing coach and training with a strength and conditioning coach while skipping his favorite carbs, such as doughnuts and the buns on his In-N-Out burgers.

At the end of the third round, Mickelson and Chris DiMarco share the Masters lead at 6 under, while Tiger is 3 over and tied for twentieth place. Asked about his position on the leaderboard, Mickelson is quick to answer, "Well, it doesn't suck," his brash honesty dissolving the press corps into fits of laughter.

Jokes aside, Mickelson takes his enduring competition with Tiger—and the specter of Tiger's three Green Jackets—very seriously. In nearly twelve years as a professional golfer, the thirty-three-year-old married father of three has become known as "the best player to never win a major."

On Sunday, April 11, he's neck and neck with Ernie Els. Mickelson mounts a charge and on his last hole ekes out his first Masters win. Mickelson raises his arms, leaps into the air, and shouts, "I did it!"

After he finished in the top two or three in eight other majors, winning one is an experience he'll remember forever. "I really don't know what to say, to tell you how awesome it feels," he says. Reflecting on his

Chapter 56

United States Army garrison
Fort Bragg, North Carolina
April 12, 2004

Tiger is the only soldier reporting for duty in a private jet.

After touching down at Pope Air Force Base, he makes a quick transfer to Fort Bragg, where he's issued a camouflage uniform tagged with his name, then meets the troops and is briefed on the installation where his father, Earl, trained during his two Vietnam tours, in 1963 and 1970.

Earl and several of his old Special Forces buddies accompany Tiger to the base. "It was the thrill of a lifetime for me," Tiger says. "To see my father's group, the 'Six Group,' which no longer exists in Green Berets, to see some of the guys my dad served with in Nam, man that was really cool."

"Tiger's interest in exploring the military firsthand means a great deal to me, especially since he's chosen my former training ground," his father says. "I will not be with him during his training exercises," Earl, who totes an oxygen tank these days, notes drily. "But I'll have plenty to talk to him about when he finishes."

Fort Bragg spokesman Lieutenant Colonel Billy Buckner admits that

Tiger isn't getting the *full* military experience. "He's not going to have a drill sergeant barking up and down at him and yelling at him to get in line," Buckner says, but he will "get some exposure and experience with how Special Forces operators conduct business."

"If I was never introduced to golf, I would be doing something like that," Tiger says in agreement. "Hopefully, something in the Special Ops arena. It's the physical and mental challenge of it all. We'll see what happens."

Earl is curious, too. Tiger, he says, is "a very independent individual, and he plays an individual sport. Quite frankly, he's not in the business of people telling him what to do." Tiger, Earl declares, will "learn an awful lot about himself, and how he can handle it. He'll come out a lot stronger than he went in."

Physical training begins that Tuesday. At 6:30 a.m. Tiger joins four hundred members of the Eighteenth Airborne Corps on a four-mile cadence-call run in full uniform, including boots. It's not too far removed from the way he trains at home. "The only difference [in the run] was yelling at the top of my lungs and singing along with the guys," Tiger says. "I'm used to running alone with my MP3 player."

He completes the run in just over thirty-one minutes—besting the standard time by four minutes. "Everyone was impressed with his physical abilities," Lieutenant Colonel Buckner says. "He's a good soldier."

"There's no physical challenge in golf," Tiger tells the Associated Press. "We walk around for 4½ hours. That's not tough. . . . These guys run miles upon miles carrying a 40-pound sack and two quarts of water and flannel and rifles. That's tough."

His job doesn't compare. "I'm just trying to hit the ball into a little bitty cup that's 400 yards away. These people here are putting their lives on the line. That to me is the ultimate dedication."

At 13,500 feet, Tiger is tethered to Billy Van Soelen, an instructor with the Golden Knights, an elite army parachute team that's also done tandem jumps with celebrities such as Chuck Norris and former president George H. W. Bush. An army photographer captures Tiger in midair, smiling in his yellow jumpsuit and goggles, arms outstretched in flight. He completes two tandem jumps, saying, "It's an experience I'll never forget. You're going 120 miles per hour, but it still feels like you're floating."

"I was so excited. I couldn't wait to go," Tiger says of the parachuting experience. "I'm one of those people who love to ride roller-coasters, so to me it's like the ultimate roller-coaster."

Earl waits for Tiger in the drop zone, and they embrace.

"Now you understand my world," Earl says. But these daytime jumps are a far cry from those done under pitch-black combat situations. "Your dad was doing tactical jumps," Van Soelen tells Tiger. "This is Hollywood."

"It's an honor to walk in my father's footsteps by training with the service men and women at Fort Bragg," Tiger says of his experience. "It's not that I didn't understand what my dad did, but to physically see what he did just shed a whole new light on it."

He ends his week by hosting the Tiger Woods Foundation's thirtieth Junior Golf Clinic and a golf exhibition on the base, which is equipped with a top golf course: Stryker, designed in 1948 by famed architect Donald Ross. Tiger emerges from his army crash course to lead a clinic on April 16 for seventy-six young golfers—giving one-on-one instruction to eight of them—then put on a skills exhibition at the 13th hole for 4,300 soldiers and their families, impressing them with a variety of shots, including a live rendition of his famous Nike ad, bouncing a golf ball on his wedge.

"He's giving something back to the community," says a local coach. "I wish more golfers would give more back."

Tiger's taking with him valuable lessons learned—about the military, about himself, about his father. A Stryker Golf Course member who, like Earl, served as a Green Beret in Vietnam assesses the impact of Tiger's military training. "He's in good shape and he's young," the retired officer says. "It won't hurt him,"

Chapter 57

Sandy Lane
The Green Monkey
St. James, Barbados, West Indies
October 4–9, 2004

The luxury resort nestled in a Caribbean mahogany grove on Barbados's Platinum Coast is preparing to host a "private party," with every detail executed to white-glove standards and with military precision.

Guards in camouflage uniforms patrol the beachside bushes. All two hundred rooms at Sandy Lane are booked, as is every helicopter in the island's only rental fleet. Hotel employees erect plywood barriers while a crane operator hoists plants large enough to block views of the hotel from prying eyes.

It's an open secret on the island of Barbados that the resort will be the site of Tiger and Elin's upcoming nuptials—the previous week, the Barbados *Daily Nation* newspaper even headlined a story TIGER WOODS TYING KNOT AT SANDY LANE—but no one will confirm officially.

Searching for a connection to Tiger leads reporters to Sandy Lane's owners, a trio of Irish investors known as the Coolmore Mafia after the County Tipperary facility where one of the co-owners, John Magnier, breeds racehorses. The other two co-owners, Dermot Desmond and JP McManus, are longtime friends of Tiger.

"It all started with Dermot [Desmond] and JP [McManus] inviting Mark and I over," Tiger recalls of his first trip to Ireland, in 1998. "I had such a great time. I've been coming here ever since. I loved fishing here. I loved hanging out at the pubs. The Irish people have actually been wonderful. It's a place that I thoroughly enjoy."

He's not enjoying Ireland quite as much as usual at this year's WGC–American Express Championship at Mount Juliet Estate, near Kilkenny. Despite being the two-time defending champion, Tiger is bested by Ernie Els on Sunday, October 3, and places ninth. Just last month, Vijay Singh superseded Tiger on the Official World Golf Ranking—ending Tiger's record 264 straight weeks at the number one position—and this latest defeat knocks him further down. Now he's number three behind Singh, at number one, and Els, at number two.

After the tournament, "Air Tiger" waits on an Irish runway along with two of Tiger's closest friends, Bryon Bell, from junior high school, and Jerry Chang, from Stanford. Tiger claims they're all going "on holiday" to Barbados, where "I'll go diving, and I'll unleash myself upon the water and try to catch some fish." As for speculation that he'll be attending a destination wedding—his own—Tiger sidesteps the question with his usual tough love for the press. "All I can say is that I'm getting married in the future. I have narrowed it down to that. I think you guys would be the last people I'd ever tell."

Just last month Tiger was forced to respond to rumors that he and Elin had split. "It's 100% false," he insisted before playing in the Ryder Cup on September 17. "Nothing's happened to us. We're still very happy."

One of the headlines is unfortunately true: seventy-two-year-old Earl's prostate cancer has recently returned, spreading to his back and behind his left eye, causing him debilitating pain.

"It's been tough," Tiger says, admitting that his dad's failing health has been preoccupying him. "It's just like it was back in '96 and '97 when my dad had a heart attack and had complications with heart surgery."

Earl says he's much improved since undergoing radiation treatments to shrink the tumors. But Tiger is wary. "He doesn't exactly take care of himself," he says of his dad. "He's still puffing away, and that's just the way it is. He's been real stubborn about everything. It's got him this far, so we'll just kind of leave him be."

"Tiger was concerned and I knew how much he was concerned," Earl tells the *Boston Herald*. "When I initially told him, he was very quiet. And he looked at me and said, 'Pop, when I was a little kid you promised me you were going to be here until [age] 84. I'm going to hold you to it.' And I said, 'You've got it. I'll be here.'"

Earl stays mum about whatever's happening in Barbados, but he makes sure to be there, too.

The bride-to-be is the most tight-lipped of all. *Sports Illustrated* likens Elin to Greta Garbo, the Swedish-American film star with a penchant for solitude. According to sources quoted in a recent *SI* profile, "When she [Elin] started dating Tiger, it was like there was an unwritten agreement she wouldn't say anything to anyone. She's still nice, but when you talk to her, you don't get anything out of her."

Tiger later reveals that he and Elin have been planning for months but "didn't tell anybody until the last minute. They all said, 'Oh it is? That soon?' Yeah, well, there you go. You can still get cheap airfare. We made sure of that." Several guests of honor are only told the specifics of their final destination upon arrival in London to catch connecting flights.

Despite Tiger's recent purchase of a $20 million 155-foot tri-deck yacht named *Privacy*—which sleeps seventeen and boasts a theater and a gym—details of the five-day wedding bash start to leak out. In addition to Tiger's parents and Elin's family from Sweden, celebrities are spotted arriving on the island: star athletes Michael Jordan and Charles Barkley, plus two of Tiger's PGA pals and Isleworth neighbors, Mark O'Meara and John Cook. CNN reports that "talk-show host and media entrepreneur Oprah Winfrey and Microsoft founder Bill Gates" are also among the guests.

Absent are Tiger's Stanford and PGA buddy Notah Begay III, unable to make the trip because of a back injury, and Jesper Parnevik, who famously introduced the couple. "There's such a brouhaha around it," Parnevik explains to a Swedish tabloid about the wedding. He and his wife "will celebrate Tiger and Elin later, a bit more privately."

At 5:40 p.m. on Tuesday, October 5, 2004, 120 guests gather at the 19th hole of the brand-new Green Monkey golf course, on a hillside overlooking the Caribbean Sea, to witness twenty-four-year-old Elin Maria Pernilla Nordegren marry twenty-eight-year-old Eldrick Tont "Tiger" Woods in a simple sunset ceremony.

The officiant oversees the exchanging of the vows and rings, but it's Earl who provides the ceremony's emotional center, moving himself, and some in attendance, to tears. Earl locks eyes with Tiger before saying to the newlyweds, "I wish you a long, rich life together."

Three official photographers and one videographer capture images of Elin, a vision in her off-the-shoulder Vera Wang gown and veil, and Tiger in his olive-beige suit. Each is supported by three attendants: the bridesmaids—including Elin's twin sister, Josefin—wearing seafoam-green dresses and the groomsmen in suits matching Tiger's.

Inside a banquet hall in the clubhouse decked with ten thousand black roses, the celebration begins with champagne and caviar as a local musician plays the steelpan between speeches. Tiger, known for his frugality in spite of his $215 million fortune, has spared no expense for his bride. Back in the States, golfer Davis Love III jokingly asks a genuine question: "What do you give for a gift for a guy who's got everything? I know I would definitely not buy a toaster."

After a sumptuous multicourse dinner, the newlyweds cut their four-tier wedding cake then gaze skyward at a brief but spectacular fireworks display, visible the length of the western coast of Barbados.

"It was very understated and very elegant, just like Tiger," wedding guest John Cook says. "People had a really good time. There was a lot of dancing [at the reception]. It went on until about 11:30. Everyone was pretty roasted—by the sun and in every other way—by the time we were through."

Hootie & the Blowfish perform a private concert for the wedding guests. Lead singer Darius Rucker and Tiger have been good friends since meeting in the mid-'90s, and Tiger even joins the band onstage at one point. "He's an awful singer," says Rucker with a laugh. "But he came on and tried to do some stuff, it was funny."

As the evening winds down, Tiger and Elin slip away to the mega-yacht *Privacy* to begin their honeymoon. When they emerge the following morning, they're greeted by the sight of a rainbow arcing over the yacht, like a good omen.

"The wedding went great," Tiger says a few days later. "It was a very special occasion. We just had a great time, with all the families there." Postwedding, he's appreciating the relaxing one-on-one time with his new bride. "We're enjoying our honeymoon," he tells the media on Friday during a planned conference call, noting that it's the first chance in a quite a while that he and Elin have had to spend time alone. "It's so nice to be on the boat. We're diving every day, being by ourselves, away from everybody. It's a lot of fun."

The future lies ahead. Tiger is certain that marriage is "not going to change the way I play golf. I've been with Elin and happy together the last two years. Just because you're married, it doesn't change the relationship," he states confidently. While it hasn't been his strongest year on the PGA Tour, "as far as off the golf course, yes, it is a great year," Tiger says.

"I just hope I can get the ball in the hole a little faster."

Chapter 58

Target World Challenge
Sherwood Country Club
Thousand Oaks, California
December 9–12, 2004

S hortly following his wedding, Tiger opens up about another relationship.

He *is* working with Hank Haney. And he *is* making another swing change.

"I felt like I could get better," Tiger says. "I'd like to play my best more frequently, and that's the whole idea. That's why you make changes. I thought I could become more consistent and play at a higher level more often.... I've always taken risks to try to become a better golfer, and that's one of the things that has gotten me this far."

It pays off on Sunday, December 12, 2004, at the Target World Challenge, the sixth outing of a charity golf event that benefits the Tiger Woods Foundation. Tiger finishes at 16 under, claiming the "Tiger" trophy, a wooden tiger with a front paw atop a golf ball emblazoned with a map of the world.

He donates his $1.25 million winnings toward the completion of the Tiger Woods Learning Center. The $25 million facility for underserved youth in Anaheim, California, is inspired by Earl—who rides a golf cart around the tournament, to the delight of his son.

"It's the first time I've seen him on the golf course following my play in a lot of years," Tiger says, smiling broadly.

As for his play, Tiger says, "Every shot I wanted to hit, I hit." It feels like a triumph. "I had to take baby steps and I did that all year," he says. "Then eventually it became nine holes and 18, then 36 and 54, now a whole tournament. It's exciting."

Mark O'Meara is already looking ahead to what Tiger will do next. "Hey, he's human," O'Meara says. "Even Tiger Woods has moments of nervousness, doubt, lack of confidence. And he's had more of those lately. But believe me, I know him and I've seen what's coming. I've seen it in practice. I guarantee you he is more complete, has more shots, has more control. We haven't seen the best of Tiger Woods."

On January 23, 2005, Tiger takes the top prize in the Buick Invitational.

In March, it's on to the Ford Championship at Doral, a suburb of Miami, on a course known as the Blue Monster, packed with thirty-five thousand fans eager to see Tiger take on Phil Mickelson in the "Duel at Doral."

March 5 is Earl's seventy-third birthday. Tiger shoots a third-round 63 and dedicates it to his ailing father. "Happy birthday, dad. I told you I would shoot a low one for you, and I did," Tiger says to Earl via NBC Sports.

In the final, Tiger eagles on 12, and Mickelson answers with birdies on 13 and 14—not enough to stop Tiger's surge to a 24-under 264, giving him his second win of the season.

With the victory at Doral, Tiger regains his number one Official World Golf Ranking, and *Sports Illustrated* applauds the return of the "Wow Factor" unique to the "Tiger Classic" style of play synonymous with the Tiger Slam era.

Tiger's confidence soars as he eyes winning a potential fourth Green Jacket at next month's Masters. On Thursday, he scores a 2-over 74, then follows with 66. Darkness suspends play after nine holes on Saturday, but Tiger's stellar play has brought him within striking distance of leader Chris DiMarco, causing reporters to ask Tiger "if he ever thought he would be only four strokes off the Masters lead Saturday night."

Without hesitation, Tiger answers, "Yes."

"You're that confident?"

"Yes," he repeats.

Tiger and DiMarco loosen up on the range Sunday morning. DiMarco, a three-time all-American golfer for the University of Florida, hits a personalized "Go Gators" golf ball fifty yards. Tiger marches into the middle of the practice ground, picks up the ball, marks it with a Sharpie, and hits it back to DiMarco. "F the Gators" the ball now reads.

The playful mood evaporates as Tiger gains seven shots to take the lead, an advantage he maintains through most of the fourth round.

On the 16th, he sinks the perfect low chip from against the second cut of rough for birdie.

"In your LIFE have you seen anything like that?!" exclaims announcer Verne Lundquist from the CBS booth.

"That was more of a creative shot, just trying to spin the ball, and it was also luck," declares Tiger. "Under the circumstances, it's one of the best shots I've ever hit."

He then bogeys the next two holes. DiMarco pars both, precipitating a playoff with the score tied at 276.

This is fun, Tiger thinks.

DiMarco pars again on the first playoff hole. Tiger birdies from fifteen feet for the win.

It's an incredible achievement—his fourth Masters and his ninth major. But the one word that most describes what he's feeling? Validation.

"Hank and I have put some serious hours into this," Tiger says of today's momentous win. "To play as beautifully as I did this entire week is pretty cool."

"That's Tiger Woods," marvels Haney. Tiger "really made a commitment to go with everything we've been working on," he says. "He weathered the storm and rode it out. He just has a real strong will and it showed."

Surrounded by cheering fans, Tiger first hugs his mother, Tida, and then kisses his wife, Elin. The two will next head off on a celebratory vacation to the Cayman Islands.

Notably missing from the 18th green is Earl, who's in Augusta but watching on live TV.

"He's not able to come out here today, or all week," Tiger says of his dad. "He's hanging in there and so that's why it meant so much for me to be able to win this tournament with him kind of struggling, maybe give him a little hope, a little more fire to keep fighting."

A tearful Tiger attempts to collect himself. "This is for Dad," he says, nearly breathless with emotion. "Every year I've been lucky enough to win this tournament, my dad has been there to give me a hug. I can't wait to get back to the house and give him a big bear hug."

By the evening awards ceremony, Tiger's smiling again. "I'm the first to win four Masters before the age of thirty," the twenty-nine-year-old says. "That's pretty neat." He's now tied Arnold Palmer's Masters record; the only person to have won more is Jack Nicklaus, who's earned six Green Jackets.

Tiger's Green Jacket is a 42 long. "The first time I got it," he says, "I made sure I got it big, because you know a lot of the guys have told me that either the jackets shrink or they might expand. So I got my jacket just a touch big."

In the warm glow of the Georgia twilight, Tiger extends his gratitude to the coach who's helped him regain his confidence and his top form. "I feel the work I've done with Hank has turned things in the right direction," he says. "I hit some beautiful golf shots this week."

Chapter 59

The 134th British Open
The Old Course, St Andrews Links
St Andrews, Scotland
July 14–17, 2005

"T he only way you don't come home with the British Open," Hank Haney tells Tiger, "is if you don't work enough on your putting."

Tiger agrees.

He putts with a Titleist Scotty Cameron Newport 2. He's used some version of this putter since the 1997 season, though this year he's switched his driver to the steel-shafted Nike Ignite 460 and his 3-wood to the Nike Ignite T60 — striking all his clubs against the Nike One Platinum TW, the high-spinning four-piece ball that's the successor to the Nike Tour Accuracy.

At noon on Thursday, July 14, Tiger's on the 14th when first-round play pauses for two minutes of silence. One week earlier, terrorists bombed England's capital city, killing fifty-two people and injuring more than seven hundred. Tiger chooses to meditate, a Buddhist practice he learned from his mother.

"Tiger and Kultida used to meditate every night in their living room as he was growing up," a family friend says. "Earl would push him hard during the day, and Kultida would help center him at night through prayer and meditation."

Tida, sixty-one, is on Tiger's mind because of her proximity to the terror attacks. "My mom was in the building right across the street from where [one of the bombs] blew up," Tiger tells *Golf* reporter Michael Bamberger. She'd been in London on vacation.

Tiger expresses gratitude for his mom's safety but doesn't pretend to know the details. "Typical mom. I went, 'Are you OK?' She said, 'Yeah, good. What are you going to do today on the course?' She likes to change the subject fast."

It's a familiar pattern, Tiger explains. "When my dad had cancer, he didn't say anything. When I had my knee surgery, I didn't say anything. We just do that. It's one of our deals of probably being a Woods, I guess."

Earl has made similar statements. "Tiger is not one to over-emotionalize things," he told reporters following one of his hospitalizations. "Neither am I. We don't have to. We just touch, and it's all said."

Tida walks the Old Course with Tiger, but many fans can't resist detouring to a special ATM. The Royal Bank of Scotland has stocked it with a limited supply of commemorative £5 notes featuring a likeness of sixty-five-year-old Jack Nicklaus. Demand is brisk—the ATM runs out of money before the Claret Jug is awarded.

Nicklaus birdies the 18th. He's shot a second-round 72, five strokes back from Tiger's 67, but it's not enough. "You know, that's my best round of the year!" Nicklaus tells Tiger. "And I still didn't make the cut."

He shakes Tiger's hand and says, "Nice playing."

"Thank you, sir."

The three-time British Open winner (1966, 1970, 1978) heads into retirement with a final crossing of the Swilcan Bridge, midway up the 18th. Spectators enthusiastically note Nicklaus's argyle sweater, reminiscent of the one he wore on the Old Course in 1978.

Scottish fans are rooting for their countryman Colin Montgomerie—another golfer touted as the best never to win a major—whom comedic commentator David Feherty famously described as "having a face like a warthog stung by a wasp." In the final round, Montgomerie pulls to within one shot of the lead when Tiger bogeys the 10th after driving into one of St Andrews's 112 pot bunkers. But after a solid back nine and a total score of 274, Tiger wins his second British Open at St Andrews, five ahead of Montgomerie.

At the Royal and Ancient Golf Club, behind the first tee, Tiger accepts the top prize of $1.26 million and the Claret Jug. Just as he did at Doral and the Masters, Tiger dedicates today's win to Earl, saying, "This is for you, dad, it doesn't get any better than this."

Following tradition, Tiger kisses the Claret Jug, the trophy every British Open winner is entitled to take home and enjoy for the following year. Tiger admits that he found many occasions to drink from the silver vessel between 2001 and 2002, the last time he had possession of the cup.

When asked if he'll continue that practice when he gets back to Florida, Tiger cheekily replies, "Why wait until I get home?"

There's a lot to celebrate. By winning the 2005 British Open, he's completed his second career grand slam and notched his tenth major.

"Man, I tell you what, when I first started playing the Tour, I didn't think I'd have this many majors before the age of thirty," Tiger says. "There's no way. No one ever has. Usually the golden years are in your 30s. Hopefully that will be the case."

Chapter 60

The 87th PGA Championship
Baltusrol Golf Club
Springfield, New Jersey
August 11–14, 2005

Charles Barkley has played with the best of the best. The Hall of Fame basketballer, who's suited up for more than one thousand NBA games and countless golf pro-ams, is a popular commentator for TNT, known for calling it like he sees it.

Best trash talkers? "Michael Jordan and Tiger Woods," Barkley says. "Michael thinks he's Tiger Woods when he's playing golf and Tiger Woods is just the greatest of all time. Michael is faking it and Tiger is just better than everyone else." He's been saying it for a long time. "I knew five years ago that Tiger was the best ever," Barkley told *Sports Illustrated* in 2002. "I've played with Phil [Mickelson] and all those guys, and Tiger does things they can't do. They're intimidated by Tiger. They're soft as s——. Black Jesus scares them."

In mid-August 2005, with temperatures hovering around one hundred degrees, Barkley takes in the carnival atmosphere at New Jersey's Baltusrol Golf Club. The 110-year-old course was named in 1895 in memory of Baltus Roll, a local farmer murdered by thieves in 1831. "I've often heard people say that the rough is so thick, it's Baltus Roll getting his revenge," says golf historian Bob Trebus. Jack Nicklaus won two U.S. Opens (1967, 1980) there, and calls the course "one of the finest in the world."

The field is determined to get revenge on Tiger, who's playing to match the feat he accomplished in 2000—winning three majors in one calendar year. On the first practice day, one bold fan parks his car in the space clearly marked TIGER WOODS, 1999, 2000 PGA CHAMPION. The car is towed by 9:20 a.m.

According to the *New York Times,* "New York's pro" is Phil Mickelson. The charm that won over fans at the 2002 U.S. Open at Bethpage is on full display here at Baltusrol, making him the sentimental favorite.

"Phil's the most talented golfer I've ever played with," Barkley declares, "but if Phil worked as hard as Tiger, he'd be there every week too."

Desert golfer Mickelson fares well in the heat, but Tiger struggles, narrowly making the cut after bogeying five holes in the second round. Mickelson tells *Sports Illustrated,* "If you're looking for me to shed a tear, it's not going to happen."

Nature takes care of that. At 2:30 on Sunday afternoon, lightning strikes halt play for close to forty-five minutes. Tiger finishes his round, scoring 68 on the day for a 2-under 278. A second storm forces suspension of the remaining play until Monday morning.

From the clubhouse, Tiger examines the leaderboard. Of the twelve players who haven't finished, three (including Mickelson) are ahead of him, and two are tied. It's mathematically possible that he could be involved in a four-way playoff for the championship, but in an uncharacteristic move, Tiger takes a calculated risk and decides to leave for Orlando on Sunday night.

Despite bogeying the 16th on Monday morning, bringing the absent Tiger to within a single stroke, Mickelson ekes out a win for his second major. Steve Elkington and Thomas Bjørn tie for second, and Tiger and Davis Love III tie for fourth.

Golfers theorize that Tiger's best move would have been to appear on Baltusrol's driving range on Monday, if only to gain a psychological advantage over his opponents heading out on the course. ESPN headlines its coverage of the "un-Tigerlike" no-show WOODS ALMOST COMMITTED COLOSSAL BLUNDER.

"Yeah, it was [risky], but also it really wasn't, either," Tiger argues. "These are the best players in the world. Look at who's on that board. It wasn't like guys who have never been there before."

The Wanamaker Trophy isn't yet engraved with Mickelson's name when he comes to his rival's defense, saying, "I hear him [Woods] getting a lot of flak for it, but my goodness, it was a nonfactor. It's over with, let it go."

Chapter 61

Isleworth Golf & Country Club
Windermere, Florida
December 30, 2005

For Tiger's thirtieth birthday, Elin gives her husband a puppy. They name the black-and-white border collie Taz.

"Tiger is a true dog person," Hank Haney observes, "and he really liked that Taz was smart, focused, and task-oriented. He didn't mind that Taz wasn't very cuddly."

The puppy will have plenty of room to run around in Tiger's other birthday gift—a nearly $40 million ten-acre oceanfront property on ultraexclusive Jupiter Island, Florida. The new residence will make them neighbors of Elin's former employers, the Parneviks, as well as other PGA stars—such as Greg Norman, Nick Price, and Gary Player—and celebrities such as Céline Dion.

Tiger is thrilled to move to the barrier island. "I miss the ocean," he says, reminiscing about having grown up near the beach in Southern California. "Being in Orlando...there's a bunch of lakes, but it's not the ocean." Though the Associated Press reports that "Woods' new property includes a 13,207-square-foot home, several guest houses and two docks, perhaps with enough space for his 155-foot yacht," it's widely assumed that Tiger and Elin will tear down the main house and rebuild.

Tiger can certainly afford the hefty price tag. He tops the 2005 money list with $10,628,024—the most a player has ever earned in a single season—adding pressure to his preparations for the ambitious 2006 PGA Tour schedule: forty-eight official events, $255 million in prize money.

Tiger's off to another good start with a January 29 win at his first tournament of the season—the Buick Invitational at Torrey Pines, in San Diego, where he outputts two-time Masters Champion (1994, 1999) José María Olazábal and tour rookie Nathan Green in a playoff for the $918,000 top prize—a win that Tiger attributes to envisioning his father, Earl, "sitting on the couch saying, 'Just lag it up there'" during his crucial playoff putt.

Kept out of the headlines is his late January stop at the Naval Special Warfare Center at Coronado, California, where he spends three days with the Navy SEALs, learning about special operations and doing basic training on weaponry and marksmanship skills.

"I wanted to be a SEAL when I was young," Tiger tells class 259, which is about to begin its Basic Underwater Demolition/SEAL (BUD/S) training. Haney suspects Tiger still harbors that fantasy, noting his continuing obsession with the video game *SOCOM U.S. Navy SEALs* (SOCOM stands for Special Operations Command) and his frequent rewatching of *Navy SEALs: BUD/S Class 234,* a documentary miniseries about the SEALs' six-month-long training course. Haney speculates that "Tiger knew the whole thing by heart."

On February 10, 2006, Tiger welcomes a former commander in chief, President Bill Clinton, to the thirty-five-thousand-square-foot Tiger Woods Learning Center, in Anaheim, California. The former president, who is there to dedicate the STEM-centered facility, tours the grounds, situated next to the Dad Miller Golf Course, where Tiger played as a

Western High School student. Clinton then steps up to the podium, next to Tiger's seat on the dais.

"It's hard to say that America can't do what we need to do with the kids we got if we give them the best life," Clinton says, echoing a cornerstone of Earl and Tida's parenting philosophy and adding, "I'm impressed that Tiger Woods decided to do this when he was 30 and not 60."

Tiger says that he was spurred to act after the events of 9/11, which "made me ask myself that if my life was to end today as it did for so many in the horrific events in New York, Pennsylvania and Washington D.C., would I have done enough to help others?"

The center has seven classrooms, a two-hundred-seat auditorium, a computer lab, a multimedia center—and a driving range and putting course. "It's not mine. It's not my family's. It's theirs," Tiger says of the students. "They created the curriculum. They watch 'CSI' [on television], hence we have a forensics lab. They want to be involved in music, hence we have a recording studio."

When Clinton marvels at a student—"The young rocket scientist had the most aerodynamically efficient hairdo I've ever seen," he says—Tiger laughs in appreciation as the young man stands up and takes a bow.

The facility was partially funded by Tiger's donation of his $1.25 million prize from the Target World Challenge in December of 2004 at nearby Sherwood Country Club. That tournament was the last time Earl managed to come out to see Tiger play in person. He's too ill to attend the dedication today.

"I talked to him last night," an emotional Tiger says of his father. "He kept telling me how proud he was of what I was able to do and proud of me for thinking of this. It's hard on all of us."

On March 5, Earl's seventy-fourth birthday, Tiger wins his forty-eighth PGA title and second consecutive Ford Championship at Doral. Tiger's practice time for the Players Championship at TPC Sawgrass is cut short when Earl's declining health takes a serious turn. He's refusing food and saying goodbye to his caretakers.

On March 21, Tiger travels by private jet to California. Over these past few months, when Earl has been able to do little more than watch television in his living room, Tiger and Elin have tried to cheer him with daily phone calls and Taz the puppy. Tida brings over bowls of healing soup. But Tiger senses that Earl is giving up. "We don't quit," Tiger urged Earl on this most recent visit. "Remember? You taught me that."

Earl's strength may be diminished, but not his sense of humor. "What the hell are you doing here?" he jokes when Tiger appears.

"It was nice to hear that," Tiger tells the press back at TPC Sawgrass on March 23. He's decided against withdrawing from the Players, reasoning, "Hopefully, I'll get on TV and hit some good golf shots, and he can watch it and give him something to look forward to every day," he says. "That's always a positive thing."

Perhaps fatefully, Tiger's first-round playing partner is Darren Clarke. Tiger and the golfer from Northern Ireland first became friendly while playing World Golf Championships; they now share the harrowing experience of witnessing a loved one — Tiger's father, Earl, and Clarke's wife, Heather — struggle with cancer for years.

"We were talking about it all day," Tiger says. "It puts things in perspective real quick. You hit a bad shot and you want to get upset, but you know what, in the whole scheme of things, it's just a golf shot." Tiger finishes the Players Championship tied for twenty-second.

That same evening, on March 26, *60 Minutes* airs an interview between Tiger and Ed Bradley.

Despite Team Tiger's mandate that Bradley keep the questions to golf, the conversation turns to Tiger's personal life. He and Elin have now been married for eighteen months.

> **Tiger:** "I have found a life partner, a best friend. She's brought joy and balance to my life. We love doing the same things."
> **Bradley:** "How do you think having children will affect your day job?"
> **Tiger:** "Family always comes first. It always has been in my life, and

always will. I may sleep a little bit less, and we have to work on that as a team."

Bradley: "Can you see yourself giving as much time to your kids as your parents gave to you?"

Tiger: "As best I can. I always want my kids to know their father."

Tiger, the defending Masters champion, is in the Augusta National press room on April 4. It's the first Masters he's ever played without Earl nearby.

When asked about his father's health, Tiger says, "He's fighting." Earl, he notes, possesses "an unbelievable will and, you know, hopefully he's passed a little bit of that on to me."

It was Earl who taught Tiger to hold focus, no matter how tough the obstacle.

"I've been dealing with it for years, so nothing has changed," Tiger tells the press about his father's poor health. "But as far as that being a distraction, no."

The course itself has again been revamped: Now further extended to 7,445 yards, it's not the same Augusta National where Tiger won last year. For once, Tiger's not the clear favorite—there's talk of a "Mickelslam" if Phil Mickelson can follow his 2005 PGA Championship win with a second consecutive major victory. To conquer the course's new length, Mickelson carries two drivers in his bag, including "the bomb driver" for maximum distance.

After weather delays push the conclusion of the third round to Sunday, April 9, Tiger briefly vaults into the lead—until bogeys on 14, 15, and 16 leave him two strokes back of Mickelson. After a three-hour break, the players return to the course.

Mickelson's prediction for the final: "It's going to be an eighteen-hole shootout."

But Tiger's putting fails him. He finishes in a five-way tie for third, one behind the second-place finisher, Tim Clark, and three behind Mickelson, who wins his second career Masters.

Caddie Steve Williams grabs Tiger's putter and, in an exaggerated gesture, extends his leg and pretends to break the offending weapon in two. "I'm probably going to go snap this putter into eight pieces," Tiger says. "As good as I hit today was as bad as I putted. I putted atrociously."

He knows Earl will agree. "I'm sure he's watching and probably a little mad at me for the way I putted," Tiger says. "I'm sure he knows what I did wrong."

Last April, Mickelson helped Tiger into his fourth Green Jacket. Today, the rivals reverse roles. "He played great," Tiger concedes. "He peaked at the right time. That's what you try to do, peak four times a year."

What Mickelson does next is an act of human kindness. In the midst of his victory speech, he looks to Tiger and asks the crowd to say a prayer for Earl, adding, "We all know how important parents are in life."

Chapter 62

Cypress, California
May 3, 2006

I'm very saddened to share the news of my father's passing at home early this morning," Tiger posts on his website on Wednesday, May 3.

A little less than a month after the Masters, Earl has succumbed to a host of health issues—chiefly, systemic cancer. "My dad was my best friend and greatest role model, and I will miss him deeply," Tiger writes. "I'm overwhelmed when I think of all of the great things he accomplished in his life. He was an amazing dad, coach, mentor, soldier, husband and friend. I wouldn't be where I am today without him."

Two days later, police surround the perimeter of the Tiger Woods Learning Center as limousines bring Tiger, Elin, and Tida to a memorial honoring the late Earl Dennison Woods. Tiger's famous friends—Charles Barkley; Nike chairman Phil Knight; volleyballer Gabrielle Reece and her surfer husband, Laird Hamilton; PGA Tour commissioner Tim Finchem; and swing coach Hank Haney—all come out in a show of support.

Tiger gives the eulogy, maintaining his composure as if he hasn't yet begun to fully grieve.

At the Players Championship back in March, Tiger had predicted, "There's a chance I might not play for a while. I mean, who knows? It all depends on how my father is doing."

Now that Earl is gone, Tiger puts away his clubs. He doesn't play. He doesn't practice. Every day he thinks of his late father. When Jack Nicklaus's Memorial Tournament opens, on May 29 at Muirfield Village, Tiger is not in the field.

Instead, on June 1, Tiger arrives at La Posta, an inland naval training center near San Diego. The area's dry, mountainous terrain resembles Afghanistan's. At the edge of a shooting facility, Tiger seeks out an instructor, Petty Officer 1st Class John Brown.

"Why are you here?" Brown asks.

"My dad," Tiger says, then explains further. "My dad told me I had two paths to choose from"—golfer or special operations officer. Right now, he's exploring the latter.

Tiger's issued camo pants, a brown T-shirt, and an M4 assault rifle that he'll use to shoot simulated ammunition to clear model combat rooms in the kill house. An instructor praises Tiger's performance under pressure. "He's not freaking out. You escalate it. You start shooting and then you start blowing s— up. A lot of people freak out. It's too loud, it's too crazy. He did well."

Tiger did better than well, one active-duty SEAL says. "He went all out. He just f—ing went all out."

It's not a goal Hank Haney can get behind. "You need to get that whole SEALs thing out of your system and stick to playing Navy SEAL on the video games," he emails Tiger after learning about the training. "Man, are you crazy? You have history to make in golf and people to influence and help. Focus on your destiny."

The next event on the calendar is a major—the U.S. Open at the historic Winged Foot Golf Club, in Mamaroneck, New York. The week before the June 15 start date, Haney visits Tiger at home in Isleworth. Tiger is amped up, but he says nothing about playing the Open.

Then Haney gets a call. "Gotta get back sometime," Tiger tells his coach. "Might as well be now."

Six weeks have passed since Earl's funeral—and nine since Tiger competed at the Masters. On Tuesday, June 13, Tiger sits for a pre-tournament interview. "The Masters loss was bitter," Tiger admits, "probably the most disappointing loss I've ever had, or ever will have. I knew it was the last major my dad was ever going to see. Just one more time. I wanted him to feel it. Why couldn't I have sucked it up and got it done on the back nine of Augusta, when he was still around?"

A reporter hits a nostalgic note, asking, "What special gift did your father have as a coach?"

Tiger answers with a single word. *Love.*

"That's basically it," he continues. "The love that we shared for one another and the respect that we had for one another was something that's pretty special."

A few other things, too: "Grip, posture, stance, alignment. Well, that's what I learned from Dad," Tiger says. Preparing to play again now, he explains, "brought back so many great memories, and every time I thought back I always had a smile on my face. As I was grinding and getting ready, it was also one of the great times, too, to remember and think back on all the lessons, life lessons Dad taught me through the game of golf."

Where Tiger wants to be isn't quite matching up with where he is emotionally, though.

In the first two rounds, Tiger's paired with the defending U.S. Open champion, Michael Campbell. "From the first tee shot," Campbell says, "Tiger just wasn't there." The New Zealand golfer, who's always enjoyed Tiger's company on the course, notices that there's "no electricity" in his partner's play. He's even more worried that Tiger "never said a word for 36 holes. Not one word in two days."

Tiger shoots two rounds of 76. For the first time since turning pro, he misses the cut in a major championship.

"No, I was not ready to play golf," Tiger concedes afterward. "Quite frankly, when I got ready for this event, I didn't really put in the time. I didn't really put in the practice."

The fans are merciful. "God bless your dad, Tiger," one shouts.

The gallery sends him off the course to heartfelt applause.

Chapter 63

The 135th British Open
Royal Liverpool Golf Club
Hoylake, England
July 20–23, 2006

At home in Isleworth, Tiger studies every moment of his disastrous performance at Winged Foot. The painful viewing gets him in a competitive mindset, ready to defend his 2005 British Open championship. As a warm-up, he competes in the Western Open at the Cog Hill Golf and Country Club and ties for second.

Not since 1967 has the Open been played at Royal Liverpool, a links course in Hoylake, England. Tiger skips his annual Irish fishing trip with Mark O'Meara and arrives in Hoylake five days early. As he and Hank Haney walk the course, Tiger determines that dry, firm, fast conditions will allow him to play his low-lofting 2-iron over his driver.

It's an unusual strategy for a player whose long drives prompted Augusta National to "Tiger-proof" the course, but it works in every practice round.

On Tuesday, July 18, Tiger enters the British Open press room.

"Does your mum offer technical advice?" a reporter asks. It's a serious question.

Tiger gets a laugh when he answers, "No, no, no, no, no, no, no, no. She usually gives words of encouragement. As you all know, she's pretty fiery. So it's more from that side of it than the technical side."

Tiger's not the only player wrestling with grief. Since the Players Championship, Darren Clarke's wife, Heather, has entered end-stage breast cancer. "Have you seen D.C.?" Tiger asks as he leaves the press room. "I need to talk to him." And less than three weeks ago, thirty-seven-year-old Chris DiMarco's mother died unexpectedly of a heart attack, on July 4. DiMarco initially plans to skip the tournament but decides to make the trip with his ten-year-old son and dad instead. "I knew my mom would have wanted me to go," DiMarco says. "And I felt my dad needed to get out of Orlando also because he was in such a bad place."

By the end of the third round, Tiger's in the lead — by one stroke — with Chris DiMarco, Ernie Els, and Sergio Garcia tied for second. On the back nine of Sunday's final round, DiMarco pulls ahead of Els and Garcia, turning the final round into a duel between him and Tiger, reminiscent of the 2005 Masters playoffs, when the two went head-to-head.

Fans are determined to capture the moment. Steve Williams tries and fails to silence the electronic clicks of camera shutters.

"We've never seen anything like this before," Tiger says when a roar goes up from 14, where DiMarco holes a fifty-foot putt. That's when Tiger summons a tactic he learned from Earl. *Block it out. Block everything out.*

"He's got an uncanny ability, when somebody gets close to him, to just turn it up another level," DiMarco says. "I made a great putt for par, which really pumped me up, and he turns around and birdies 14, 15 and 16. It's just — it's hard to catch him."

By two strokes, Tiger wins back-to-back British Open championships and his eleventh major.

"When you are playing Tiger, especially when he's at the top of his game, it's so difficult," DiMarco says. "I shot 16 under par in the British Open and didn't win. That's kind of crazy, to tell you the truth." But he's at peace, saying, "I know my mom would be very proud of me right now.

The hardest part is that I know I'll never see her again, but if I close my eyes, I see her."

Tiger is overcome with his own emotion, dissolving into sobs and, for several minutes, hugging Steve Williams the way he hugged Earl after his greatest wins. When Tiger is ready to walk off the course, Williams points to the sky above the 18th green.

"After my last putt," Tiger explains, "I realized that my dad is never going to see this again." Instead of his typical stoicism, "it just came pouring out of me, all the things my dad meant to me, and the game of golf. I just wish he could have seen it one more time."

"Tiger was fantastic during the [winner's] speech. He talked about the fact that we both played with heavy hearts," DiMarco says. "When he came off the 18th and into the tent we had a little embrace and shed a tear for my mom and his dad."

"He would have been very proud, very proud," Tiger says of Earl. "He was always on my case about thinking my way around the golf course and not letting emotions get the better of you, because it's so very easy to do in this sport. Just use your mind to plot your way around the golf course, and if you had to deviate from the game plan, make sure it's the right decision to do that.

"He was very adamant I play like that my entire career."

The now three-time British Open champion (2000, 2005, 2006) accepts the winner's check for $1,228,430 and retains custody of the Claret Jug. "This jug will be filled up, I'll tell you that," Tiger promises. "Beverage of my choice, and not just once."

First, Tiger has a heartfelt message for Rich DiMarco, Chris DiMarco's father. With the trophy in one hand, Tiger wraps his other arm around Rich and whispers, "I know exactly what you're going through. My dad was my best friend. I know your wife was your best friend."

A few hours later, Tiger celebrates on board his private jet. He fills the Claret Jug with champagne and drinks from it, then passes it to Hank Haney and his fellow passengers. Victory has never tasted sweeter.

*   *   *

Playing a major championship takes an emotional and physical toll.

Phil Mickelson tells *Sports Illustrated* that three days in bed is his typical post-majors routine.

Tiger can't rest. In his next five starts following the British Open, he achieves consistent results: in his terms, "getting the W."

The Buick Open.

The PGA Championship.

The WGC-Bridgestone Invitational.

The Deutsche Bank Championship.

The WGC-American Express Championship.

The statistics are astonishing. Six wins in a row at an average score of 18 under and a cumulative 109 under par. With the latest addition, his third PGA Championship, Tiger is now a twelve-time major winner, two-thirds of the way to matching Nicklaus's record.

Sportswriters draw comparisons to Tiger's record-breaking 2000 season. "If you compare the two years, I think this year would have to be better because of, obviously, things I've been dealing with off the golf course," Tiger says. "In 2000, I didn't have to deal with that. Hey, life is full of mysteries and you've got to deal with things as they come. Who's to know that if Dad didn't struggle and end up passing that I wouldn't have played that well in the summer."

On December 17, days before his thirty-first birthday, he notches one last 2006 win at the Target World Challenge, where two years ago Earl last came out to watch him play. He once again donates the $1.35 million in prize money to the Tiger Woods Foundation, to be divided between the learning center and the Start Something program.

Tiger has endured tragedy to soar in triumph. After hoisting the "Tiger" trophy, he says, "This has been a year of two halves really."

Chapter 64

John Nichol's Field
San Diego County, California
December 30, 2006

The cake, topped with a skydiver figurine, reads HAPPY BIRTHDAY, TIGER! The only other decoration in this room in the Tac Air building is the Navy SEAL flag that hangs on the wall. Tiger and Elin began his thirty-first birthday with a drive through the desert to John Nichol's Field, where he practiced advanced air maneuvers with the SEALs, who are now singing "Happy Birthday."

Dressed in a navy-issue blue-and-white jumpsuit, Tiger blows out the candles. He's already gotten his wish. The USPA A-level license he earned last month allows him to jump from a plane without an instructor in tandem.

"The dude's amazing," one SEAL says of Tiger's ability to process the tutoring he receives between jumps. "He can literally think himself through the skydives."

Elin and Tiger have also taken another leap. They're starting a family.

On New Year's Eve — the day after Tiger's thirty-first birthday and the day before Elin's twenty-seventh — United Press International reports from Orlando: WOODS REVEALS WIFE'S PREGNANCY ON BIRTHDAY.

"Obviously, we couldn't be happier and our families are thrilled," Tiger writes on tigerwoods.com. "I have always wanted to be a dad. I just wish my father could be around to share the experience."

He soon finds a new way to honor Earl's memory. On February 28, Tiger visits Capitol Hill with breaking golf news: He's bringing a PGA event to the nation's capital. Perfectly timed between the U.S. and British Opens, the "Woods-Washington" event during Fourth of July week looks to be a major draw.

Plans come together quickly in Washington. By March 7, the tournament has a date, a name, and, with the Tiger Woods Foundation, a cosponsor. "I'm thrilled the AT&T National is helping facilitate my foundation's East Coast expansion," Tiger says. "We plan to make a lasting impact in this community—both on and off the course."

Tiger envisions an Earl Woods Memorial Pro-Am honoring the military. During tournament week, active-duty service personnel will be welcomed onto the grounds of the Congressional Country Club, where during World War II the Office of Strategic Services trained troops in espionage and parachute jumping.

"It's just a small way of saying thank you," Tiger says. Still, there's an unspoken disconnect to overcome. Earl's military career was indisputably authentic. Tiger can't make that claim.

According to the SEAL who runs the Nichol's Field training facility, "Tiger Woods never got wet and sandy." He *has* completed a free-diving course—with a personal-best free dive of one hundred feet (the record is more than three times that depth)—but that was during a Caribbean vacation on his yacht, *Privacy*. "Tiger Woods," he'd introduced himself to his free-diving class. "My whole deal is to go deeper and longer so I can shoot bigger fish."

And to build a bigger frame. Tiger's bulked up his six-foot-one-inch body with twenty pounds of muscle. He's agreed to an interview and cover photo shoot for *Men's Fitness* magazine. But with his weight hovering near 190, Tiger's trainer and surgeon urge him to ease the stress on his joints by losing between ten and twenty-five pounds.

Tiger ignores their warnings. He increases his workouts and makes more trips to Southern California, where he perfects SEAL strength-training routines by logging the graveyard shift at Gold's Gym. At home, he runs for miles through the secluded streets of Isleworth.

Neighbor, friend, and fellow PGA player John Cook reacts with awe to Tiger's enhanced physique. "I would be on the back of the range, beating balls," says Cook, "and Tiger would come up after an eight-mile run: no shirt, hat backward, sunglasses, body soaked with sweat. He would grab my 2-iron and start hitting these missiles. How you going to beat that? You can't beat that."

Even so, some PGA players begin to chip away at Tiger's long-held edge.

On April 8, American golfer Zach Johnson wins the 2007 Masters, his first major. Tiger finishes two strokes back, in a three-way tie for second.

Expectations surrounding Tiger's level of play have never been higher. Hank Haney worries that Tiger's focus isn't where it needs to be to stay ahead of rising talent.

He has two months to prepare for this year's U.S. Open, three months for the inaugural AT&T National—and he's still talking about becoming a SEAL.

"For as long as I've known him, Tiger's had a huge interest in the military," says caddie Steve Williams. "He always read a lot of military books and watched war documentaries on The History Channel and liked military movies. And when Earl passed away, maybe Tiger thought it was a good thing to indulge in a bit more of what Earl went through."

Williams has been noticing "more mood swings" and "a sense of loneliness" lingering in Tiger since Earl's death but bites his tongue. "There are times in people's lives when you have to be more understanding," he says.

Tiger tells the *Charlotte Observer* that he commemorated the exact one-year anniversary of Earl's death, staring at a clock in a hotel room to mark the minute. "I just wish I could talk to him, hear his voice and ask him for advice on certain things," Tiger says.

Physical trainer Keith Kleven is especially concerned with the impact military drills might have on Tiger's vulnerable left knee. When Haney notices Tiger coming in from a run wearing combat boots, Tiger explains that even in heavy tactical footwear, "I beat my best time."

Warning bells are clanging for Team Tiger.

During bunker practice one day at the Isleworth country club, Haney confronts him. "Are you out of your mind? What about Nicklaus's record? Don't you care about that?"

"No," Tiger says. "I'm satisfied with what I've done in my career."

Chapter 65

The 107th U.S. Open
Oakmont Country Club
Oakmont, Pennsylvania
June 14–17, 2007

Nike Golf has an early Father's Day present for Tiger: a thirty-second spot that debuts on the Golf Channel and NBC Sports and airs throughout the U.S. Open. Filmed at Nike Golf's research and development facility, in Fort Worth, Texas, the ad shows the team that created Tiger's clubs hard at work on a custom set of tiny clubs that they place in a golf bag embroidered with the words BABY WOODS.

The spot cuts to Tiger—dressed in a Stanford T-shirt—opening his front door to receive the box marked NIKE GOLF.

"Hey, perfect," he says to the delivery driver. "Thanks, man."

Tiger's eager to become a dad and carry on some of the memorable traditions Tida and Earl created. "My parents always told me they loved me every night, every time we said goodbye. I was never afraid to fail, because I knew that I would always come home to a home of love. . . . I was lucky to have that my entire life."

Though Jesper Parnevik points to his own record—"as soon as we had our first child, Peg in 1995, I won five tournaments the next three or four years"—Tiger refuses to speculate how fatherhood might change his game "because I've never gone through it before. But I do know Elin and I are excited, and that this is far more important than the game of golf."

Most people who know Tiger scoff at the idea of anything slowing him down. "Hah!" says John Cook with a laugh. "Tiger is able to do more things well by flipping a switch nobody else has. When it's time for golf, he's all golf. When it's time for family, it will be all family."

Elin is due in early July.

Although Oakmont Country Club, where this year's U.S. Open is being held, has been called "the hardest course in major championship history," Tiger's not feeling intimidated. "I've had success on difficult golf courses before, yes."

"Felt good vibrations from Tiger Woods," says Johnny Miller, a PGA champion turned NBC commentator, in agreement. "He looks like he's right on his game."

The U.S. Open ends on June 17—Father's Day. It's a tight competition. Tiger ultimately ties with Jim Furyk for second place, losing to Angel Cabrera, an Argentinian former caddie and father of two, by a single stroke.

It's going to take a while to get over this one, Steve Williams assumes as Tiger silently boards the plane back to Florida. What Williams doesn't realize, though, is that as soon as they arrive back in Orlando, Tiger goes straight to the facility endowed by Arnold Palmer and his wife: Winnie Palmer Hospital for Women & Babies.

It's close to midnight. Elin is already there.

The news breaks the next morning: Elin and Tiger's first child has arrived two and a half weeks early. "Elin and I are delighted to announce the birth of our daughter, Sam Alexis Woods. Sam was born early on Monday morning, June 18th," Tiger posts to his website. "Both Elin and Sam are doing well.

"Landed in Orlando, went straight to the hospital," he says. "And next thing you know, we have Sam Alexis in our arms." More details come out a few weeks later, when Tiger is at the Congressional Country Club, in

Bethesda, Maryland, promoting the A&T National. Elin, he reveals, had begun experiencing pregnancy complications on June 14 while home in Florida, at the same moment that Tiger was playing round 1 of the U.S. Open.

"It wasn't life-threatening or anything," Tiger explains, "but she just had a few problems and had to be admitted. It wasn't easy. It was not easy, because I wanted to be there. And the doctor and Elin said, 'There's nothing you can do. So go out there and just get a 'W.' Well, came close. But that night was infinitely more rewarding than any 'W' ever could have been."

Tiger's friend Notah Begay III offers some context, highlighting Tiger's famous ability to block out distractions. "When he's on the golf course, he's a golfer. And once he steps off, then he's a celebrity, he's a father, he's a husband," Begay says. "I think in that particular instance, he was so focused on winning that golf tournament and knowing that his wife was strong enough to deal with the things that she was dealing with. Give her some credit, too."

The new parents easily agreed on what to name their daughter.

"We wanted to have a name that would be meaningful," Tiger says. The name Sam "just happened to fit. My father had always called me Sam since the day I was born. He rarely ever called me Tiger. I would ask him, 'Why don't you ever call me Tiger?' He says, 'Well, you look more like a Sam.'"

Golf Digest publishes exclusive photos of the newly expanded family, including one of Tiger holding Sam in his left arm while balancing Yogi, their blond Labradoodle, on his lap while border collie Taz and Elin look down at the sleeping baby.

"It's something that Elin and I talked about on our first night," Tiger says about the joy of new parenthood. "How can you love something so much that didn't exist the day before?"

Once Sam is a few weeks old, Tiger even tries putting a golf club into her tiny hands. She "couldn't quite hold it," Tiger admits. "But it was there," he adds with a grin.

*   *   *

On the Fourth of July, President George H. W. Bush walks the grounds of the Congressional Golf Club. Just as Tiger had planned, American servicemen and servicewomen take part in the opening ceremony of the Earl Woods Memorial Pro-Am.

Tiger places sixth at the inaugural AT&T National, but according to *Golf Digest,* pulling together the successful event in a record 116 days has significantly raised his leadership profile. "Tiger Woods has D.C. in the palm of his paw, turning on this city more than any presidential candidate, more than any Washington Redskin, National, Capital, more than Michael Jordan when [he] tried to resurrect the Wizards. It's like he's become the adopted sport star, in a city looking for one."

Less successful is Tiger's bid for a third consecutive win at the British Open, instead returning from Carnoustie, Scotland, with a tie for twelfth place.

Tiger's left knee is badly injured. He's somehow torn his ACL. Tiger claims it must've happened while he was running on a golf course at Isleworth, but caddie Steve Williams finds the situation "something of a mystery" and isn't convinced. Hank Haney suspects that the injury occurred when Tiger was kicked in the knee during a Navy SEALs training exercise.

Tiger decides against surgery. He continues to talk about joining the SEALs, telling Haney that even though the SEALs have a twenty-eight-year age limit and he's over thirty, it's "not a problem" because "they're making a special age exception for me."

Mark Steinberg, Tiger's agent at IMG, assures Haney that there's no chance Tiger will move forward with these military fantasies. "He's not going to do that," Steinberg says. "There is no way. He can't. He's got obligations. He's got to pay for that sixty-million-dollar house."

*   *   *

On August 5, Tiger does what only two golfers in the modern era—Jack Nicklaus and Sam Snead—have done before: he wins six times on the same course.

"I just got in my own little world," Tiger says of that day's victory over South African golfer Rory Sabbatini at the WGC–Bridgestone Invitational on the South Course at Firestone Country Club, in Ohio, where he also won in 1999, 2000, 2001, 2005, and 2006. "I just…let my clubs do the talking."

The following week, Tiger competes in Tulsa, Oklahoma, for his fourth PGA Championship, defending his 2006 title. As daily temperatures upwards of ninety-nine degrees send two hundred spectators and crew to seek medical treatment, Tiger faces his fiercest opponent: the blistering heat. Only five players manage to finish the tournament under par.

The course at Southern Hills Country Club is a five-mile walk. Tiger's peak physical condition carries him through the four-day endurance test, which ends on August 12, when he notches a thirteenth major victory, two strokes ahead of journeyman golfer Woody Austin and three up from key rival Ernie Els.

He continues to gain on Nicklaus's record. "When you first start your career, 18 is just a long way away," Tiger says. "And even though I'm at 13, it's still a long way away. You can't get it done in one year. It's going to take time."

Maybe so, but as the *Denver Post* points out, "This win gives him more major championships than the rest of the players in the world's top 10 combined."

The first faces Tiger sees in the scoring tent belong to Elin and Sam. Elin's dressed the two-month-old baby in Sunday red, like her father. "To have her here brings chills to me," says the besotted new dad.

"It's a feeling I've never had before, having Sam there and having Elin there," Tiger says. "It used to be my mom and dad. And now Elin, and now we have our own daughter. It's evolved.

"This one feels so much more special than the other majors."

He enjoys everything about his baby girl, even when she fusses and cries. "I don't sleep well, anyway," Tiger claims. "I'll be up all night. Doesn't really change from that aspect." Now, he says, "When she wakes up at 2 a.m., I get on the leg-press machine and put her on my lap. Six hundred reps later, she's out."

He's warming up for a stellar finish to the season. In mid-December, Tiger once again wins the "Tiger" trophy in the Target World Challenge at Sherwood Country Club, in California.

On the 18th green, Tida creates a special winner's circle. The new grandmother holds up Sam for Tiger to kiss, and he adds one for Elin. After he once more donates his $1.35 million check to the Tiger Woods Foundation, the family is going Christmas shopping.

"On the golf course, it's been a great year," Tiger declares. "Off the golf course, it's been the greatest year I've ever had."

Chapter 66

Tiger Woods Learning Center
Anaheim, California
January 21, 2008

A photographer poses Kultida, Tiger, Elin, and seven-month-old Sam Woods against a larger-than-life backdrop: an eight-foot bronze statue of Earl and Tiger, arm in arm. As Tida holds Sam in her arms, the child gives her thirty-two-year-old father an adoring smile.

It's an emotional day at the Tiger Woods Learning Center. "I have yet to go a day without thinking of my dad," says Tiger. "I always thought my dad would live forever," he admits. "I thought he was immortal. Obviously, we all know that's not the case. But I wanted to be sure that I truly appreciated these days with my daughter."

"Now that I've had Sam, it's amazing how I keep reflecting on the things he taught me. I can't wait to pass that on."

Tiger's set a personal goal for 2008: winning the calendar grand slam.

It's raining in La Jolla on Sunday, January 27, but the stars line up for Tiger. He wins the Buick Invitational by eight strokes, tying him with Arnold Palmer's sixty-two PGA Tour victories, behind only Ben Hogan (sixty-four), Jack Nicklaus (seventy-three), and Sam Snead (eighty-two).

From Orlando, the seventy-eight-year-old Arnold Palmer offers his congratulations. "I'm sure that there are many, many more coming in the future," Palmer says. "There isn't any question about that. I wish him all the luck in the world."

Two more come quickly. In February, Tiger wins the WGC–Accenture Match Play Championship, and in March, with the King looking on from the 18th green at Bay Hill Club & Lodge, Tiger sinks a twenty-five-foot birdie to win the Arnold Palmer Invitational for the fifth time.

He removes his hat and spikes it into the ground in a victory celebration. "I was so into the moment of the putt going in and winning the golf tournament," Tiger says, that when Steve Williams picks up his hat and returns it to him, Tiger asks his caddie a genuine question: "How in the hell did you get my hat?"

From the TV broadcast booth comes the call: "The perfect season is still alive." Tiger has now surpassed Palmer and pulled even with Ben Hogan's record.

Palmer and Tiger embrace. "It felt different than other years," Palmer says. "Tiger's father had passed away in 2006, and his relationship with his dad was as strong as mine was with Pap. Perhaps that came through when we shared that hug, and that in some small way he looked upon me as a father figure of sorts."

At Isleworth, Tiger's intense physical training continues to concern Team Tiger. He ignores an email from Hank Haney that asks, "You are already the fittest guy on the planet. Isn't that enough?"

Tiger keeps watching Navy SEALs DVDs and incorporating the exercises into his routines. He trains with a former NFL defensive back.

Wearing a weighted vest, he runs sets of ten sixty-yard wind sprints on the Isleworth practice tee.

Halfway through one set, Haney interrupts. "Tiger, you're limping. C'mon, what are you doing?"

"No, I'm fine. This helps me build up [body] speed."

His clubhead speed approaches 130 miles per hour.

During lunch at the Isleworth clubhouse, Tiger sees Shaquille O'Neal.

"How are you doing?" Tiger asks his friend and neighbor.

O'Neal missed thirty-nine games for the Miami Heat when he had surgery on his left knee during the 2006–2007 NBA season. In 2008, the knee is still sore.

"Trying to get through this thing with my knee," O'Neal says.

Tiger nods in a silent show of understanding.

Visions of a 2008 calendar grand slam end at Augusta National.

Tiger finishes three strokes back from South African golfer Trevor Immelman, who bags his first major and second win on the PGA Tour.

"You have good weeks and bad weeks. Certainly, this was not one of my best," Tiger says of this year's Masters. He makes a decision that sends sportswriters chasing a new story: WOODS HAS ARTHROSCOPIC KNEE SURGERY reads a United Press International headline days later. In Park City, Utah, Tiger is under the care of Dr. Thomas Rosenberg, who performed Tiger's previous procedure, in 2002.

"The upside is that I have been through this process before and know how to handle it," Tiger says. The arthroscopic procedure—an interim step before reconstructive surgery, planned for the offseason—will need four to six weeks to heal.

Tiger pushes to get back into competitive form. "I work out. I lift, do my cardio, like I always do. Ice, yes. Stretch, yep. So it's the same." Though with his left knee unstable, the strain causes two stress fractures to the tibia in Tiger's lower leg.

Hank Haney visits Tiger in Isleworth. Simply standing up from the dinner table puts enough stress on Tiger's knee to send him doubling over in pain.

That's not a good sign, Haney thinks. But Tiger is steadfast: he'll play at the U.S. Open in mid-June.

Tiger's agent, Mark Steinberg, confides in Mike Davis, CEO of the USGA, regarding the severity of the situation. "Mike, I need to share with you that Tiger has fractured his leg in a few places."

Davis can't believe what he's hearing. "What?"

"Yeah, and he's going to try to play," Steinberg says. "I would ask you not to share that information with anybody."

"So he's going to play on a broken leg?" Davis is incredulous.

Tiger flies west to California, where he tries playing with a knee brace. It doesn't work. On the drive from Newport Beach to San Diego, he tosses the brace from the car window.

Chapter 67

The 108th U.S. Open
Torrey Pines
La Jolla, California
June 13–16, 2008

At 7,463 yards, Torrey Pines is the longest course in U.S. Open history. The 4.25-mile walk was manageable for Tiger back in January, when he won his fourth straight Buick Invitational here, but his practice round is so excruciating that he needs a golf cart.

He knows he can't use it during competition—joking after the first round, "I can walk 18 holes. I don't need a cart yet"—though he concedes that his knee is sore. He scores a 1-over 72, but caddie Steve Williams is anything but convinced. "Tiger, you are going to have a lot more U.S. Opens to play in. You're probably damaging your leg even more here. We're close to the clubhouse. Maybe it's time to call it quits."

Not only does Tiger refuse, he also declares his intention to win.

When not on the course, he's in his fifth-floor room at the Lodge at Torrey Pines, where numerous medical personnel are providing treatment.

Tiger articulates exactly where and how much it hurts as well as how he manages to ignore it on the course. "I just keep telling myself that if it grabs me and if I get that shooting pain, I get it, but it's always after impact. So go ahead and just make the proper swing if I can."

His attitude is "You just keep going…there is no finish line. You keep pushing and pushing."

Early in the third round, that strategy is sorely tested. After Tiger tees off on the 2nd, a fan spots him limping off the tee box—using his club as a cane. He somehow finds the strength to continue, then closes decisively, landing an eagle on 18.

He now holds a one-stroke lead over England's Lee Westwood. Two strokes behind is forty-five-year-old Rocco Mediate. Ranked 158th in the world and enduring a nagging back injury, Mediate is a fun-loving American "everyman" with a peace sign on his belt buckle.

As Tiger walks off the course, Mediate—whom Tiger calls "one of the nicest guys you'll ever meet"—dares to ask the obvious question. "Excuse me, Mr. Woods," he says. "Are you out of your mind what you're doing out there? Come on."

As always, the final round of the U.S. Open coincides with Father's Day—Tiger's first as a dad. He credits his daughter with speeding along his recovery. "There's no way I could have gotten through this without Sam being there," Tiger says.

On Sunday morning, June 15, twenty-five thousand spectators turn out hours early for the final round. A chant of "Let's go, Roc-co!" rises up from the gallery as Mediate comes off the course leading the tournament at 1 under. "Win it for the old guys, Rocco," someone yells.

Tiger needs to birdie the par-five 18th to force a playoff.

"I want Tiger to make that putt," Mediate tells an NBC Golf reporter. "I want to win the U.S. Open, but I want him to make that putt. I want him tomorrow."

"Don't check out of your hotel room, Rocco," NBC's Johnny Miller says from the broadcast booth.

Tiger surveys his twelve-foot putt. The course goes silent as the ball begins to move. "That ball went in by a hundredth of an inch," Miller says. "That ball could have easily lipped out just as easy as it went in."

After four rounds, they're tied at 1-under 283, necessitating a playoff round on Monday, June 16. Tiger wears red and black, his typical Sunday power colors.

So does Mediate, though he claims coincidence. "I had no intention of getting Tiger's attention," he says of his own red-and-black outfit on Monday. "It was my last clean shirt."

Tiger once again has to birdie the 18th to stay even; he does, and for the first time since Ernie Els won at Oakmont in 1994, the players go to sudden death.

The 19th hole is the par-four 7th. Mediate bogeys and Tiger makes par, winning his fourteenth major championship and screaming at the sky in joy.

As fans burst through the gallery ropes, Tiger is whisked away in a golf cart. He later enjoys a photo op with Sam, dressed in red-and-white stripes. On June 18, Sam will celebrate her first birthday.

What will Tiger tell his daughter when she's old enough to hear the story of the 2008 U.S. Open?

"I got a 'W,'" he says.

But his season is over. "I'm going to shut it down for a little bit here and see what happens," he tells reporters.

The physical and emotional cost of this epic victory is beyond description. Tiger, who's held the number one Official World Golf Ranking for five hundred total weeks, is now facing reconstructive surgery on his left knee to repair the ACL he tore in 2007, followed by eight months of rehab.

There's no easy path through the recovery process. But Hank Haney is optimistic, telling the Associated Press that Tiger has "been playing way less than 100 percent for a long, long, time. It has limited him a lot in practice. He's going to come back better than he's ever been."

Chapter 68

Orlando, Florida
August 2008

Jimmy Buffett calls his longtime pal Carl Hiaasen. He has a dinner invite—and a dilemma. Buffett may be a multiplatinum recording artist, but golf isn't his strongest subject.

Especially when the person he's meeting for dinner is none other than Tiger Woods.

That's where Hiaasen comes in. The bestselling novelist and *Miami Herald* columnist's latest book, *The Downhill Lie: A Hacker's Return to a Ruinous Sport,* is a hilarious collection of self-deprecating golf stories that the *New York Times Book Review* calls "all too familiar to anyone who has ever flailed at the ball in futile attempts to conquer a sport that mercilessly strips us of our dignity." If there's any slack in the conversation, Hiaasen will have it covered.

He and Buffett have been friends for decades, sharing a love of Florida, fishing, and environmental activism. "In Florida, Carl Hiaasen is the literary equivalent of Jimmy Buffett," the English-department chair at a local college told the *Orlando Sentinel* in 2002. Buffett produced—and wrote the soundtrack for—the film of Hiaasen's middle-grade book *Hoot* in 2006 and even plays a couple of scenes as the character Mr. Ryan. Hiaasen got to cameo in the movie, too.

The musician and the writer meet up in Vero Beach, Florida. From there, they travel together to a steak house in Orlando, where they are shown to the restaurant's private dining room and a table set for three. Tiger Woods is already seated.

Hiaasen notices right away what a quick and dry sense of humor Tiger has, the way his face lights up when he talks about his just-turned-one-year-old daughter, Sam.

He tells warm and funny stories about the toddler and how much he's been enjoying the extra time at home with her. It's a thrill watching her grow, learning to walk—and run. If only Tiger could chase after her.

But the thirty-two-year-old father is still limping along postsurgery. He doesn't much want to talk about golf tonight. He's more interested in taking advantage of this unusual down time and asks Buffett about his tour schedule.

Jimmy Buffett has named his 2008 tour the Year of Still Here. He'll be playing the MGM Grand Garden Arena, in Las Vegas, in mid-October. Tiger, who knows Vegas well, offers Buffett entrée to the exclusive world of Vegas high-roller gambling, the kind that takes place behind velvet ropes.

Buffett thanks him without reminding Tiger that he'll be in Vegas to perform, not to bet. But he's happy to give Tiger tickets to the show.

The three men do share a couple of passions. A love of nature, the ocean. And fishing. The conversation takes an interesting turn when Tiger mentions that he spearfishes for yellowfin tuna in the Bahamas. Buffett and Hiaasen have never heard of anyone spearfishing yellowfin for kicks. These fish measure up to six feet in length and weigh up to four hundred pounds, though yellowfin are smaller than Atlantic bluefin tuna, which max out at thirteen feet and two thousand pounds.

Tiger details his kill strategy. He jumps off the boat, shoots the tuna with a speargun, and lets the fish pull him behind as he keeps his head above water.

Eventually, the fish tires out and dies, but there's a huge risk of its passenger drowning, especially if the speared tuna chooses to go deep and drags the diver down with it.

Buffett and Hiaasen exchange a glance, a shorthand between close friends as Tiger stands up from the table. He's noticeably limping. *How would you like to be the captain who has to keep Tiger Woods alive?*

Tuna fishing happens in deep water with no oxygen tanks. But it turns out that Tiger is also a talented free diver as well as an avid spearfisherman. Back in 2002, he even skipped a tournament in Chicago, blaming "an unspecified illness" later revealed to be a spearfishing trip on a boat called the *Jolly Roger II*.

Tiger can hold his breath under water for up to four minutes. It's better when he free dives and doesn't use a regulator, he says, so that the fish aren't scared off. "The only problem is that when you don't make any bubbles, the sharks come around, too."

Not that Tiger is necessarily afraid of sharks. Fellow PGA player Charles Howell III vacationed with Tiger off the coast of Cape Town, South Africa, and recalls that Tiger was eager to go cage diving with the great white sharks native to the area.

"We chummed the water for seven or eight hours, but there's not a shark to be seen," says Howell. "Tiger is bored out of his mind. He's wearing a wet suit to dive into the cage in case any sharks come, and suddenly he just jumps into open water."

As Tiger swims over to investigate a nearby island where seals congregate, "the guys on the boat are going nuts, shouting for Tiger to come back, but he just keeps swimming, through all the chum," recalls Howell. Oblivious to the concern, "Tiger is having a great time. After what seems like an eternity, he swims back and casually gets on the boat.

"He's just different from normal people," Howell decides. "Completely fearless."

Tiger enjoys the thrill. "I love every day of living life to its fullest," he says.

Like Navy SEAL training, spearfishing provides the kind of adrenaline rush Tiger yearns for. Something outside of golf.

He looked for it in New Zealand, when in 2006 he twice leaped 440 feet from the world's third-highest bungee-jumping platform, the Nevis Highwire. He chased it when he took up celebrity stock car racing—and won. He's thrown himself out of airplanes and attempted underwater spelunking, much to the teeth-gnashing of his sponsors and—especially—his friends and family.

A few weeks later, Tiger attends Jimmy Buffett's concert in Las Vegas. Buffett closes the show with a fan-favorite encore from his album *Coconut Telegraph:* "Growing Older but Not Up."

Not long after the steak dinner in Orlando, Jimmy Buffett starts playing a lot more golf.

Chapter 69

Isleworth Golf & Country Club
Windermere, Florida
September 2008

I have some wonderful news to report," Tiger posts on his website on September 2. "Sam is going to be a big sister." His two children will be less than two years apart, Tiger's dream scenario. "I want them to be close in age," he's said. "I want my kids to grow up close."

The baby is due in early 2009, around the time Tiger expects doctors to clear him to return to the PGA Tour.

"I can't rotate the knee until then," he says. But he can still dream of the Masters in April. If he could play one or two events before then, that would be ideal. In an interview with the *Los Angeles Times,* he says, "I can walk, the knee is good, we are right on schedule. There is no pain, and the work is on strength and mobility."

He pauses, rolling his eyes. "Oh, man," he says. "There is lots of work, hours a day. Man."

Unable to play, Tiger turns his attention to course design. His first project: Punta Brava ("wild point") Golf & Surf Club, a $100 million private golf course on a seven-mile peninsula in Cabo San Lucas, Mexico, seventy miles south of San Diego, where players will be able to see the Pacific Ocean from every tee, fairway, and green.

"I told myself I would play on every continent before I started designing," Tiger says. "I guess I have missed the Antarctica Four Ball, but otherwise, I've done it...I've learned a lot, thought a lot about it, used the experiences I've had as a player."

Tiger's schedule is up in the air as 2009 begins and he awaits clearance from his doctors and the arrival of his second child. He's been waiting nearly nine months for both and anticipates "a hectic spring."

"I'm taking it tournament to tournament," Tiger writes on his website on February 4. Though he admits to going "full-bore" in practice sessions, he says he needs to work on his stamina, and "a lot depends on the baby, which is due pretty soon." Baby number two "takes precedent over anything I do golf-wise."

On Sunday, February 8, Elin gives birth to Charlie Axel Woods at Winnie Palmer Hospital, in Orlando, where she also delivered big sister Sam twenty months earlier.

"We had a couple names and Charlie just fit," Tiger reveals. Though many expected a name that commemorated his late father, baby Charlie's name is a nod to Tiger's surrogate grandfather, Charlie Sifford. "As far as the Axel, that's Elin's brother's name so we wanted to make sure it stayed in the family."

Axel also means "father of peace," which seems fitting.

"I didn't realize how much I loved being home and being around Sam and E and now Charlie," Tiger gushes to reporters. "That's something that was a blessing in disguise, to be away from the game and have an opportunity to be a part of Sam's growth and development."

He feels mentally ready to get back on the links, though.

"I must admit, I am also excited about returning to competition," Tiger says. "Early on, I didn't miss golf because I enjoyed staying home with Elin and Sam and I knew I wasn't physically able to play."

Now it's just a question of which PGA tournament he chooses for his return.

"We're hopeful he'll make the Accenture Match Play Championship his first event back," says tournament director Wade Dunagan. Tiger is defending champion, "but he may want to stay home for another week now that the baby is born."

Tiger decides to play. He arrives at the Golf Club at Dove Mountain, at the Ritz-Carlton in Marana, Arizona, for a "Hello (Again) World" press conference on Tuesday, February 24. He's been sorely missed.

"Welcome back, Tiger!" a fan shouts from a gallery on the 7th green. Tiger's practice round today draws more spectators than did tournaments played during his recovery.

"The game just hasn't been the same without the world's best player—hasn't been as interesting, hasn't been as compelling, hasn't been nearly as much fun," notes sports columnist Ray McNulty.

"We are starved for him," says player turned NBC Golf announcer Roger Maltbie. "The year seems flat. I don't mean to be unfair to any of the other guys, but a lot of people can play the fiddle. Only one guy is Itzhak Perlman."

"I felt good," Tiger says in a post-round television interview. "I got off to a good start, which certainly helped. It didn't feel like I was gone."

The feeling vanishes in the second round, when Tiger is eliminated by Tim Clark—a South African golfer who's never won on the PGA Tour. Still, his leg is getting stronger: "No pain at all. Zero," he says.

"I have been blessed, more than most people are blessed," he adds. "I love being a husband and father. It's who I am."

Chapter 70

Arnold Palmer Invitational
Bay Hill Club & Lodge
Orlando, Florida
March 26–29, 2009

H ey, golf world, Tiger Woods is back," the *Los Angeles Times* declares. Nine and a half months after Tiger won his last tournament, he not only wins the Arnold Palmer Invitational—for the sixth time—but also overcomes a five-stroke deficit to do so. He sinks a sixteen-foot birdie putt to win by a single stroke, reminiscent of his victory here last year.

At the course, outside Orlando, Florida, local fans root for their hometown hero.

"Reel him in, Tiger!"

"Catch up, buddy!"

"We have faith in you!"

"This win definitely validates all the things I've been trying to do," says Tiger.

It's not all smooth sailing. At the Masters, he ties for sixth, then gives a ninety-second press conference, stating, "I hit the ball terrible out there." He's been having trouble controlling his temper, swearing and throwing his clubs in anger.

On Sunday, June 22, instead of defending his history-making 2008 U.S. Open title, Tiger finishes sixth there, too.

On July 16, he misses the cut—by a single stroke—at the British Open at Turnberry, in Ayrshire, Scotland. "This is surprising," says five-time Open champion Tom Watson, who finishes second. Despite high-profile losses, "it seems like [Tiger's] been playing awfully well this year."

He's had a fair number of wins, following the Arnold Palmer Invitational on March 29 with wins at the Memorial Tournament on June 7 and the AT&T National on July 5.

But when he hit bad shots at Turnberry, he angrily reacted with a move ESPN columnist Rick Reilly calls a "Turn and Bury," raising his club and slamming it into the ground.

"In every other case," Reilly writes, "I think Tiger Woods has been an A-plus role model. Never shows up in the back of a squad car with a black eye. Never gets busted in a sleazy motel with three 'freelance models.' Never gets so much as a parking ticket. But this punk act on the golf course has got to stop."

Tantrums are more characteristic of kids. Sam, who just turned two on June 18, "doesn't like for me to help her hold a golf club," Tiger says. "She'll figure it out herself." It's wild to recall that Tiger was roughly the same age when he putted with Bob Hope on *The Mike Douglas Show,* a reporter points out.

Tiger concurs. "It's hard to believe that I was swinging a club at that age."

Four-month-old Charlie is too young to take up the game just yet, but his dad is looking forward to it. "I love to teach," he says, hoping he can soon "start teaching Charlie a few things, that's fun. I live to be able to do that."

Tiger strings together another two wins in August—in a single week notching both the Buick Open on August 2 and the WGC-Bridgestone Invitational on August 9.

Then on August 16, at the PGA Championship at Hazeltine National Golf Club, the unthinkable happens. Tiger's never lost when leading on a Sunday—until an unlikely thirty-seven-year-old challenger named Y. E. Yang, who's barely cracked the top five hundred in the Official World Golf Ranking ("Who the heck is Y. E. Yang?") prevails over him.

Tiger's soon back on top with his fifth BMW Championship on September 12, dominating the field with a 19-under 265 at Cog Hill, in Illinois. It's his sixth win of the season and his seventy-first PGA tournament win, bringing him to within two of Jack Nicklaus's seventy-three career wins.

"It's one of my best years, there's no doubt about that" is Tiger's perspective. "I haven't won as many times as I did in 2000 and didn't win any majors this year, but certainly I've never had a year where I've been this consistent either, this many high finishes and the number of events I've played."

He's definitely been well paid, ending the season with $10,508,163 in prize money and once again topping the PGA Tour money list. His take is nearly double the $5,332,755 in earnings that puts Phil Mickelson at third.

When the money list is published, in mid-November, Tiger is in Melbourne, Australia, playing in the Australian Masters at Kingston Heath Golf Club, located in the Melbourne Sandbelt. "All the guys have raved about this golf course and I understand why," Tiger comments. "I enjoy all the sandbelt courses really, because it brings back shotmaking and it's something that we don't see enough of in the States."

IMG runs the tournament, cosanctioned by the PGA Tour of Australasia and the European Tour, and funds half of Tiger's $3 million appearance fee. The Australian government picks up the other half. Tiger's multimillion-dollar appearance fee is controversial—it's double the tournament's total prize money—but when Kingston Heath sells one hundred thousand tickets, the event is declared a success, generating an estimated $20 million return to the local economy.

"He over-delivered," says Australian Ian Baker-Finch, the 1991 British Open champion turned analyst for CBS Golf.

An unprecedented crowd of twenty-five thousand turns out for the final round. Tiger and two Australian golfers are in a three-way tie for the lead when they start the final round. On the 13th hole, a cameraman presses uncomfortably close, twice snapping photos just as Tiger executes his approach shot.

When the ball bounces off the green and lands in the rough, Tiger turns and angrily tears into the photographer: "That got me right on my downswing." He spikes his Nike club into the ground with such force that it boomerangs into the gallery, packed ten deep, narrowly missing the heads of several spectators.

Tiger retrieves his club but bogeys the hole.

It's a momentary lapse. He recovers his composure to win the tournament by two shots.

"I got a W," Tiger says. "That was the goal this week."

Winning the Gold Jacket—the Australian Masters' equivalent of Augusta National's Green Jacket—also expands his international achievements. "Now I have won on every continent, except for Antarctica," he notes.

From Australia, Tiger flies to Asia, stopping in Dubai, where he's designing a new golf course. From there, it's a quick stop home in Orlando to scoop up his wife and kids, bringing them with him to Northern California.

This time it's not for golf: it's for the Big Game, the annual football match-up between the Stanford Cardinal team and the California Golden Bears of the University of California at Berkeley.

The 112th Big Game at Stanford Stadium "is going to be pretty special," says Conrad Ray, who once hosted Tiger as a Cardinal recruit and now coaches the Stanford men's golf team. Tiger will be inducted into the Stanford Hall of Fame, act as honorary football captain for the game, and do the pregame coin toss.

On Saturday, November 21, Tiger carries Sam with him as he gives an on-field pep talk to the Cardinal team. He calls heads in the coin toss and wins it for his former school.

"It's a great honor to be included in the 2009 Stanford Athletics Hall of Fame class," Tiger says. "The university helped me grow as a person and an athlete, and I will always be grateful."

"Tiger belongs in [the Stanford Hall of Fame], that's for sure," Ray says. "Everyone here is excited."

Not the Cal fans. They interrupt Tiger's halftime speech with a chorus of boos. Tiger pauses, then delivers his closer. "The second half is ours."

The prediction wins cheers, but not results. Cal pulls off an upset, 34–28.

"I don't care what school you went to. You can't boo Tiger Woods," a coanchor marvels on ABC's *After the Game*. "How do you boo Tiger Woods?"

That's a question only Tiger can answer.

Chapter 71

Isleworth Golf & Country Club
Windermere, Florida
Friday, November 27, 2009, 2:25 a.m.

From ESPN News:

TIGER WOODS INJURED IN CAR ACCIDENT
OUTSIDE HIS FLORIDA HOME THIS MORNING

Windermere police chief, Daniel Saylor: My two officers arrived at the scene and noticed Tiger Woods laying on the ground in front of his vehicle with his wife over him rendering first aid. My officers immediately exited their vehicles, went to Mr. Woods and began rendering first aid to him at that time.

Reporter: How did you get there?

Saylor: From what we understand, his wife came out of the house when she heard the accident, him hitting the fire hydrant, used a golf club, is what we were told, to break out the rear window to gain entrance to the vehicle, removed him from the vehicle, and laid him down on the street.

* * *

Dispatcher 1 [Orange County Sheriff's Office dispatcher]: 911 what's your emergency?

Caller: I have a neighbor, he hit the tree. And we came out here just to see what was going on. I see him and he's laying down.

Dispatcher 2 [Orange County Fire Rescue dispatcher]: There was an auto accident?

Caller: An auto accident, yes.

Dispatcher 2: OK, is he outside or inside his car?

Dispatcher 2: Sir, your phone broke up. I heard inside. You there? Your phone broke up there. Can you repeat your phone number for me?

Dispatcher 2: Is he unconscious?

Caller: Yes.

Dispatcher 2: OK, are you able to tell if he's breathing?

Caller: No, I can't tell right now.

Dispatcher 2: OK. We do have help on the way. What color is his car, too?

Caller: It's a black Escalade.

Background, woman yelling: WHAT HAPPENED?

Isleworth Golf & Country Club: There's been some speculation [around the club] that since he doesn't always sleep well, he might have been going to work out. It's hard to tell at this point. He's not the type to go out late and be irresponsible or anything like that.

Florida Highway Patrol: VI [VEHICLE I] DRIVER HAD JUST PULLED OUT OF THE DRIVEWAY AT HIS RESIDENCE, LOCATED AT 6348 DEACON CIRCLE. AS VI BEGAN TO DRIVE ON DEACON CIRCLE, VI STRUCK A FIRE HYDRANT. THE FRONT OF VI THEN STRUCK A TREE LOCATED AT 6342 DEACON CIRCLE. THE DRIVER WAS TRANSPORTED TO HEALTH CENTRAL HOSPITAL. THE CRASH REMAINS UNDER INVESTIGATION AND CHARGES ARE PENDING.

Chapter 72

Isleworth Golf & Country Club
Windermere, Florida
December 1, 2009

What happened?
      That had been Tida's voice wailing in the background, caught on the 911 recording.

The answer is still unraveling.

On Thursday, November 26, Tiger and Elin had hosted Tida for a family Thanksgiving in Isleworth. Their daughter, Sam, is two and a half years old, and their son, Charlie, is ten months, just starting to take his first steps and toddle around.

There's been a simmering tension in the air for the last several days, after twenty-nine-year-old Elin first learned that the *National Enquirer* would be publishing a cover story about thirty-three-year-old Tiger and another woman. Tiger had downplayed and denied the allegations, and Elin wanted to believe him. It made no sense at all.

Tiger has long criticized the media, pointing out that "a lot of things they write are fabrications. Sensationalism sells: Don't let the facts get in the way of a good story." Elin knew that to be true—she'd been victimized by it herself, when Irish tabloid *The Dubliner* published nude photos they claimed to be of her. Besides, Elin loved and trusted her husband. They'd just celebrated their fifth wedding anniversary last month. She'd always "felt safe" with Tiger, and until these past few days she had never once doubted him—the very idea of his cheating on her was hard to stomach. It had to be a mistake.

But once Elin started looking, there was far too much evidence to ignore.

Tiger's going to have to pay.

"With the issuance of this citation, the Florida Highway Patrol has completed this investigation," says Major Cindy Williams on December 1.

The damage assessments: Windermere property, $3,200; Tiger's SUV, $8,000. He's cited for reckless driving, assigned four points on his driver's license, and fined $164.

There's a much bigger debt looming in terms of his public image, however. The first athlete to earn $1 billion, according to *Forbes,* has a PR "bill" that's years overdue.

The *Wall Street Journal* has been investigating suspicions that Tiger's atypical appearance on the August 2007 cover of *Men's Fitness* was a negotiated trade-off with American Media, parent company to both the lifestyle magazine and the Florida-based *National Enquirer.* The *Enquirer* had planned to run a story about Tiger cheating on Elin with the hostess of a local restaurant, based on shadowy but provocative photos of the two having sex in a car in a church parking lot.

In 2007, Tiger's expert PR team managed to make a "catch and kill" deal—the *Enquirer* dropped the salacious story, and soon afterward, readers of *Men's Fitness* instead learned about the strength training behind Tiger's "wonderful swing" and that "he and Elin often worked out together."

But the latest *National Enquirer* headline—TIGER WOODS CHEATING SCANDAL—hit newsstands two days before Thanksgiving. The piece centered on thirty-four-year-old Vegas and New York City nightclub hostess Rachel Uchitel, whom *Enquirer* reporters had witnessed entering Tiger's hotel suite in Australia last month. The article quoted her telling a friend, "It's Tiger Woods! I don't care about his wife! We're in love!"

Aware of the imminent article, Tiger made a wild play the day before it was published, setting up a call between Uchitel and his wife so Uchitel could assure Elin that the entire story was a lie.

"We talked about how I knew Tiger, how I knew his friends. How and why I was in Australia," Uchitel said of the phone call. After half an hour of conversation, Elin seemed convinced. When the article hit newsstands the following day, no one appeared to give it any credence.

Oh my god, we're going to slide right over this, Uchitel thought as she and Tiger texted each other on Thanksgiving Day. "We had gotten away completely unscathed in what could have been a complete nightmare."

Their mutual celebration was premature.

Late Thanksgiving night, after Tiger took an Ambien and went to sleep, Elin picked up his cell phone. She wasn't as convinced of his innocence as she'd let on.

Scrolling through Tiger's phone, she soon found plenty of incriminating information—romantic and sexual texts to *several* women, including one to Uchitel sent earlier that day: **You are the only one I've ever loved.**

Elin sent out a lure around one in the morning. "I miss you," she texted Uchitel from Tiger's phone. "When are we seeing each other again?"

Uchitel responded right away, which was all the confirmation Elin needed. She immediately placed a call to the mistress.

"Hey babe, I thought you went to sleep," Uchitel answered, expecting Tiger.

"I knew it was you," spat Elin. "I know everything."

"Oh f—," said Uchitel, then hung up.

A groggy Tiger woke to an incensed Elin. He quickly grabbed his phone and locked himself in the bathroom. Not realizing how much Elin had already learned, Tiger texted Uchitel a heads-up, then called another of his mistresses, twenty-four-year-old Los Angeles cocktail waitress

Jaimee Grubbs, pleading with her in a voicemail message to "please take your name off your phone? My wife went through my phone and, uh, may be calling you. . . . just have it as a number on the voicemail. OK? You got to do this for me. *Huge.* Quickly. All right, bye."

Tiger's warning came too late. Elin had already found some texts and had left a message on Grubbs's voicemail before dialing Uchitel. "You know who this is," Elin said, "because you are f—ing my husband."

After heated words were exchanged between the married couple, Tiger grabbed his keys and ran out.

"The latest news," National Public Radio reports at 9:00 a.m. on Sunday, November 29, "is that Florida Highway Patrol investigators hope to be able to speak to golfer Tiger Woods and his wife Elin today. They're still trying to pin down exactly what happened early Friday morning."

Elin told police that shortly after Tiger drove off, she'd heard a loud crash, so she raced over in a golf cart. Finding her husband slumped inside his locked Cadillac Escalade, which had run into a fire hydrant and a tree about 150 feet away, she'd taken a golf club from the cart and smashed out the back windows to reach him. Tiger wasn't wearing shoes—or his seat belt—when Elin pulled him out.

The noise brought out the neighbors. "Help us," Elin cried, asking them to call an ambulance.

When the police arrived, they found Tiger "unconscious and unresponsive," though they were able to momentarily revive him. Elin denied that her husband had been drinking but showed police his bottles of prescription Ambien and Vicodin.

The public demands answers. Why didn't Tiger speak to the police upon being treated and released from Health Central Hospital? Why was "no" checked next to "alcohol related?" on the police report prior to any actual investigation? More than 1,600 people email the Florida Highway Patrol.

"I've seen better work by a mall cop," one writes.

"WHAT THE HELL ARE YOU PEOPLE DOING," another email rages. *"The FHP in this incident is being bullied, and mocked by Tiger Woods. . . . Shame on You FHP and get back to business."*

Six years ago this same weekend, the papers had all been breathlessly reporting news of Tiger and Elin's engagement. Now they can't stop speculating about Tiger's infidelities. His first post-crash statement is inadequate against the onslaught. "Although I understand there is curiosity, the many false, unfounded and malicious rumors that are currently circulating about my family and me are irresponsible" is his feeble response.

"How differently would this story have unfolded had an agent or P.R. person said at eight a.m. the next morning, 'Mr. Woods was involved in a minor traffic accident coming out of the driveway of his home,'" says the Windermere mayor, Gary Bruhn. Instead, the lack of information only fanned interest. "Two hundred paparazzi and everyone from CBS to CNN to Al Jazeera! Paparazzi hanging from the trees! TMZ wanted to know what golf club Elin used."

Citing unspecified injuries sustained in the crash, Tiger withdraws from the Chevron World Challenge, set for December 3–6, which he'd been scheduled to host and play in to benefit the Tiger Woods Foundation. Ticket holders are offered refunds. *USA Today* reports from California that opening-day attendance is 6,893, around half what it was two years earlier, in 2007, when Tiger won the tournament.

Though the withdrawal protects Tiger from facing the press at Sherwood Country Club, the news cycle is inescapable. While some of his colleagues take the high road—including Jack Nicklaus, who says that Tiger's issues are "a private matter for him and his family"—others are more blunt.

Swedish golfer Jesper Parnevik states that he's "lost all respect" for the man he introduced to Elin, whom he considers a little sister. "My heart goes out to her," he says. "Elin is having a very tough time." Parnevik's feeling especially upset about the situation "because me and my wife were at fault hooking her up with him.

"I vouched for the guy," he laments. "I told her this is the guy that I think is everything you want. He's true. He's honest. He has great values. He has everything you would want in a guy. And uhh, I was wrong."

Chapter 73

Isleworth Golf & Country Club
Windermere, Florida
December 11, 2009

Tiger Woods hasn't been seen in public since the night of the accident.

On Friday, December 11, two weeks after the infamous car crash, he puts out a statement on his website admitting to his infidelities and taking full blame. "I am deeply aware of the disappointment and hurt that my infidelity has caused to so many people, most of all my wife and children," he posts. "I want to say again to everyone that I am profoundly sorry and that I ask forgiveness. It may not be possible to repair the damage I've done, but I want to do my best to try."

It's a fairly standard mea culpa except for a surprise announcement:

"After much soul searching, I have decided to take an indefinite break from professional golf. I need to focus my attention on being a better husband, father and person."

The mention of "an indefinite break" sends the golf community into overdrive, speculating on Tiger's career.

"I think he's been really great," the Nike cofounder and chairman, Phil

Knight, says, minimizing the current situation and stating confidently that in the future, "you'll look back on these indiscretions as a minor blip, but the media is making a big deal out of it right now."

Actually, it's the public who appears most upset with Tiger: The media—or at least the sports editors and writers who've been in the midst of their year-end voting as the news cycle churns—seem willing to separate the scandals rocking Tiger's personal life from his legacy as an athlete. On December 17, the Golf Writers Association of America names Tiger its Player of the Year for the tenth time in thirteen seasons, and that same day, the Associated Press announces: "Tiger Named AP Athlete of the Decade."

Mike Strain, sports editor of *Tulsa World,* states, "The only reason I wouldn't vote for Tiger Woods is because of the events of the last three weeks. And I didn't think that was enough to change my vote. I thought he was a transcendent sports figure."

It's the same with Stu Whitney, sports editor of the Sioux Falls *Argus Leader,* who notes that "despite the tsunami of negative publicity that will likely tarnish his image, there's no denying that Woods' on-the-course accomplishments set a new standard of dominance within his sport while making golf more accessible to the masses."

Though sensational personal revelations are "part of the game" with athlete-endorsers, the costs are significant. In an interview with the *Los Angeles Times,* a Syracuse University sports management professor and former chief marketing officer for the United States Olympic Committee says, "If you asked anyone at any company two months ago who was the cleanest, safest athlete in the world, most people would have said Tiger Woods." But now, the wholesome "fortress" that Tiger's agent, Mark Steinberg, has built around him—"this impenetrable image to make Tiger seem superhuman," as one insider put it—is quickly crumbling. The abrupt about-face his reputation takes has had immediate real-world financial implications.

According to *Harvard Business Review,* the portfolios of Tiger's sponsors, especially Nike, Pepsi, and video game partner Electronic Arts, have lost $12 billion, their market value initially plunging by 2.3 percent. Tiger's $120 million in endorsement deals—from companies such as Titleist, Nike, American Express, Rolex, Tag Heuer, Buick, General Mills, AT&T, and Accenture—are all jeopardized. On December 13, Accenture is the first to cut ties, stating that Tiger "is no longer the right representative for [our] advertising"; AT&T follows shortly thereafter, wishing Tiger well but publicly ending its sponsorship agreement. Gatorade and Gillette both decline to continue using Tiger in their marketing programs.

Tiger's once sterling image continues to quickly tarnish as more allegations and affair partners come forth, what Fox Sports calls an "onslaught of porn stars, strippers, escorts, and party girls"—more than a dozen women claiming sexual relationships with Tiger.

Elin is stunned and devastated. "The word betrayal isn't strong enough," she reveals. "It seemed that my world as I thought it was had never existed. I felt embarrassed for having been so deceived."

She's been keeping a low profile, hunkered down with her two kids and her mother and her twin sister, Josefin, who've both flown in to offer their support. "I never suspected—not a one," Elin says. "I felt stupid as more things were revealed—how could I not have known anything?"

A child of divorce herself, Elin wants to save the marriage...but she's not sure if they can weather this crisis.

In January, the *National Enquirer* finds and photographs Tiger in Hattiesburg, Mississippi, where Pine Grove, a sex, alcohol, and drug addiction center, is located.

A few weeks earlier, Elin was also photographed by paparazzi while at a gas station, her bare ring finger a source of major speculation. Public consensus suggests that she was making an intentional statement. "She knew what she was doing when she stepped out and pumped gas without her wedding rings," an unidentified source tells MSNBC. "There are plenty of people who would have filled the tank for her so she wouldn't even have to be photographed."

The banner at the bottom of the TV screen reads LIVE FROM PONTE VEDRA BEACH.

"It was like church, very somber," says AP reporter Doug Ferguson of the atmosphere in the clubhouse on February 19, 2010, at TPC Sawgrass, where Tiger is about to give a press conference, his first public appearance since Thanksgiving.

Tiger won the Players Championship here at Sawgrass in 2001, but today he's surrounded not by tour competitors but by forty friends and relatives plus three reporters—one from Reuters, one from Bloomberg News, and one from the Associated Press.

A mile away, three hundred more reporters and photographers cluster in the Champions Ballroom at the Sawgrass Marriott Golf Resort & Spa, reluctantly complying with conditions set by Team Tiger. "We were not happy with the terms. We wanted more people in there and we wanted to ask questions," says Bob Harig, an ESPN.com staff writer who is also vice president of the Golf Writers Association of America. Harig says the organization that two months ago anointed Tiger as the 2009 PGA Tour Player of the Year is boycotting today's event on principle.

Tiger steps to the clubhouse podium. Instead of his familiar golf shirt and cap, he's wearing a dark sport coat and a light blue dress shirt with an open collar. "Tiger Woods forgets his tie," comments men's fashion blog *Dappered*, which deems the look too casual, though it's clear that no detail of this long-awaited public appearance has been left unconsidered.

Tida sits in the front row, Tiger's Stanford teammate Notah Begay III nearby.

Elin and the children are not in attendance.

"I was unfaithful. I had affairs. I cheated," Tiger tells the assembly and the cameras, heaping blame on himself while praising Elin for her "enormous grace and poise" and for her wisdom. "As Elin pointed out to me," he says, "my real apology to her will come not in words. It will come from my behavior over time."

Tiger admits to having believed that his celebrity status exempted him from censure, that getting "to enjoy all the temptations around me" was something he somehow deserved. "I was wrong. I was foolish. I don't get to play by different rules."

He knows the criticism is deserved. "Parents used to point to me as a role model for their kids. I owe all those families a special apology."

Tiger reveals that he's spent the last forty-five days "in inpatient therapy receiving guidance for the issues I'm facing. I have a long way to go. But I've taken my first steps in the right direction."

This press conference is part of his treatment. He's making public amends.

After speaking for close to fifteen minutes, Tiger crumples into his mother's arms. She returns the embrace, whispering tenderly, "I'm so proud of you. Never think you stand alone. Mom will always be there for you and I love you."

When Tiger was young, Tida would warn him, "You will never, never ruin my reputation as a parent, because I will beat you." Today she fiercely defends him. "I am upset the way media treated him like he's a criminal. He didn't kill anybody, he didn't do anything illegal," she insists. "As a human being, everyone has faults, makes missteps and learns from it."

His tour colleagues are supportive. "It sounded heartfelt to me," says Stewart Cink. "He handled it very professionally," John Daly tells CNN. "I've always said the toughest major he's got is keeping his family together, but it looks like they're doing it."

Just last week, Tiger spent $3 million to buy his wife *Solitude*—a sixty-one-foot boat "designed for Elin, who loves the sport" of scuba diving, according to a source in *Parade* magazine, who optimistically speculates that the boat may help bond the couple. "Romantic sea air can do wonders for a troubled marriage."

The biggest challenge for Tiger, muses Nick Faldo, will be whether he "can, emotionally, look at Elin and say, 'You and the family—that's it— are my big kick. When I come off and I've won the tournament, pumped up full of adrenaline, I can come home and be a family man.'"

PART 6

Comeback

Chapter 74

The Woods Jupiter
Jupiter, Florida
December 30, 2015

Tiger Woods is turning forty.

It's been a long six years since his crash—both literal and metaphorical—over Thanksgiving weekend of 2009.

By the spring of 2010, it was clear that the damage he'd done to his marriage was insurmountable; that summer, he and Elin were finalizing settlements and custody arrangements for Sam and Charlie. "All that really matters is I have two beautiful kids, and I'm trying to be the best dad I can possibly be," Tiger told reporters. "That's the most important thing of all."

After he and Elin finalized their divorce, in August of 2010, Tiger moved to the Jupiter Island property they'd bought together in 2006 and built his "dream home"—an island mansion set on a property stretching from the Intracoastal Waterway to the Atlantic Ocean. Jupiter Island (population nine hundred) is an enclave of greater Jupiter (population fifty-five thousand): like Isleworth, it is a mecca for professional athletes. According to the *Wall Street Journal*, nearly thirty PGA Tour players live nearby, including Ernie Els and LGPA star Michelle Wie, who own homes in the Bear's Club, the luxury golf community designed by long-time South Florida resident Jack Nicklaus. In 2013, Serena Williams also bought an "extremely private" lot in the club, and Michael Jordan built a 43,000-square-foot home there.

Elin chose to settle thirty minutes away in North Palm Beach, where she purchased a 1.4-acre property with two hundred feet fronting the ocean, and built her own luxurious home.

Tiger had offered Elin *Privacy* in the divorce, but she declined the 155-foot yacht.

"Money can't buy happiness," she told *People* in 2010 of her reported $100 million settlement. "Or put my family back together." It took her some time to make peace with their new reality. "It's hard to think you have this life, and then all of a sudden—was it a lie?...Initially, I thought we had a chance, and we tried really hard," she explained, but once it became clear that the trust between them was irrevocably broken, they turned their focus instead to what was best for Sam and Charlie. "I will always have a working parent relationship with Tiger," Elin declared. "Tiger loves the children, and I want them to have regular and good contact with both of us."

"We both know the most important things in our lives are our kids," Tiger says in a 2015 sit-down interview with Lorne Rubenstein for *Time* magazine ahead of his fortieth birthday, adding, "I wish I would have known that back then."

He's tackled explaining to Sam and Charlie why their parents are no longer together. "I've taken the initiative with the kids," Tiger explains, "and told them up front, 'Guys, the reason why we're not in the same house, why we don't live under the same roof, Mommy and Daddy, is because Daddy made some mistakes.'"

He's even reconciled to not being his children's favorite sports hero.

While golf has always been Tiger's number one sport, the junior Woodses have fallen in love with another sport: soccer. *USA Today* goes as far as to call the siblings "soccer-obsessed."

Recently, golf reporter Steve DiMeglio good-naturedly roasted Tiger while covering the 2015 Hero World Challenge, which benefits the Tiger

Woods Foundation. During the tournament, held earlier this month at the Albany Bahamas resort—the "Monaco of the Caribbean," home to the course where Tiger's hosting the event—DiMeglio asked Sam and Charlie, "Would you rather be Lionel Messi on the pitch or Tiger Woods on the golf course?"

"Messi," eight-year-old Sam answered. She smiled and giggled, but like any superfan, she knew the twenty-eight-year-old Argentinian soccer legend's 2015 stats: fifty-two combined goals for club and country in sixty-one appearances.

"Messi," six-year-old Charlie chimed in, then added a zinger. "He's playing."

"Well," Tiger said with a laugh, dramatizing his kids' teasing by hanging his head in mock shame, "he's right." Their dad has not been playing.

Tiger shocked the press assembled for the Hero World Challenge (won this year by Bubba Watson—the 2012 and 2014 Masters winner, who in 2013 bought Tiger's Isleworth house) when he revealed that a "chip shot left-handed" is the only golf ball he's hit in two months. Tiger hasn't played in a tournament since August. His primary pastime nowadays is playing video games.

Is this how he wants it? Not at all.

To "really be a part of my kids' life in the way that I want to be part of it physically, not just as a cheerleader" was the goal he named, with the "first step" being "getting healthy enough to play soccer" with Sam and Charlie.

A *Washington Post* article, headlined TIGER WOODS'S LATEST PRESS CONFERENCE IS A MASTER CLASS IN SADNESS, quoted Tiger as saying that "the hardest part for me is there's really nothing I can look forward to, nothing I can build toward."

In December of 2011, Tiger *did* win the Hero World Challenge, his first victory since the 2009 Australian Masters. The twenty-six tournaments he'd played in between had yielded only frustrating results—and had led to his parting ways with Steve Williams, his caddie of a dozen years.

In 2012, Tiger managed three PGA Tour wins: the 2012 Arnold Palmer Invitational (his first since the 2009 BMW Championship) followed by the Memorial Tournament and the AT&T National.

In 2013, though injuries prevented him from playing at 100 percent, Tiger had five victories: He led the Tour money list with $8.5 million and was named, for the eleventh time, PGA Tour Player of the Year. It had felt like the start of a real comeback, even though none of the wins was a major.

Then came the dark day on his home practice course when "I hit a flop shot over the bunker, and it just hit the nerve. And I was down."

He collapsed, unable to get to his feet and unable to call for help without his cell phone. He remained there until his daughter, Sam, came wandering out in search of him.

"Daddy, what are you doing lying on the ground?" Sam asked.

"Sam, thank goodness you're here," Tiger said. "Can you go tell the guys inside to try and get the cart out, to help me back up?"

"What's wrong?" Sam asked.

"My back's not doing very good."

"Again?"

"Yes, again, Sam. Can you please go get those guys."

He's since had no tournament wins at all in 2014 or 2015, his year-end outlook bleaker than ever while hosting the Hero World Challenge in the Bahamas.

"Where is the light at the end of the tunnel?" he asked rhetorically. "I don't know."

There's been one bright spot: Tiger's new relationship with Olympic gold medalist Lindsey Vonn.

"Something nice that's happened off the course was meeting Lindsey Vonn," Tiger said in March of 2013, confirming that he and the beautiful blond skier were dating and noting that he hoped to continue their relationship "privately, as an ordinary couple."

"Our relationship evolved from a friendship into something more," said Vonn, "and it has made me very happy." She deemed Tiger "an amazing father," adding, "You know, I feel privileged to be along for the ride, and I help as much as I can. They're great kids—I love 'em."

Tiger and Vonn, who won gold in women's downhill skiing at the 2010 Vancouver Winter Olympics and has a record-setting number of World Cup victories, are well matched. Even Elin approves.

"You'd think it would be weird," an unnamed source tells *Us Weekly*, "but Elin loves Lindsey and they talk all the time. Elin likes that Lindsey is a strong woman." Another source assures *Page Six* that Elin "really likes Lindsey and thinks she is a very good influence on Tiger."

Elin and Tiger get along well as exes, even occasionally double-dating. "As years and years have gone by," Tiger remarked, "we're like best friends. It's fun. She talks to me about her life, I talk to her about my life."

"My relationship with Tiger is centered around our children and we are doing good—we really are—and I am so happy that is the case," Elin told *People*. "I'm happy for Tiger," she said about Vonn. "I'm happy that there's somebody else loving my children."

Following their divorce, Elin focused on finishing her college degree, graduating from Rollins College, in Winter Park, Florida, on May 10, 2014, with a bachelor of arts in psychology and a 3.96 GPA, though she admits that she could have been a better student in one particular subject. "It was right after I had taken Communications and the Media that I was unexpectedly thrust into the media limelight…and I probably should have taken more notes in that class," Elin notes wryly.

Tiger and Lindsey Vonn dated for nearly three years before announcing an amicable parting on May 3, 2015. Vonn put the blame on their "incredibly hectic lives that force us to spend a majority of our time apart," and Tiger likewise stated that "we lead very hectic lives and are both competing in demanding sports. It's difficult to spend time together."

As Vonn said, and Elin knows all too well, "Generally, it's really difficult to date anyone in the public eye."

The timing is especially unfortunate for Tiger, coinciding with the "just brutal" anniversary of his father's death. "It's tough. There's no doubt. I'm not going to lie about that," he admits in the days following the breakup. "And on top of that, this time of the year is really, really hard on me."

The following month, in June of 2015, Tiger played solo in the fourth round of the Memorial Tournament, hosted by his childhood idol, Jack Nicklaus. There was an odd number of players, which led to the stark visual, broadcast on national television, of Tiger walking the Muirfield Village course alone. His tournament score of 302 included a career low point: a third-round 85 that ended with a quadruple bogey on 18.

With a mixture of bravery and defiance, Tiger commented on PGA.com: "When you're on, no one is going to slow you down. When you're off, no one is going to pick you up, either. It's one of those sports that's tough. Deal with it. This is a lonely sport."

That feeling stalked him all season long as he missed the cut in three of four 2015 majors and finished the PGA season at 292 on the Official World Golf Ranking.

The reaction on tour was a bitter cocktail of disappointment, astonishment, and sympathy. "It's hard to watch the greatest player of this generation be a middle of the pack hack," said former PGA pro turned ESPN golf analyst Paul Azinger after a British Open in which Tiger himself was "a little angered" by his bogey-ridden play.

Azinger, who'd played with Tiger in the second round of his historic 1997 Masters win, voiced the inescapable question: "Who are you and what have you done with Tiger Woods?"

Tiger, a lifelong fan of dressing up for Halloween, had the answer.

He chose a self-deprecating "costume," telling his friend Notah Begay III: "I'm going as a golfer formerly known as Tiger Woods."

Tiger did manage to best international soccer superstar Lionel Messi on one count in 2015: becoming a restaurateur.

"Enough with the trophies, it's time to own restaurants," CBS Sports declared of Messi's planned 2016 restaurant opening in Barcelona. Tiger's restaurant, the Woods Jupiter, a 5,900-square-foot space the *Orlando Sentinel* called a "swanky new restaurant" with a new American menu and the *Broward Palm Beach New Times* praised as the "classiest sports bar ever," welcomed its first guests in August.

It's at the Woods Jupiter where Tiger now sits for his birthday interview with sportswriter Lorne Rubenstein of *Time* while holding an ice pack to his aching back. "I don't need another surgery, period," Tiger tells Rubenstein. "Seven's enough. Four knees, three backs, that's enough."

The pain has been unmanageable at times. To treat pinched nerves in his back, he underwent two microdiscectomy procedures, one in April of 2014 and another in September of 2015, plus a follow-up neurosurgery six weeks later, on October 28. On days when he is able to practice, he plays the four-hole tournament-level minicourse behind his home.

It's been a while.

But for now, he's appreciating what he has more than what he's lost. He throws himself a party at his restaurant for his fortieth, complete with a private concert by his longtime friend Darius Rucker of Hootie & the Blowfish.

Had a great time celebrating my 40th with family & friends at The Woods Jupiter last night, he tweets out the following morning. **Thanks @dariusrucker for a fun show.**

Thanks everyone for the wonderful birthday wishes. 40 is cool.

Chapter 75

Lost Tree Village
North Palm Beach, Florida
February 25, 2016

Had a few friends over tonight to talk The Ryder Cup 2016 #teamusa, tweets seventy-six-year-old Jack Nicklaus on a Thursday night in late February, accompanied by a photo of him and his wife hosting a gathering at their home for more than twenty-five PGA players—including Tiger Woods, Phil Mickelson, and Davis Love III.

The forty-first Ryder Cup isn't set to start until late September, but Nicklaus has wasted no time gathering prospective US team members together for a dinner party to discuss how to reverse the wildly lopsided record of the last ten biennial competitions—Europe: eight; America: two.

There's steak and lobster to eat, Jack Nicklaus–branded wine to drink, and Jack Nicklaus–branded ice cream for dessert—as well as food for thought.

"We all learned something for sure," says Love, who will captain the twelve-man team. "We got to see Tiger, Phil and Jack, all in the same room, talking to each other and asking each other questions. We had an awful lot of wins sitting there for some young guys to listen to."

Though Tiger lives just a few miles north of Nicklaus, his appearance at the gathering comes as a surprise to some of the new players on the tour. "It was cool to see Tiger for sure," says Keegan Bradley, a Vermonter who joined the PGA Tour in 2010. "I didn't expect him to be there."

Nor did Billy Horschel, who entered the PGA Tour in late 2009. Just two months ago, at the Hero World Challenge, Tiger had been "in rough shape," but now he looks "really good" and tells Horschel that he's "excited to be progressing and hopefully he'll get back out here and kick our ass."

Yesterday, Tiger posted a video of himself swinging a 9-iron. Caption: "Progressing nicely."

Surprised fans and sportswriters watch the video on repeat. It launches its own whirlwind of sports conspiracy theories. *Is it really Tiger in the video? Or a body double? When exactly was the video taken?*

CBS Sports's Kyle Porter tweets that he **can't believe I'm breaking down a golfer on a simulator like it's the Zapruder film**, but questions remain even after ESPN's Bob Harig shares an official statement: "Tiger's agent Mark Steinberg said the video of Tiger swinging was from this morning—just before 9 a.m."

It's widely believed that Tiger isn't well enough to be out and about, let alone in form to play. So when Jimmy Walker, an Oklahoman who in 2001, while he was still in college, first played a hole with Tiger, jokes at the Ryder Cup dinner, "Wow, you're standing up and you're not dead," the gallows humor isn't lost on Tiger.

"I know," Tiger says, quick with the comeback. "That's how everybody thinks I am now—dead."

As a matter of fact, he's showing signs of life. Even if Tiger isn't fit enough to play in the Ryder Cup, he'll still serve as one of the team's four vice captains. Taking on a leadership role like this is a new experience for Tiger, but he's all in. "I think we have the blueprint," he tells ESPN of the US team's developing strategy. "I think we have the right people in place, and I think we set up really well for [winning] Cups down the road."

Tiger may well play on one of those future teams himself if he can continue his return to form. His new caddie, Joe LaCava—who succeeded Steve Williams on Tiger's bag in 2011, after twenty-two years of caddying for the 1992 Masters winner, Fred Couples—has gotten numerous offers to leave but has turned them all down, expressing his confidence that Tiger is "going to continue to do well and win."

In a March 22 interview with the BBC's *5 Live Golf,* Steve Williams is similarly optimistic about Tiger's future, saying, "I don't doubt he will come back to the winner's circle."

Williams is publicizing his new book, *Out of the Rough,* which chronicles his and Tiger's former professional partnership. During their twelve years working together, Tiger won thirteen of his fourteen major titles (Fluff Cowan caddied Tiger's 1997 Masters win, his first major). Though the two men were once close enough for Tiger to serve as best man at Williams's 2006 wedding, Williams says his shock over the revelations about Tiger's personal life left their relationship "stretched to the max." Still, he praises Tiger as "a great competitor" with "an incredible work ethic," though noting that his former boss "might question some of the gym work that he might have done that, you know, had all these injuries escalate."

It's Tiger's lingering back injury that sidelines him at the 2016 Masters. On April 1, he announces that he won't be competing but does intend "to attend the Champions' Dinner and see a lot of old friends."

True to his word, Tiger shows up in support of the defending 2015 Masters champion, Jordan Spieth, who in January tied one of Tiger's records by winning seven PGA Tour titles before his twenty-third birthday. "When I turned pro, I think Jordan was still in diapers," Tiger jokes.

It's clear that the twenty-two-year-old has real talent, and his April 5 Champions' Dinner menu takes the event to another level. Tiger describes Spieth's Texas barbecue spread as "unreal" and "amazing." A few minutes later, he tweets, **Pretty cool that at dinner tonight 3 of us sitting next to each other have won a combined 14 green jackets.** That's enough of a clue for the Golf Channel's Tim Rosaforte to identify

Tiger's dinner companions as six-time Masters winner Jack Nicklaus and four-time winner Arnold Palmer.

One day earlier, Tiger registered for the U.S. Open, to be held in June at Oakmont, clearly feeling hopeful about his chances. The United States Golf Association reports that it received his entry at 4:33 p.m. on April 4, twenty-seven minutes ahead of the 5:00 p.m. deadline. But in early June, Tiger releases a statement on his website explaining that he's not ready to play and is withdrawing from the U.S. Open. Then at the end of the month, he confirms that he won't be playing in the British Open at Troon. Finally, on July 19, the PGA of America breaks the news. "We have been in contact with Tiger's agent, Mark Steinberg, and he informed us today that our four-time PGA Champion will be unable to join us at Baltusrol Golf Club next week for the 98th PGA Championship."

Tiger's broken a record he never intended to break. For the first time in his professional career, as the rehabilitation of his back stretches into ten months, he'll miss all four majors in the season.

"I am getting better," Tiger recently told the *Washington Post*. He's finally achieved one dearly held goal, being "able to play with my kids and play soccer with them and ride bikes and do all that kind of stuff." Yet his body is still recovering, unable to withstand the rigors of competitive golf.

On September 25, 2016, word comes that the King, Arnold Palmer, has died at age eighty-seven from heart complications.

"It's hard," Tiger says of the loss. "It hurts." He'll never forget the man who mentored him from his junior golf days and whose philanthropy helped fund the Winnie Palmer Hospital for Women and Babies, where Tiger's two kids were born. "You have all the golf stuff but all the life stuff as well. He absolutely loved being Arnold Palmer. He just loved it. He was probably one of the most comfortable people in their own skin," Tiger reflects.

Tiger's warming up to the rewarding feeling that comes from being a mentor and a coach. As Ryder Cup vice captain, he's at the Hazeltine National Golf Club, in Chaska, Minnesota, when the news about Palmer breaks. Few know Hazeltine better than Tiger, twice a PGA Championship runner-up when the tournament was played there in 2002 and 2009.

Before play begins, on September 30, the 2016 squad—which the captain, Davis Love III, calls "the best golf team maybe ever assembled"—honors Arnold Palmer.

On the first tee stands the golf bag Palmer used when captaining the 1975 Ryder Cup. It's a good omen. In the Friday morning foursomes session, it's America 4, Europe 0, an identical start to that of Palmer's 1975 team.

As vice captain, Tiger's issued a red-and-white golf cart and a communications earpiece, the kind typically associated with his security detail. When he's not speaking directly with team members, he's doing one-on-one tutorials.

Before the tournament, Tiger accompanies twenty-six-year-old Patrick Reed, a five-time winner on tour, on the Hazeltine back nine. Of their one-of-a-kind practice round, Reed says, "That alone could save me so many shots throughout my career." Tiger's openness with younger players dispels his reputation as a reclusive champion. "He'll answer any question," Reed says, "whether it's about golf, on the golf course, off the golf course, anything."

"It's great to have him out here, with all the experience that he's had," says J. B. Holmes. This is Holmes's second Ryder Cup, but Tiger's played in seven. He calls Tiger both "an icon" and "a team player" who's all in for the US team. "It's been a lot of fun."

"I think he's enjoying it, I really do," says Jimmy Walker. "He looks like he's having a great time." He and Tiger have spent hours talking golf, being "just all kind of golf nerd" this week. "I think he's happy to be here and happy to be a part of it."

The 2016 American team celebrates a decisive 17–11 Ryder Cup victory on October 2, breaking Europe's winning streak and notching Tiger's first win as a team leader.

The question that's been burning for fifteen months—*When is Tiger going to play again?*—is soon asked and answered by the man himself.

On Tuesday, November 29, reporters pack the press tent in the Bahamas ahead of the Hero World Challenge, where last year Tiger was pessimistic about his chances of *ever* playing again.

This year, he's joining the eighteen-man field once more.

The conference is interrupted when a fierce tropical storm descends. The rain lashing the tent makes it difficult to hear, but Tiger's message resonates powerfully.

"Would I like to play a full schedule every year for the next decade-plus? Yeah, that would be great. Can I? I don't know. We'll see."

Chapter 76

Farmers Insurance Open
Torrey Pines
La Jolla, California
January 27, 2017

The Farmers Insurance Open—where Tiger's won an astonishing seven titles (1999, 2003, 2005, 2006, 2007, 2008, and 2013)—is a tournament in which "fans loved to see Tiger really romp and smash us and win by a lot," says 2009 British Open Champion Stewart Cink.

It's played every year at Torrey Pines, the same course where in 1982, Earl brought six-year-old Tiger to the Andy Williams–San Diego Open (as it was then known) to watch Johnny Miller beat Jack Nicklaus by a single stroke. Tiger also won six Junior World Golf Championship division titles here as well as the historic 2008 U.S. Open, where he triumphed despite the shredded ACL and the several stress fractures on his left leg.

His previous wins here bring Tiger a jolt of confidence, but history does not repeat itself. He misses the cut at Farmers after shooting a 76 in the opening round and making what he calls "dumb mistakes" in the second.

"Playing tournament golf is a little bit different than playing with your buddies at home in a cart," Tiger admits. "I need to get more rounds under my belt, more playing time, and that's what I'm trying to do."

Less than two weeks later, Tiger watchers spot a disturbing sign. At a pre-tournament interview for the Dubai Desert Classic, in Abu Dhabi, United Arab Emirates, Tiger settles uneasily into his chair, clearly in pain.

Citing back spasms, Tiger withdraws after the first round, then withdraws from the next two PGA events, the Genesis Open and the Honda Classic. Back in January at Torrey Pines, Tiger told reporters he was preparing to play the Masters in April. A season barely begun already seems in jeopardy.

Tiger confides in Jack Nicklaus, who recommends a physical therapist. The practitioner would be only the latest to administer a yearslong battery of ineffective treatments. "I tried everything," Tiger says. "I tried stem cell. I tried Lidocaine. I tried Marcaine, nerve block. Nothing took the pain away."

The forty-one-year-old may have to consider a fourth surgery on his back. Now that the previous microdiscectomy procedures have failed, that leaves spinal fusion. He's resistant to the idea, considering it "a very negative thing," Tiger says. "It would mean the end of my career. The word fusion means you're done."

Yet his options to live a pain-free life are dwindling. The feeling of swinging a golf club is as excruciating, he says, as "playing the game bloody knuckles…the uncomfortableness of when you hit your funny bone, how much that hurts…now do that 1,000 times per day and see what that feels like."

On April 4, Tiger dons one of the four Green Jackets he's won and joins fellow members of the "Masters Club" for this year's Champions' Dinner. Ben Hogan started the winners-only society in 1952, and the yearly tradition continues in the upstairs dining room at the Augusta National clubhouse.

Tonight's Champions' Dinner is the first since 1959 without Arnold Palmer. Despite the prime-rib menu, inspired by the traditions of

England, homeland of the defending Masters champion Danny Willett, everyone is missing the charismatic King.

Decades before the crowds that gathered for Tiger Woods, there was "Arnie's Army," the legions of fans who lionized Palmer and even helped popularize his favorite drink—half iced tea, half lemonade—as "an Arnold Palmer."

"I'll have a Mr. Palmer," was how the man himself ordered his signature beverage—always with a wink.

Three-time Masters champion Nick Faldo is planning a sartorial tribute, saying, "I'm wearing his clothes all week," including "a fancy gray outfit" (Palmer's favorite color) for the lighthearted pre-tournament Par 3 Contest. Palmer especially enjoyed reminding younger golfers that he was the 1967 Par 3 champion.

In *The 1997 Masters: My Story,* Tiger's instant *New York Times* bestseller, he fondly recalls making a hole in one on the 9th while playing with Mark O'Meara and Arnold Palmer in the 2004 Par 3. "I still have the scorecard with Arnold Palmer's signature on it," Tiger says. "I just thought it was the coolest thing in the world that I made a hole-in-one with Arnold."

Tonight, the mood is somber. Memories are shared around the table. So is one seismic secret:

"I'm done. I won't play golf again," Tiger whispers to a fellow Masters champion.

His spinal fusion surgery is scheduled for a little less than two weeks away.

On April 17, Dr. Richard Guyer of the Texas Back Institute performs L5/S1 spinal fusion surgery. The anterior lumbar interbody fusion procedure involves removing a degenerated disc, replacing it with a metal cage, and then fusing the surrounding spinal bones together to add stability and diminish severe back and leg pain.

Tiger is recovering from the surgery that May when Jack Nicklaus gives an interview to Golf.com that touches on revelations from the April 4 Champions' Dinner. Without naming Tiger's confidant, Nicklaus confirms the conversation that occurred in Augusta National's private dining room.

Tiger, Nicklaus tells the reporter, "won't be back."

"Why's that?"

"He's in too much pain. He can't stand for 10 minutes." Nicklaus goes on to explain that "it's nerve pain. It's not going away that easy."

But the procedure, which *Golf Digest* describes as a "medical Hail Mary," has the makings of a miracle.

When Tiger awoke following surgery, Dr. Guyer gave him a surprising instruction. *Stand up.*

"Are you kidding me, stand up? You just cut me open," Tiger protests.

The medical team reassures him. "You're ok to stand up now. It's good."

Tiger takes his first tentative step and is astonished to discover "that nerve pain that I had been feeling for what seemed like an eternity, that was gone. My right leg was working again."

On May 26, the Friday of Memorial Day weekend, Tiger posts a hopeful progress report to his website, describing his recent surgery as "instant nerve relief" and saying, "I haven't felt this good in years."

Chapter 77

2999 Military Trail
Jupiter, Florida
May 29, 2017

A black Mercedes is stopped in the right lane of Military Trail, a north-south road that runs forty-six miles between Palm Beach and Broward Counties. It's 2:03 a.m. on Monday, May 29, when Officer Matthew Palladino of the Jupiter Police Department spots the car, which appears to have veered into the bike lane. The brake lights and right turn signal are on; the car is still running but not moving. There's some damage visible; both driver's-side tires are flat, and the passenger-side taillight is out.

Officer Palladino approaches the Mercedes. He spots a Black male asleep at the wheel. Once awakened, the man identifies himself as Tiger Woods and groggily manages to hand over his driver's license, insurance card, and registration.

Through all these tasks, Officer Palladino notes Tiger's "extremely droopy" eyes, "extremely slow" movements, and his "slurred and mumbled speech."

Police backup appears, including Officer Christopher Fandrey.

"Where are you coming from?" asks Officer Fandrey.

"L.A.," replies Tiger. When questioned, he clarifies that he's on his way down to Orange County in California.

"Do you know where you're at right now?" asks Officer Fandrey.

"No," says Tiger. "I have no idea."

Tiger's informed that he's in Jupiter, Florida, about fifteen miles from home. He denies having had anything to drink, but he says he is on medication. Then, complying with police procedure, he exits the vehicle. He's unsteady on his feet, and his shoes are untied.

"Do you want to tie your shoes?" Officer Fandrey asks.

"No," Tiger answers. "I can't get down that far." He chooses to remove them instead.

Tiger agrees to undergo Standardized Field Sobriety Testing but has trouble following the instructions. Like Officer Palladino, Officer Fandrey notices Tiger's "extremely droopy" eyes and "dilated" pupils. He's in a state of confusion. Instead of reciting the alphabet, Tiger thinks he's been asked "not to sing the national anthem backwards."

The officers arrest Tiger on suspicion of driving under the influence and double-lock handcuffs around his wrists. Two separate Breathalyzer tests administered at a breath-alcohol testing facility both come up 0.000 — detecting no alcohol in his body.

Tiger is handed over to the Palm Beach County jail, then released from custody. On Tuesday, May 30, he issues a statement: "What happened was an unexpected reaction to prescribed medications. I didn't realize the mix of medications had affected me so strongly." He's disappointed in himself. "I would like to apologize with all my heart to my family, friends and the fans. I expect more from myself too."

Comparisons to Tiger's November 2009 car accident — and the question of whether he'd been driving under the influence that night, too — are inescapable. Also inescapable is the unflattering booking photo released by the Palm Beach County Sheriff's Office. Tiger's heavy-lidded image dominates the news cycle, along with the sensational details of his arrest. One ABC News report includes a stark reminder of Tiger's current position on the Official World Golf Ranking: 876.

There is no comment from the PGA or from Tiger's agent, Mark Steinberg (now a partner at Excel Sports Management), but Tiger's friends rally around him.

"I'm a fan of Tiger's. I'm a friend of Tiger's. And I feel bad for him," says Jack Nicklaus. "I think that he's struggling. And I wish him well. I hope he gets out of it and I hope he plays golf again. He needs a lot of support from a lot of people...And I'll be one of them."

Longtime friend Notah Begay III can especially relate to Tiger's current situation, unfortunately. The men—whose friendship as junior golfers deepened when they became Stanford teammates and players on the PGA Tour—now share the experience of a DUI arrest. In Begay's case, two of them. During his second PGA season, in 2000, Begay won two consecutive tour events...and then committed his second DUI offense in five years. After he'd struck a parked car outside an Albuquerque bar, his blood alcohol level was found to be more than twice the legal limit in New Mexico. The incident landed Begay in jail, where he served seven days of a 364-day sentence.

He understood that his actions would forever follow him. "This isn't the type of incident that's going to be forgotten quickly," Begay said upon his release. "It will be written about leading into a story. It will always be a part of my career."

Begay stopped drinking, and in 2013 he left the PGA Tour to become an analyst for the Golf Channel and NBC Sports. So he speaks from hard-won experience when he says, while broadcasting on the Golf Channel at the NCAA men's golf championship, "It's embarrassing for Tiger, something that you can't go back and change. I've been there myself...But it was a turning point in my life. Hopefully, it's something he'll learn from, grow from, take responsibility for and use it to make some changes."

Of Tiger's latest public downfall, Olympic swimmer Michael Phelps says, knowingly, "I feel like that's a massive scream for help."

Phelps won a record-setting number of medals for Team USA in three Olympic Games (five gold and two bronze medals at Athens in 2004;

eight golds at Beijing in 2008; and four golds and two silvers at London in 2012) before his own DUI arrest in 2014 and subsequent rehab.

Begay, who'd reached out to Phelps when the swimmer was in treatment, now connects Phelps with Tiger. "Michael can provide honest and direct feedback, and that's what athletes of their caliber need the most."

Phelps understands what Tiger is going through. In 2004, shortly after the Olympic Games in Athens, he pleaded guilty to driving under the influence, and ten years later, in 2014, he made the same plea after being stopped exiting a Maryland traffic tunnel driving eighty-four miles per hour.

At the time, Phelps admitted to being "in a really dark place" and "not wanting to be alive anymore." Forty-five days of inpatient treatment provided the reset he needed, though he admits that in the beginning, "it's probably the most afraid I've ever felt in my life." Once he came to view rehab as a new competition to crush, he was on his way to staging an inspiring comeback at the 2016 Olympics in Rio, where he won another five golds and one silver.

These days, Phelps speaks publicly about mental health. He offers himself as a private counselor to Tiger. That doesn't mean the conversations are easy. The two talk "on and off" until, Phelps finds, "there's more of a comfort level."

As a new dad to a one-year-old son, Boomer, Phelps feels especially sympathetic about Tiger's missed family time. "Not having the freedom to see your children whenever you want," Phelps says — "it's heartbreaking."

Elin strongly considers taking legal action against Tiger for breaking a clause in their divorce agreement that prohibits him from causing public scandals, raising the possibility that Tiger would lose shared custody of Sam and Charlie. On June 12, Tiger checks in to the Jupiter Medical Center, reserving the male inpatient unit for his sole use.

"It doesn't matter whether you're Tiger Woods or Joe Blow down the street," says Australian Olympic gold–medal swimmer Grant Hackett, whom Phelps also helped recover from substance abuse and the pressures of fame. "We're all just people trying to work through stuff."

A week later, Tiger tweets: I'm currently receiving professional help to manage my medications and the ways that I deal with back pain and a sleep disorder. I want to thank everyone for their amazing outpouring of support and understanding especially the fans and players on tour.

"May 29 shook him up quite a bit, as it should," Tiger's agent, Mark Steinberg, tells the *New York Times* on June 20. "He's been in just immense pain for so very long that taking prescribed medication was a must, just to be able to get up and move," Steinberg says, adding the qualifier, "I don't think it's fair to say there is an addiction."

On Monday, July 3, Tiger tweets that he has completed the treatment program, renewing his thanks to all those who have offered their support. He's next seen on July 29 at the El Clásico soccer match at Hard Rock Stadium. The trip to Miami to watch Spain's top La Liga rivals, Real Madrid CF versus FC Barcelona—featuring star players Lionel Messi and Luis Suárez—is a special treat for soccer-mad Sam and Charlie.

After Barcelona wins the game, Tiger arranges for a locker-room visit and posts a group photo with Messi and Suárez, all in Barcelona jerseys, while Suárez posts one of just him and Tiger captioned: "Finishing the tour with a victory, also a great photo with an idol !!!!!!!!!"

As they pose with Messi, Tiger says to Sam, "Isn't it neat to meet a living legend?"

"Yeah. We live with one," replies Sam.

It's a surprising reminder that his kids are aware of their dad's celebrity, even if his last PGA win was four years ago, in August of 2013, when Sam was six and Charlie was four. "Most of the stuff they've seen has been on highlight packages," says Tiger. "I never thought my kids have understood what I've been able to do in the game because they always think I'm the 'YouTube' golfer."

It's a heady night being in the company of top professional athletes at the top of their game. Whatever it takes to get back on the PGA Tour, Tiger is up for it.

"I want them to see what I've been able to do my entire career," he says of his kids and his hopes of playing again. "I want them to come to a few events. I want them to feel it. I want them to understand it a little bit more.

"I recently spoke to my surgeon and he's very pleased with how my fusion is healing," Tiger tells the Associated Press. "I'm right on schedule. I'm now doing some light lifting, riding a stationary bike and putting a little."

But on August 16, the release of the incident report from the Palm Beach County Sheriff's Office yanks the news cycle back to the events of May 29. The *New York Times* reports, TIGER WOODS HAD 5 DRUGS IN HIS SYSTEM AFTER ARREST. The list includes Vicodin and Dilaudid (for pain), Xanax (for anxiety), Ambien (for sleep), and THC, the psychoactive ingredient in cannabis.

Tiger's made a plea deal with Jupiter authorities, who lower the DUI charge to reckless driving (the same conviction he received in 2009) and fine him $250. After an arraignment on October 25, he'll begin a year of probation, enroll in a community service program, and participate in a "victim impact panel" led by people whose lives have been changed by impaired drivers.

Though there's some grumbling that Tiger's gotten a light sentence, "he wasn't treated differently than anybody else," the Palm Beach County chief assistant state attorney tells ABC News.

It's the universal struggle that's perhaps the most captivating aspect of Tiger's story. On September 26, the capacity crowd at the Liberty National Golf Club, in Jersey City, New Jersey, cheers at the sight of Tiger riding a golf cart, his friend Notah Begay III at the wheel. The 2017 Presidents Cup opens in two days. Tiger is one of three assistant captains for the American team, reprising a leadership role after last year's win at the 2016 Ryder Cup.

When Tiger emerges onto the driving range, autograph seekers eagerly approach. As *Golf Digest* reports, TIGER WOODS, DESPITE YEAR FROM HELL, REMAINS GOLF'S BIGGEST DRAW — even when the tournament's VIP attendees include three former US presidents (Bill Clinton, George W. Bush, and Barack Obama) as honorary chairmen.

The POTUSes' joint appearance ahead of the first tee time at the Presidents Cup marks the first time that three former US presidents have attended together. After American team member Phil Mickelson shakes the hands of presidents number 42, 43, and 44, then poses for an impromptu photo, his brother tweets it out under the caption: **When you can take a selfie with three US Presidents, you do it!!**

Mickelson's seize-the-day mentality is understandable. Every professional athlete operates with full knowledge that the physical gifts available today could vanish tomorrow, and Tiger's recent issues serve as a stark reminder.

On October 1, the American team wins the 2017 Presidents Cup 19–11. More history is made when the forty-fifth president, Donald Trump, appears at the final round to hand-deliver the trophy to the winners, the first sitting US president ever to do so.

Despite these notable moments, it's Tiger who still captures the attention of the media. He dominates the pre-tournament press conference, where reporters direct the majority of their questions to the assistant captain.

"Why do you need competitive golf still?" asks Karen Crouse of the *New York Times*.

Tiger pauses before offering the noncommittal answer, "I think it's fun."

Alex Miceli, veteran golf writer and founder of Golf.com, digs deeper, asking, "Could you see a scenario where you could not come back?"

That's when Tiger delivers an answer that lingers throughout the offseason.

"Yeah, definitely," he says. "I don't know what my future holds for me."

Chapter 78

TOUR Championship
East Lake Golf Club
Atlanta, Georgia
September 20–23, 2018

It's happening. Everything's coming true.

"We got to be there," Ethan Cimma says to his grandfather.

From their home in Kentucky, the two Tiger Woods fans have been following their favorite player's progress all season, his first full slate on the PGA Tour since 2013, when he won five events and was named PGA Tour Player of the Year.

It's been impossible to look away. "I got a second chance on life," Tiger posted to his website in late March about the "last resort" spinal fusion surgery he underwent the previous spring. "I am a walking miracle."

"I am loving life now," Tiger told reporters at the Hero World Challenge late last year. "I've come out the other side and I feel fantastic. A lot of friends have helped me," he said, acknowledging that "It's just hard to imagine that I was living the way I was living with my foot not working, my leg not working, and then the hours of not being able to sleep because of the pain." The "neatest thing" is that he's "able to get out of bed and I can grab a club and not use it as a crutch," Tiger said. "Now I'm able to take a swing. That's so exciting; you have no idea how exciting that is, and I'm just so thankful that I've had this procedure and gotten to this point."

At the lead-up to the Hero World Challenge, Tiger enjoyed showing off a bit for Sam and Charlie.

"How do you see that golf ball?" Sam asked her dad as he hit balls hundreds of yards away.

"It's only going about 320," Tiger told her, later admitting he was "just being a complete smartass about it" since she "just thought it was so cool I was hitting it where she couldn't see it." Charlie was also impressed: Tiger says his son "wants to compete, he wants to play with me, those are things that are special."

Could he ever return to the level of that legend on YouTube?

"That's going to be hard," he said with a knowing grin. "I mean, I was pretty good."

He's certainly on an upward trajectory. Following a thirty-second-place finish at the Masters and a missed cut at the U.S. Open, he finished tied for sixth at the British Open and in the runner-up spot at the PGA Championship. The TOUR Championship is the final event of a season he began at number 1,199 on the Official World Golf Ranking and ended at number 21, earning the right to compete today in a field of thirty that contains eighteen of the top twenty PGA golfers.

Tiger shoots three sizzling rounds—65-68-65—birdieing six of the first seven holes on Saturday. "You play a lot like that golfer Tiger Woods," NBC's on-course reporter, Roger Maltbie, tells Tiger, who holds a three-stroke lead going into the final round on Sunday.

As the Tiger faithful well know, he's a perfect 23–0 when starting a fourth round with a lead this size or greater. His record is unmatched.

It's been 1,877 days, and 268 Sundays, since Tiger won the 2013 WGC–Bridgestone Invitational at Firestone Country Club, in Akron, Ohio. Five years since his last win.

That's the point when Ethan Cimma turns to his grandfather. "I live in Kentucky, and on Saturday night I'm watching sports recaps and see what Tiger's doing," he says. Cimma immediately knows that he and his grandfather need to be present for this moment. "So we got in the car at 5:30 a.m. and head down," he tells *Golf Digest*. It's a seven-hour drive to Atlanta's East Lake Golf Club. They devote another few hours to securing seats in the stands, but "after watching a few holes, I realized I needed to be on No. 18," says Cimma.

"See, this is the guy I have been telling you about," parents say to their kids. The excitement has the effect of turning back the clock. "I'm going to be like a little kid out there screaming for him," one Tiger booster says.

Tiger's playing partner is Rory McIlroy. The twenty-nine-year-old golfer from Northern Ireland has won four major championships as well as the TOUR Championship in 2016. "It was sort of the first time I'd really been in that position with him," McIlroy says of sharing the final tee time with Tiger, "who's such a hero for a lot of us out here.

"You dream of situations like that," he remarks.

On the front nine, Tiger opens with a birdie followed by eight straight pars, steadily increasing his lead to five strokes. While McIlroy struggles with the frustration of "not being able to conjure up your best stuff when you need it," Tiger's competing against Billy Horschel's number one position on the leaderboard, with a clubhouse target of 9 under.

Even with his own win in jeopardy, Horschel is in awe of the energy that Tiger brings. "There's always that extra buzz, that extra energy around the course when he's here."

Tiger keeps hitting the fairway until he bogeys 15, then 16, diminishing his lead to two strokes. The margin holds on 17. Bogey on 18 will suffice for the win.

Today's crowd is standing ten to fifteen deep behind the gallery ropes, collectively hoping—praying, even—for redemption. "It's an American story of a comeback" is how one fan explains the urgent energy. "He's earning his way back. It feels like the heyday of Tiger Woods out here today."

"Things were tense," says NBC reporter Roger Maltbie. "There wasn't a person that wasn't pulling for Tiger in that moment. It felt like we were about to watch someone perform open-heart surgery."

Tiger tees it up on 18 and drives the ball 350 yards.

Chants rise up from the gallery.

"Ti-ger! Ti-ger!"

"U-S-A! U-S-A!"

Ethan Cimma and his grandfather see Tiger coming down the fairway and realize, *It's happening. Everything's coming true.*

In their collective euphoria, thousands suddenly burst through the ropes and form a human wave surging behind Tiger and Rory McIlroy. A Georgia state trooper turns to Maltbie and says, "What are we going to do about these fans?"

"Son," Maltbie says, laughing, "ain't no way you getting that puppy back on the porch." But the chaos is happy, not dangerous. "It was beautiful pandemonium."

Especially when play is still ongoing.

On the 589-yard par-five 18th, Tiger and McIlroy are both struck by the parallels to one of golf's greatest moments: JACK IS BACK read the scoreboard at the eightieth U.S. Open, thirty-eight years ago, when Jack Nicklaus won his first victory in two years—his fourth U.S. Open and his sixteenth major championship.

"This is like Jack in '80 at Baltusrol," McIlroy says.

"Yeah, I just didn't have the tight pants and the hair."

Tiger bunkers his approach.

Whatever you do, he tells himself, *don't blade this thing out of bounds.*

He wedges out to around eight feet, missing the birdie putt before tapping in—two strokes ahead of Billy Horschel.

Six million viewers are tuned to NBC, watching as Tiger wins his eightieth PGA tournament.

The crowd explodes, jumping up and down, cheering and screaming for joy.

Rory McIlroy makes his own final putt, then mouths a message that tells the story of the day in three short words: "That was awesome."

"Tiger Woods has done so much for the sport," says Maltbie. "That Sunday at East Lake, the way everyone—and I mean everyone—showered him with love, it was the game's way of finally thanking him."

Accepting the TOUR Championship trophy, Tiger says, "I just can't believe I pulled this off."

Chapter 79

The 83rd Masters
Augusta National Golf Club
Augusta, Georgia
April 9, 2019

Tiger has two dinner invitations in the days before the 2019 Masters. On Tuesday, April 9, he turns up in his Green Jacket at the Augusta National clubhouse, where Patrick Reed, winner of the 2018 Masters, is hosting this year's Champions' Dinner. The golfer, known as Captain America for his devotion to Ryder Cup and Presidents Cup team play, is serving an all-American menu with "prime bone-in cowboy rib-eye" as the main course.

Two years ago, Tiger had been in such physical distress that even sitting at the Champions' Dinner required an injection of pain medication. "I couldn't sit. I couldn't walk. I couldn't lay down without feeling the pain in my back and my leg." He recalls wondering, *Is this how the rest of my life is going to be?* "I didn't have much of a life there for about two years," he tells the Golf Channel. "I couldn't get out of bed, I couldn't go out for dinner because I couldn't sit, I couldn't drive a car."

He confirms that at the 2017 Champions' Dinner he'd said, "I'm done." That was then. He recounts his recovery journey since, pointing out that after his spinal fusion surgery he "was able to start to walk again. I was able to participate in life, to be able to be around my kids again, to go to their games, go to their practices, take them to school again."

Of Sam and Charlie, he says, "The only thing they've seen is my struggles and the pain I was going through. Now they just want to go play soccer with me. Man, it's just such a great feeling."

Now he's "on the good side" again, and in two days he'll play in the eighty-third Masters.

On Wednesday, April 10, the Golf Writers Association of America hosts its forty-seventh annual awards dinner. Tiger swaps his Green Jacket for one in navy blue to receive a prize—but not the same Player of the Year award he's received eleven times. This year, the seven hundred members of the nonprofit organization announced in January that Tiger Woods is being presented with the Ben Hogan Award, named for the legendary Texas golfer. The award has been presented annually since 1954 to golfers who have overcome physical handicaps or injuries and continue to play.

On February 2, 1949, Hogan had been driving down a road in rural Texas with his wife, Valerie, when their car was struck by a Greyhound bus. Hogan's instinct to shield Valerie with his body saved both their lives, though his several fractures and life-threatening blood clots were medically regarded as career-ending injuries.

"People have always been telling me what I can't do," said Hogan, who helped support his widowed mother and siblings on golf-caddie wages. Doctors underestimated Hogan's determination to make it through a grueling rehabilitation that left him too weak to swing a club throughout 1949. "I guess I have wanted to show them. That's been one of my driving forces all my life."

Prior to the accident, Hogan had won three majors: two PGA Championships (in 1946 and 1948) and the 1948 U.S. Open. Defying predictions that he would never walk again, much less compete as a professional athlete, he entered the 1950 U.S. Open, at Merion Golf Club, in Pennsylvania, and won the event in an eighteen-hole playoff.

Hogan went on to win five additional majors, including two Masters (in 1951 and 1953), two U.S. Opens (also in 1951 and 1953), and one British Open (in 1953), but when asked his favorite, Hogan always cited the "Miracle at Merion" because, he said, "it proved I could still win."

Tiger and Hogan are two of only five golfers (along with Gary Player, Gene Sarazen, and Jack Nicklaus) to win all four majors. But now, that's not the only way their names are linked in the minds of sportswriters. Receiving the Hogan Award, Tiger says, "is very special," knowing "what Mr. Hogan went through and what he did and what he was able to accomplish post-[accident]."

Ahead of his 2018 TOUR Championship win, journalists asked Tiger if a victory to close out that season would "complete one of the greatest comebacks in all of sports." Tiger deferred to Ben Hogan, but in the lead-up to the 2019 Masters, he's asked again.

His answer is fundamentally the same: "One of the greatest comebacks in all of sports is the gentleman who won here, Mr. Hogan," he says. "I mean, he got hit by a bus and came back and won major championships. The pain he had to endure, the things he had to do just to play, the wrapping of the leg, all the hot tubs, and just how hard it was for him to walk, period . . . One of the greatest comebacks there is and it happens to be in our sport."

Hogan's comeback included a 1953 win at the eighty-second British Open at Carnoustie, Scotland. Tiger narrowly missed repeating Hogan's feat when at the 147th British Open last July, also at Carnoustie, he briefly topped the leaderboard during Sunday's final round. It was a breathtaking moment for everyone watching; *Golf Digest* noted the thrill of "the mere sight of Big Cat in Sunday red."

Also watching at Carnoustie and dressed in their dad's traditional red and black were Sam, then eleven, and Charlie, then nine. Their presence was the most important aspect of the tournament to Tiger. "I know that they know how much this championship means to me and how much it feels good to be back playing again," he said. "It's just so special to have them aware because I've won a lot of golf tournaments in my career, but they don't remember any of them."

On the Golf Channel, sportswriter Tim Rosaforte reported Tiger telling him, "I want [my kids] to see dad do what he's done most of his life and make them feel and watch what their father can do."

It's a sentiment shared by younger players on the tour as well, many of whom were still kids themselves when forty-three-year-old Tiger turned pro, in 1996.

"Tiger being back in the mix," said Rory McIlroy, who won the Open four years earlier, in 2014, at age twenty-five, "was great, just to be a part of it and hear the roars." Seeing Tiger's name atop the leaderboard made the twenty-four-year-old defending champion, Jordan Spieth, turn to his caddie and remark, "This is what you dream about."

The dream quickly dissolved on the back nine after a double bogey and a bogey. Tiger ended up in sixth place, three shots back from his Italian partner, Francesco Molinari, who emerged as that year's winner.

"I had a chance starting that back nine to do something, and I didn't do it," Tiger admitted. "I know that it's going to sting for a little bit here, but given where I was to where I'm at now, I'm blessed."

Put in perspective, the disappointment is "a teachable moment" for him and his children, who ran up to the 18th green to tightly embrace him. "They gave me some pretty significant hugs there and squeezed."

"Well, you weren't going to win," was the kids' blunt analysis.

"I know I wasn't going to win, but that doesn't stop me from grinding," he told them. "Sometimes you can't always see that on TV." He added, "Hopefully you're proud of your pops for trying as hard as I did."

The outstanding outcome of Tiger's surgery, according to a one prominent spinal surgeon, has been "like winning the lottery."

Tiger is going to play those odds right through Masters Week.

Chapter 80

The 83rd Masters
Augusta National Golf Club
Augusta, Georgia
April 11–14, 2019

A hopeful Sam and Charlie fly in from Orlando, Florida, to Augusta, Georgia, in time to catch the final round of the 2019 Masters. They'll be watching from the gallery with Tiger's mom, Tida, and his girlfriend of the past two years, Erica Herman, all rooting for Tiger to achieve what could be his greatest "W."

They're far from the only ones.

In North Augusta, South Carolina—just across the Savannah River from Augusta National Golf Club—Tiger's friend Darius Rucker and fellow members of Hootie & the Blowfish are all glued to a TV in their dressing room, whooping and hollering whenever Tiger makes birdie. "It's funny, the parallels in our lives," notes Rucker as the band preps for a reunion tour. "We haven't done this in 11 years, and he hasn't won a major tournament in 11 years."

Jack Nicklaus calls in to NBC Sports's *Live from the Masters*. He's watching this Sunday, April 14, from a fishing trip in the Bahamas, but the distance doesn't dull the spark the six-time Masters winner sees as Tiger competes for what could be his fifth Green Jacket.

Going into the final round, Tiger's two behind Francesco Molinari, the 2018 British Open champion, and tied for second place with Tony Finau. A poor weather forecast forces an adjustment to the groupings, expanding the traditional couples into threeballs and pushing planned start times several hours earlier. Molinari, Finau, and Tiger are the final grouping, at 9:20 a.m.

Tiger wakes at 4:00 a.m. to get into his routine. The early tee time and the threesome aren't the only differences from previous Masters; he's also never won when coming from behind on a Sunday.

For Finau, a twenty-nine-year-old of Tongan-Samoan descent who grew up in Salt Lake City, Utah, today's reality borders on the surreal. "I dreamed since I was a kid of competing against Tiger, playing against him in the final group, being paired with him in the final group of a Masters or a U.S. Open," says Finau.

Just as watching Jack Nicklaus win the 1986 Masters made an indelible impression on ten-year-old Tiger, watching Tiger win the 1997 Masters inspired seven-year-old Finau. "The way he fist-pumped, the red shirt, his power compared to the other players, the way he made the fans go crazy, and the rawness of it all seemed larger than life. I thought, *I want to be like that.* It's impossible to overestimate Tiger's influence on kids like me, or the impact he's had on golf in general. He's an icon, absolutely one of a kind," Finau tells *Golf Digest.*

He and Tiger, both Nike pitchmen, wear custom golf shoes: special-edition Nike Air Max 1s for Finau; chrome-soled black Nike Air Zoom TW71s with a green snakeskin pattern for Tiger, who's also wearing a Nike TW Vapor mock-neck polo in Sunday red, a throwback to the one Tiger wore fourteen Aprils ago—in 2005, the last time he won the Masters.

"This is a man possessed," Nicklaus says of Tiger. "He's possessed to win a golf tournament. He's absolutely under total control and he's going to get it done."

"Molinari fended off Tiger at Carnoustie in Scotland. But this is America. The support for Tiger is monumental, the noise will be monumental," says Nick Faldo on the CBS telecast. One noise that will be absent, however, is the sound of cell phones—there's a ban on them at Augusta National, to Tiger's delight. "The art of clapping is gone, right? You can't clap when you've got a cell phone in your hand," he points out. The Masters, though, "is so different, and is so unique. It's *pure* golf. You know, it's just player and caddie out there playing."

When the threesome reaches 12—part of what's known as Amen Corner at Augusta after the number of prayers sent up there—the winds are swirling. Rick Reilly of *Sports Illustrated* says, "The best hole in the country is the 12th at Augusta National," calling it "a hellacious, wonderful, terrifying, simple, treacherous, impossible, perfect molar-knocker of a par-3" and quipping, "More green jackets have been lost at the 12th than at the Augusta City Dry Cleaners."

Amen Corner lives up to its fierce reputation. Both Molinari and Finau hit draws that send their balls into the water of Rae's Creek for double bogeys. Tiger, however, plays "the prettiest little cut shot, right over where he should put it, over the center of the bunker, the left side of the bunker, into the middle of the green," says Nicklaus, declaring, "Tournament's over. It doesn't make any difference what anyone else is going to do. Somebody is going to make enough mistakes, and Tiger won't make any."

He's now tied for the lead.

"Game on!" yells a fan. *"Game. On."*

But as Tiger tees off on 13, a heavy rain is falling. The round spikes on his Air Zooms lose traction on the wet ground, where the grass is worn after four previous rounds. "Ahhh, I f—ing slipped," Tiger says, watching his ball's flight as he tosses his blue chewing gum into an azalea bush.

He's pulled the ball left into some trees, but it bounces back out and winds up splitting the fairway.

Tiger birdies 15 and claims the outright lead for the first time.

"The Tiger has hunted them down and now he's going for the kill," says Faldo.

On 16, the 173-yard hole named Redbud, he hits 8-iron off the tee. Two other players—Bryson DeChambeau and Justin Thomas—both scored aces on that same hole earlier today. Tiger looks good to be the third.

The cameras cut to the crowd's reaction. The *Golf Talk Canada* TV and radio announcers make a celebrity sighting in the gallery. "Right behind him [Tiger]. Who's that? Look, Michael Phelps, wearing that white visor. Another great."

The twenty-three-time Olympic gold medalist is attending his first Masters to cheer Tiger on. His prime spot in the gallery? That, he tells NBC's *OlympicTalk,* is courtesy of "a couple of nice people who had gotten to the gate early, at 3:30 a.m.," and who invited him to join them at the 16th.

"I did not notice Michael was back there," Tiger admits. "I was locked into what I was doing." The crowd behind him is on their feet, cheering in anticipation.

"Come on! *Come on!*" Tiger urges the ball, waiting to see where it will come to rest on the green.

"Of course it's exciting back there on the tee to watch the people stand up. Now you know it has a chance to go in, which is fun," says caddie Joe LaCava. But Tiger's "got to keep his emotions in check. That's probably as calm as I've ever seen him on a golf course. Not that I've ever seen him antsy. But there was certainly a calmness and a confidence that he was going to get this thing done."

The ball rolls about a foot past the hole. Not an ace, but close enough for an easy tap-in.

Tiger steps to 17 with a two-shot lead.

I've been in this position before, he remembers, flashing back to the 2005 Masters, when he went bogey, bogey to lose his lead over DiMarco. *Let's go ahead and pipe this ball right down the middle. Hit a little flat squeezer out there,* he tells himself.

He smokes it for par and keeps his two-shot lead.

"That was the best shot of the tournament," says LaCava.

After the defending U.S. Open and PGA Championship winner, Brooks Koepka, misses his birdie opportunity on 18, the tournament's left wide open for Tiger.

He's still got the lead but can't let himself relax until the very end, even when he's walking up to the green and seeing his family and friends gathered on 18. "I started to get a little bit emotional and I had to rein it back in and say, 'Hey, it's not quite over yet. I've had this putt before. Let's go ahead and make this putt.'"

He bogeys the hole, but it's still enough for him to win by a single stroke.

The typically sedate Augusta crowd of ten thousand erupts in chants of "Ti-ger! Ti-ger!" as a euphoric Tiger raises his arms in triumph. "WOOOOOOO!!!"

"We did it!" Tiger tells his caddie—"That meant everything to me," says LaCava—then strides over to tightly embrace his family, Charlie running to meet him first.

It's a full-circle moment. Earl is absent but deeply felt in the family celebration on the 18th green.

"I never thought we'd see anything that could rival the hug with his father in 1997, but we just did," Jim Nantz says from the CBS broadcast booth. "That hug with his children. If that doesn't bring a tear to your eye, and you're a parent...you're not human."

"That will be the greatest scene in golf, forever," says three-time Masters winner Nick Faldo, who helped Tiger into his first Green Jacket, in 1997. "We will never see anything as exhilarating as that."

A line of past Masters champions, wearing their own Green Jackets, comes out to congratulate Tiger. After Tiger signs his scorecard, Patrick Reed, the 2018 defending champion, helps Tiger slip into his own Green Jacket. "To put the jacket on him was unbelievable," says Reed. "The only thing I could think of when I did that was to not mess it up. I reminded myself to make sure I put the jacket on him correctly. And we got that job done. But it was a special moment."

Forty-three-year-old Tiger becomes the oldest Masters winner since forty-six-year-old Jack Nicklaus won his record sixth Green Jacket, in 1986. Nicklaus, who accurately made his final-round prediction from the Bahamas, tweets his congratulations: **A big 'well done' from me to Tiger. I am so happy for him and for the game of golf. This is just fantastic!!!**

In his post-tournament interview with CBS, Tiger, the now five-time Masters champion, says, "I'm really at a loss for words. This would be up there. It was one of the hardest I've ever had to win just because of what has transpired the last couple of years, trying to come back and play.

"You couldn't have had more drama than we all had out there. And now I know why I'm balding," he says. "This stuff is hard." On a more serious note, he's most grateful for his children's love and support. He's especially proud of showing eleven-year-old Sam and ten-year-old Charlie that he's more than "just Dad"—"Daddy has won golf tournaments, and he's not the YouTube guy," the 2019 Masters champion says. "I can still do it."

"This game was taken away from me for a few years there," Tiger says. "Now I'm able to play golf again, and do it at an elite level again, which is something I'm just very blessed to be able to have that opportunity again."

"It means the world to me" to be able to share this victory with his children, Tiger says. "They were there at the British Open last year when I had the lead on that back nine and made a few mistakes and cost myself a chance to win the Open title," he adds. "I wasn't going to let that happen to them twice."

"So to have them experience what it feels like to be part of a major championship and watch their dad fail and not get it done, and now to be a part of it when I did get it done, I think it's two memories that they will never forget," he says. "They know how I felt and what it felt like when

I lost at Carnoustie. To have the complete flip with them in less than a year, it was very fresh in their minds."

"For them to see it, feel it, and feel the electricity of the crowd—and for me to see Charlie, there as the first one…it gives me chills."

"Just to have them there and then now to have them see their Pops win, just like my Pops saw me win here, it's pretty special."

En route home to Florida, Tiger's delighted to see his kids arguing over which one of them gets to wear his jacket. "Just watching them fight over the green jacket on the airplane was pretty funny," Tiger says. "'I want to wear it; no, I want to wear it.' That's something I certainly will never forget."

Chapter 81

White House Rose Garden
Washington, DC
May 6, 2019

President Donald Trump tweets: **Spoke to @TigerWoods to congratulate him on the great victory he had in yesterday's @TheMasters, & to inform him that because of his incredible Success & Comeback in Sports (Golf) and, more importantly, LIFE, I will be presenting him with the PRESIDENTIAL MEDAL OF FREEDOM!**

At 6:00 p.m. on May 6, three weeks after winning his fifth Masters—his fifteenth major—Tiger stands before the president in the White House Rose Garden as Trump fastens the Presidential Medal of Freedom around the golfer's neck, calling him a "true legend."

The award is given to individuals who have made "especially meritorious contributions to the security or national interests of the United States, to world peace, or to cultural or other significant public or private endeavors," according to the White House.

After accepting America's highest civilian honor, Tiger says, "I've battled. I've tried to hang in there, and I've tried to come back and play the great game of golf again." He thanks his family and supporters, saying,

"You've seen the good and bad, the highs and lows, and I would not be in this position without all of your help."

Tiger's words evoke a standing ovation from the Rose Garden audience.

At forty-three, Tiger is the youngest golfer to receive the Medal of Freedom, but he's not the first: President George W. Bush awarded the first two to Arnold Palmer and Jack Nicklaus in 2004 and 2005 respectively, while President Barack Obama honored Charlie Sifford, the "Jackie Robinson of Golf," in 2014.

"I always called him Grandpa, because he was like the grandpa I never had," Tiger says of Sifford. "I ended up becoming so close with him that I ended up naming my son, Charlie, after him. And so to have been chosen as the next golfer after Charlie is truly remarkable."

While Tiger's relative youth was no deterrent to receiving the Presidential Medal of Freedom, the age limitations governing the World Golf Hall of Fame may push his seemingly inevitable induction far into the future.

In Pebble Beach on June 9, the class of 2019 is inducted ahead of the U.S. Open, where next week Tiger will be competing on the Pebble Beach Golf Links. New members include Dennis Walters, who as a twenty-four-year-old amateur golfer survived a car accident that paralyzed his legs, then ingeniously taught himself to swing a club from a cart and made a career of making trick shots at golfing exhibitions—more than three thousand of them—sometimes performing alongside Tiger.

In an acceptance speech charting experiences ranging "from the depths of despair to golf's ultimate destination," Walters asks the audience with genuine wonder:

"Can you believe I'm in the World Golf Hall of Fame before Tiger Woods?"

On October 28, 2019—three months after a fifth operation on his left knee—Tiger plays the first PGA Tour event ever staged in Japan, the inaugural Zozo Championship at the Accordia Golf Narashino Country Club, around half an hour east of Tokyo.

"It was a cool atmosphere. I loved being there," says Tiger's first-round playing partner, twenty-eight-year-old English golfer Tommy Fleetwood. Tiger's first postsurgery tournament begins slowly. "He hit it in the water off the first, hooked a tee shot off the next, and then he bogeyed the next," says Fleetwood. "You could tell he'd not been in contention for a little while." But things pick up after the third hole, and from then on "it probably is the best round of golf I've ever watched.... very, very impressive."

At the end of round 1, he shakes Tiger's hand. "Tiger, that was really good today."

Tiger grins. "How about that, huh?"

He keeps up the momentum and shoots 64-64-66-67 to win the tournament by three strokes.

The victory brings Tiger's tally of career PGA wins to eighty-two, tying the record Sam Snead set back in 1965.

"Obviously it was cool for him to get to 82," says Fleetwood, "but I know deep down he wants 83."

The thirteenth Presidents Cup takes place a month and a half later, from December 12 to December 15, in Melbourne, Australia. Tiger has decided to be a playing captain, the first in twenty-five years. "The Zozo Championship was a big event. It validated that I could still play and that I could help the team," Tiger says.

He chooses four players as "captain's picks": himself, his 2019 Masters final-round playing partner, Tony Finau; the 2018 Masters champion, Patrick Reed; and the 2019 U.S. Open champion, Gary Woodland.

The United States has a dominant record, but the one place they've lost before is the Royal Melbourne Golf Club, where they'll play again this year. Tiger was part of that 1998 team, too.

The Internationals put up a tough fight, but the United States pulls off a win on December 15, largely courtesy of Tiger's match-play victories.

"It was an honor for me as a player and even more of an honor to be their captain," Tiger says. "This cup wasn't going to be given to us. We had to go earn it, and we did."

"We were kind of against the odds, but we are very inspired to play for Tiger, with Tiger, and it's so satisfying to win this cup because of that," says Finau.

It's been a remarkable comeback year as Tiger's forty-fourth birthday approaches. "I'm enjoying this opportunity again because…there was a time when that was not a reality," he says. "I don't know how long it's going to be. How long am I going to do it for? And so however long that is, I'm going to keep giving my best. And when it's time to quit, then it's time to call it a day and I would have said that I would have had a good career."

That said, when asked if it's still a possibility that he could reach or surpass Jack Nicklaus's record of eighteen major titles, Tiger answers, "I think it is. I think it is." After all, as he's said before, "Who knows what the future holds?"

Chapter 82

Jupiter Island, Florida
April 5, 2020

It's the Sunday before the 2020 Masters in Augusta. At least it's supposed to be.

From his home on Jupiter Island, Tiger calls his friend Justin Thomas, a twenty-six-year-old fellow PGA Tour member and the 2017 PGA Championship winner. Thomas lives nearby, in mainland Jupiter, but with COVID-19 lockdowns, everyone is staying home.

The defending Masters champion would normally be in Augusta, Georgia, as he has been every April for the last twenty-five years. But with the PGA schedule in flux, so are Tiger's feelings, which he describes to Thomas as "energetic" and "wired" on the high end and "irritable" on the low end. Tiger's struggling to "unwire those circuits," which are firing an urgent message: "Subconsciously I knew I was supposed to get up there. My body was ready to go."

The tournament's been rescheduled for November 12–15, the first major move in a PGA season upended by the coronavirus pandemic. Only World War II, which suspended Masters play between 1942 and 1946, has had as big an impact.

On a February 25 pre-Masters conference call, Tiger had answered an ever-popular media question: What's on the menu for the Champions' Dinner? His plan for 2020 was to go retro. "I'm going back to what I had in 2006," he'd said. "Being born and raised in SoCal, having fajitas and sushi was part of my entire childhood," Tiger explained. "So we'll have steak and chicken fajitas, and we'll have sushi and sashimi out on the deck, and I hope the guys will enjoy it."

For dessert, another throwback, this one to the first Champions' Dinner he'd hosted: "I'm debating whether or not to have milkshakes as desserts because that was one of the most great memories to see Gene Sarazen and Sam Snead having milkshakes that night in '98."

But on Tuesday, April 7, instead of hosting a dinner at the Augusta National clubhouse for the fifth time, Tiger—sporting a quarantine beard—dons his Green Jacket over a red Nike shirt, sets out his Masters trophy as a centerpiece, and gathers with Sam, Charlie, Erica, and the family dogs (Bugs and Lola, a border collie and a springer spaniel mix) at their Jupiter Island dinner table to enjoy the planned SoCal menu.

He tweets out a photo captioned: **Masters Champions Dinner quarantine style. Nothing better than being with family.**

After the meal, the evening ends in a family food fight, Tiger tells NBC Sports, though he assures them, "I did take the jacket off."

Tiger and Charlie, who's working on his game, hit the backyard practice area and putting green. Bugs and Lola fetch stray golf balls the way Boom-Boom used to do when young Tiger was practicing on the Navy Golf Course.

Tiger tries not to offer golf advice unless Charlie asks. "My job is to get them prepared for life, not sports," he says, echoing sentiments shared by both his parents. But he follows in Earl's footsteps as a parent more than in Tida's. "My mom's tough. Very, very tough. Very vocal" is Tiger's description. "My dad was more cerebral, and liked to plant seeds that wouldn't germinate for years—but then it was like, 'Oh yeah.' That's what I like to do."

He thinks Earl would approve of him nowadays. "Pops would be proud," he says. "I mean, he'd say, 'Yeah, you—you've made your share of mistakes. We all do. And you bounce back, learn from 'em.'

"And, you know, that's what I've done," Tiger says. "I've done a lot of meditation, a lot of thinking, a lot of analyzing," adding, "And here we are, come full circle."

Family time isn't the only benefit to emerge from the pandemic pause. "I feel a lot better now than I did then," Tiger says in an interview with Discovery. "I've been able to turn a negative into a positive and been able to train a lot and get my body back to where I think it should be."

On Sunday, May 24, Tiger is seen holding an oversize check for $20 million. He's one of four headliners in The Match: Champions for Charity golf tournament, held to raise money for coronavirus relief. At Tiger's home course, the Medalist Golf Club, in Hobe Sound, Florida, Tiger and Peyton Manning defeat Phil Mickelson and Tom Brady, the new quarterback for the Tampa Bay Buccaneers.

Tiger hasn't played since February 16, but any bitterness over that last-place finish at Riviera Country Club, in Los Angeles, is overcome by today's good work for an important cause—and some classic trash talk.

On the 5th hole, three-time U.S. Open champion Tiger landed a zinger on the six-time runner-up, Mickelson. "You want me to mark with a U.S. Open medal?" Tiger asked.

"Do you have one? I have some silver ones," Mickelson answered.

Yet neither makes the cut at the 120th U.S. Open, rescheduled from June to September of 2020 at Winged Foot Golf Club, in Mamaroneck, New York.

Twenty-seven-year-old Bryson DeChambeau wins his first major at 6 under. The Southern California golfer and college physics major name-checks Tiger in his victory speech as the motivation behind his strength-training regimen.

"Tiger inspired this whole generation to do this, and we're going to keep going after it. I don't think it's going to stop."

Tiger returns to Augusta National to defend the title he's held for nineteen months, thanks to the delayed 2020 schedule. Thoughts of his 2019 victory have never left him. "I'm getting chills just thinking about it," he says on Tuesday, November 10, as he hosts the Champions' Dinner—minus the milkshakes he'd originally considered for dessert.

On Saturday, November 14, his alarm wakes him at 3:30 a.m. A first-round weather delay that stretched into Friday has him playing twenty-six holes today. It's a twelve-hour session, a supreme test for a back that's vulnerable to stress. And pain.

The next day, Tiger's wearing his Sunday red, but his body doesn't have what it takes to deliver the green. After what has to be an embarrassing septuple bogey, with three shots in the water (and a bit of bad luck on the first two, which roll back off the green), Tiger birdies 13, pars 14, then birdies 15, 16, 17, and 18 for a final-round score of 76. "You've got five green jackets and you made a 10 on the 12th hole. You got it all covered," Tiger's caddie, Joe LaCava, says in consolation. In a stark contrast to last year's mobbed victory celebration, Covid restrictions mean only a few spectators are waiting on the 18th green to watch him tap in—in thirty-eighth place.

"I hit a few too many shots than I wanted to today, and I will not have the chairman be putting the green jacket on me," Tiger says. "I'll be passing it on."

There's ample time for reflection. More than a full hour passes before Tiger's called upon to put the Green Jacket on the 2016 U.S. Open winner and first-time Masters champion, Dustin Johnson. With an unmatched 20-under score of 268, the thirty-six-year-old Johnson broke the record Tiger set in 1997 by two strokes.

Though earning the Green Jacket is more important than who passes it along, "having Tiger put it on was awesome," Johnson says of Augusta National's most coveted prize. "It's an incredible feeling. Dreaming about winning the Masters as a kid and having Tiger put the green jacket on you; it still feels like a dream.

"You wouldn't want it any other way."

The tournament formerly known as the Father/Son Challenge has a new name and two players new to the twenty-team field, Tiger and eleven-year-old Charlie—the youngest (by a year) to compete in the tournament since it began, in 1997.

Walking with Team Tiger at the Ritz-Carlton Golf Club in Orlando, Florida, during the weekend before Christmas are thirteen-year-old Sam and her mother, Elin. It's the first time Elin has been seen at an event with her ex-spouse since their 2010 divorce.

Justin Thomas—who's won three PGA events this year—and his father, Mike, win the PNC Championship, with Team Singh (Vijay and Qass) taking second and Team O'Meara (Mark and Shaun) third.

"This is a big stage, to bring Charlie out at 11 it could be a little intimidating, but we witnessed something really special in the way they played," Mark O'Meara says.

"I'm trying to make sure Charlie is in the right environment," Tiger says, "so he can practice and play" rather than worry about the publicity that comes with having a famous parent. "Making sure he's able to have fun just playing the game of golf."

Charlie more than holds his own, hitting every fairway in the first round. **Youngest competitor in the field**, the PGA Tour tweets. **Biggest trash-talker.**

"Draw hole" reads the note Justin finds in the sand after he bunkered his ball on the 13th.

It's from Charlie.

Team Tiger finishes in seventh place. Tiger's been known to get emotional when a win eludes him. Today the source of his feelings is different.

"I don't think words can describe it," he says. "Just the fact that we were able to have this experience together, Charlie and I, they are memories for a lifetime."

It's an intersection of the past and the future.

"I know my dad would have been proud with how Sam and Charlie turned out, I just wished he could have been here for all of this," Tiger says. "My mom has been, she's been a part of their lives, I wish my dad would have been."

Chapter 83

Jupiter Island, Florida
January 19, 2021

Tiger and Notah Begay III are exchanging text messages about a favorite topic: hitting golf balls.

On December 23, three days after playing with Charlie in the PNC Championship and a week before his forty-fifth birthday, Tiger underwent a microdiscectomy—his fifth—to treat a painful "pressurized disc fragment" in his back.

As Begay tells ESPN on January 19, Tiger was "back on his feet" the next day, and though not "ripping drivers" on the range, he was testing his swing, and texting Begay the results.

"I think they were trying to clean a couple little bits up," Begay says. "Obviously he won't be playing for the next couple of months, but he should be back for the Masters, if not before that. So yeah, I think he'll be just fine."

It must have been some big celebrity who crashed.

That's what a resident of Rancho Palos Verdes, California, thinks as he watches police activity on Tuesday, February 23, at Hawthorne Boulevard and Blackhorse Road, a downhill intersection locally regarded as a "speed trap."

The area has been swarming with activity since shortly after 7:12 a.m., when a resident called 911 upon spotting an unconscious man inside a Genesis SUV that had crossed two lanes of oncoming traffic before colliding with a median and rolling several times. At 7:18 a.m., Los Angeles County sheriff's deputy Carlos Gonzalez is first on the scene.

It's dark inside the damaged car, but Gonzalez can see that the driver's eyes are now open.

"Hey, can you tell me your first name?" he asks.

"Tiger."

Oh, yeah, Gonzalez realizes. *You're Tiger Woods.*

Gonzalez observes Tiger "stuffing the deployed airbag back into the steering wheel" and, concerningly, notices that he "has an open fracture mid shaft on his right leg below the knee."

Tiger can move his legs from under the steering mechanism, displaced by the crash, but he can't get out of the car under his own power. Deputy Gonzalez calls for assistance. "Do we have an ETA for fire [department rescue units]?" comes the radio dispatch at 7:25 a.m. "We have a rollover with someone trapped."

Using a pry bar and an ax, firefighters extract Tiger through the shattered windshield and rush him to the nearest trauma center, Harbor-UCLA Medical Center, in Torrance, California. While doctors are stitching a gash in Tiger's chin, Deputy Kyle Sullivan interviews him and notes that "Woods did not remember being involved in a traffic collision and thought he was currently in the state of Florida."

Tiger's actually been in California for the last week. Though his recent back surgery kept him out of play at the 2021 Genesis Invitational, held at the Riviera Country Club, in Pacific Palisades, he'd continued in a role he'd taken on in 2017: host. He has a sentimental connection to Riviera Country Club, where in 1992 he played his first PGA tournament as a sixteen-year-old amateur.

On Sunday, February 21, during the final round of the Genesis Invitational, Tiger revealed to CBS's Jim Nantz his immediate goal: to overcome his lingering back injuries and compete for his sixteenth major at this year's Masters.

"God, I hope so. I've got to get there first," Tiger said when asked if he'd be well enough to play by then. "A lot of it is based on my surgeons and doctors and therapist and making sure I do it correctly. This is the only back I've got; I don't have much more wiggle room left."

Following the Genesis, Tiger had stayed in Los Angeles to shoot an instructional video for GolfTV and *Golf Digest*. Yesterday he'd worked with actors Jada Pinkett Smith and David Spade plus NBA star Dwyane Wade. Director Peter Berg says Tiger "was charming, giving and full of love. He was professional and f—ing awesome." This morning, he'd been making the twenty-minute drive in his tournament courtesy car from Terranea Resort, where he's staying, to the Rolling Hills Country Club for a second day of filming when the accident occurred.

Now he's in emergency surgery.

A little before 1:00 p.m., his agent, Mark Steinberg, releases a statement to the media: "Tiger Woods was in a single-car accident this morning in California where he suffered multiple leg injuries."

These injuries are detailed on Tiger's website by Dr. Anish Mahajan, Harbor-UCLA Medical Center's chief medical officer and interim CEO. Tiger's right leg and foot, the doctor explains, have been surgically stabilized by a rod as well as with screws and pins.

At 6:00 p.m., CNN broadcasts a news conference with the Los Angeles County sheriff, Alex Villanueva, who explains that Tiger was wearing his seat belt and that the SUV's "interior was more or less intact, which kind of gave him the cushion to survive what otherwise would have been a fatal crash."

It's the third time in a dozen years that police have been called to the scene of a single-car accident to find a semiconscious Tiger Woods behind the wheel of a wrecked car. Skeptical reporters press for information on Tiger's condition in the moments preceding the accident.

Question: "When you say no evidence of impairment, what exactly—what impairments are you looking at?"

Villanueva: "Well, we're looking at signs of influence—under the influence of either narcotics, medication, alcohol, odor of alcohol, all these different things that would give you an idea and their behavior, but there was none present."

At the Concession Golf Club, in Bradenton, Florida, PGA Tour players are prepping for this week's WGC–Workday Championship.

According to Xander Schauffele, Team USA's 2020 Olympic gold medalist in golf, "Everyone I've talked to has been in a strange mood due to the news."

Bryson DeChambeau compares Tiger to the legendary Ben Hogan, who miraculously survived a 1949 car crash. DeChambeau says of Tiger, "I have no doubt in my mind he'll be back."

Others, like Justin Thomas, remove golf from the equation entirely. "I'm sick to my stomach. It hurts to see, now one of my closest friends get in an accident, and I just hope he's alright," Thomas says. "I'm just worried for his kids. I'm sure they're struggling."

Phil Mickelson, father of three, observes, "I thought Rory McIlroy said it well when he said that we are just lucky and appreciative that his kids didn't lose their father. We are hoping and praying for a speedy recovery. We're thankful that he's still with us."

On February 24, the Los Angeles County sheriff, Alex Villanueva, briefs the press. "We don't contemplate any charges whatsoever in this crash," he announces. "This remains an accident. An accident is not a crime. They do happen unfortunately." Although a supplemental collision report identifies the contents of the SUV—including a backpack containing an empty unlabeled prescription pill bottle—the sheriff addresses only the question of whether alcohol was involved. "He was not drunk," Villanueva says. "We can throw that one out."

Throughout the final round of the WGC–Workday Championship on Sunday, February 28, more than a dozen PGA golfers pay visual tribute to Tiger. Phil Mickelson, Tony Finau, and many others turn up in Tiger's traditional Sunday red, wear caps hand-lettered TW, and strike TIGER-stamped golf balls.

It's a moving display of solidarity and support.

Tiger watches the broadcast from his room at Cedars-Sinai Medical Center, where he was transferred two days ago to receive ongoing orthopedic treatment in the hospital's top-rated sports medicine department.

"It is hard to explain how touching today was when I turned on the TV and saw all the red shirts," Tiger posts on Monday, March 1. "To every golfer and every fan, you are truly helping me get through this tough time."

Tiger's injuries are extensive—both the tibia and fibula bones are broken in several places—and there's concern that he might lose his right leg entirely. But on March 16, after three weeks of hospital care, he posts a milestone change of venue: he's back in Florida. **Happy to report that I am back home and continuing my recovery . . . working on getting stronger every day.**

Though he's no stranger to postsurgical rehabilitation, this time is different—startlingly so. "It's altered," Tiger says of his physical symmetry. "My right leg does not look like my left, put it that way."

County sheriff Alex Villanueva holds another press conference in LA. With Tiger's permission, he's released the full results of the police investigation into the February 23 crash.

"The primary causal factor for this traffic collision was driving at a speed unsafe for the road conditions and the inability to negotiate the curve of the roadway," the sheriff states.

Today's date—Wednesday, April 7—is significant. Tomorrow begins the first round of the 2021 Masters. Tiger, who's played in the tournament for four consecutive decades, will be missing his third Masters since 2014.

Justin Thomas, who visited Tiger at home last week, shares his friend's state of mind. "It's kind of starting to set in," Thomas tells a reporter at Augusta. "He's bummed he's not here playing practice rounds with us, and we hate it too."

Rory McIlroy gives another insight into Tiger's state of mind. During a recent visit with Tiger, McIlroy caught sight of the living-room trophy cabinet and did a double take. Only Tiger's fifteen major trophies were on display. What happened to his other sixty-seven PGA Tour trophies?

"I don't know," Tiger said.

"What?" McIlroy asked, incredulous.

"Yeah, my mom has some, and a few are in the office and a few are wherever."

On the drive home, McIlroy thought, *All he cared about were four weeks a year. The other stuff must have been like practice.*

During Masters Week, ESPN airs an emotional tribute to Tiger narrated by broadcast journalist Gene Wojciechowski. Closing out the video is the poignant reminder of the absence of an icon. "Augusta National has a long memory. It remembers those who have added to its legacy and no one has done that more often than Tiger Woods."

On November 21, 2021, Tiger posts a video captioned "Making Progress" that shows him hitting a golf ball. It's a new installment of the "Making Progress" video he posted on October 15, 2017, when he was recovering from spinal fusion surgery.

Tiger's wearing a black compression sleeve on his right leg; the crutches he's been relying on are nowhere in sight. He describes this recovery, which began with three months in bed, as "an entirely different animal. I understand more of the rehab process because of my past injuries, but this was more painful than anything I have ever experienced."

The response to the new video is overwhelming.

Tiger keeps pushing. But he does set limits, in November telling *Golf Digest*: "Something that is realistic is playing the tour one day, never full time, ever again, but pick and choose, just like Mr. Hogan did."

Days before Christmas and the week before his forty-sixth birthday, Team Tiger makes its latest return.

It's been a harrowing year since Tiger and Charlie placed seventh in the 2020 PNC Championship at Orlando's Ritz-Carlton Golf Club. Twelve-year-old Charlie Axel Woods walks the course while his father rides a cart. Luckily, the generational tournament is operated in collaboration with the PGA Tour Champions (golf's "senior" tour for players over fifty), which allows the use of carts.

Dressed in red for the final round, Team Tiger birdies eleven straight holes to place second, two strokes behind winning Team Daly (John and John II).

"Charlie was hitting the ball unbelievable," a proud Tiger boasts to NBC. As for himself, he's just grateful for the progress he's made. "I still have my own leg, which was questionable for a while. And it's functioning. I'm just really tired. I'm not used to this. I think this might be my fourth or fifth round of golf [this] year. I'm a little worn out."

Still, "the competitive juices, they're never going to go away," Tiger says. "This is my environment, this is what I've done my entire life. I'm just so thankful to have this opportunity to do it again."

Tiger reminds reporters, "Remember what I said at Pebble Beach in '97?" Back then, his attitude was "Second sucks."

Not today. Today, it feels like a miracle.

Chapter 84

PGA Tour headquarters
Ponte Vedra Beach, Florida
March 9, 2022

Cameras are rolling as Tiger, Sam, and Charlie walk the red carpet outside the PGA Tour's "global home," in Ponte Vedra Beach, Florida.

Tiger's looking effortlessly cool, wearing dark sunglasses, a turned-backward ball cap, a Nike long-sleeved T-shirt, and coordinating shorts and sneakers. The navy-blue-and-white color palette is a preview of the formal wear he'll sport when it's time to get glammed up tonight for the World Golf Hall of Fame induction ceremony.

He's known this day was coming for the past two years. In March of 2020, members of the selection committee for the World Golf Hall of Fame had cast their ballots, selecting Tiger Woods for the class of 2021.

Tiger issued a statement calling the Hall of Fame nod "the ultimate recognition to never give up and keep chasing." But he'd had to wait an extra year to be officially inducted into the elite, soon-to-be-164-member society when the ceremony planned for 2021 was delayed by the COVID-19 pandemic.

Fourteen-year-old Sam Alexis Woods has put considerable thought into her speech, but the color of her outfit was a no-brainer. That's easy. Her dad's colors are red and black, and so are the clothes her grandmother Tida and brother, Charlie, are wearing. Tida and her grandkids are seated in the front row of the PGA's event space.

In a red sleeveless minidress and red heels decorated with butterflies, Sam steps to the presenter's podium. Over the next four minutes, her words wing their way into the hearts of all who hear them. The capacity crowd of five hundred includes PGA golfers as well as attendees such as Tiger's longtime childhood friends Bryon Bell and Jerry Chang, all here to witness a career-capping moment for a golfer who needs no introduction.

"It's been at the soccer fields and golf tournaments over the years that Charlie and I have begun to realize how famous he actually is," Sam says of her father, gently teasing. "I mean, how can a guy who still FaceTimes his friends to discuss Marvel-DC timelines and who goes to Comic-Con dressed as Batman be one of the greatest golfers that ever lived?"

The Hall of Fame has mounted a commemorative display of Tiger's career. The memorabilia fills three cases—hardly enough space to tell his story, one that's grown more remarkable by the year. But it's telling that many of the items Tiger has chosen to display date from his remarkable amateur years.

"Train hard, fight easy," Sam says, invoking the words of another family member, her grandfather Earl Woods, who died in 2006, the year before she was born.

Tiger nods knowingly as Sam addresses her father directly, saying, "You've defied the odds every time."

She bravely touches on the near-fatal car crash in faraway Los Angeles County, when the family worried and wondered, along with the rest of the world, if the seemingly insurmountable odds against recovery would defeat a competitor as fierce as Tiger Woods. "We didn't know if you'd come home with two legs or not," Sam says. "Now, you're not only about to be inducted into the Hall of Fame, but you're standing here on your own two feet. This is why you deserve this.

"Dad," Sam says, "I inducted you into Dad Hall of Fame a long time ago. But today, I am so proud to present, my dad, Tiger Woods, into the World Golf Hall of Fame."

Onstage, Sam holds an engraved plaque in her hands. Tiger walks over, on the legs that nearly failed him, to accept it. The moment is awe-inspiring—even to the legend himself.

"Crap, I just lost a bet to [Steve] Stricker that I wouldn't cry," Tiger begins. The opening is unrehearsed perfection.

Starting "kind of retro," Tiger recalls his formative years in the sport in riveting personal detail. The list of those who inspired and influenced him features corporate titans, his childhood dog Boom-Boom, and a who's who of golfing greats, including the incomparable Charlie Sifford, whose memory lives on in Charlie Woods. Echoing Sam's words, Tiger also invokes Earl's mantra, "Train hard, fight easy."

Team Tiger made it look that way.

Now it's Tiger's turn to directly address a particular member of the audience.

Through fresh tears, he looks at Tida and says:

"So without the sacrifices of Mom who took me to all those junior golf tournaments, and Dad, who's not here, but who instilled in me this work ethic to fight for what I believe in, chase after my dreams, nothing's ever going to be given to you, everything's going to be earned.

"I've had two amazing parents. I had amazing golf instructors, unbelievable caddies, friends that I've had for a lifetime," he says. "I know that golf is an individual sport. We do things on our own a lot for hours on end, but in my case, I didn't get here alone.

"This is an individual award, but it's actually a team award. All of you allowed me to get here. I just want to say thank you very much from the bottom of my heart."

* * *

On March 29, Tiger watchers identify his Gulfstream G550 jet—tailnumber N517TW—en route from South Florida's Martin County Airport to Augusta Regional Airport.

At Augusta National, Tiger and Charlie hit the driving range and then play a practice round, thirteen-year-old Charlie's first on the hilly course where Tiger's won five championships.

Will he try for another in April? It would be his twenty-fifth Masters start.

As of Sunday, April 3, 2022, his status remains a "game-time decision."

If he's going to play, he needs the right equipment. "My apparel is an extension of me," he told Golf Galaxy in February. It's important that all parts of his game, from his golf balls and clubs "to my apparel, to my footwear, my glove, my lid, everything," work in unison. "I don't want to feel uncomfortable. Because when we're out there competing, we're in a very uncomfortable environment. The last thing you want to do is have something that's nagging at you."

On Thursday, April 7, Tiger steps to the first tee. It's been 508 days since he played competitive golf.

The television cameras reveal a monumental equipment change. Gone are the Nike Air Zooms he wore from 2019 to 2021.

On his feet are 2022 FootJoy Premiere Series Packard spikes.

In a pre-tournament press conference, Tiger discussed the reason he changed shoes, despite his decades as a Nike ambassador. "I have very limited mobility now with the rods and plates and screws that are in my leg," he explained. "I needed something different, something that allowed me to be more stable. That's what I've gone to."

Tiger's mobility issues, *Golf* magazine surmises, may require a shoe that keeps his foot flatter on the ground than the more padded Nike soles do.

"Like golf fans around the world, we are delighted to see Tiger back on the course," Nike said in a statement, making no mention of the shoes. "As he continues his return, we will work with him to meet his new needs."

Endurance will be his first need, with a marathon four-round tournament underway. Social media buzzes with the initial results. **A first-round -1 for Tiger is truly remarkable. What a treat for all of us. Miracle of doctors and medicine, and his hard work back**, one fan posts on Twitter.

But Tiger's right leg isn't fully healed, and the prospect of completing all four rounds is daunting—and so painful that throughout the back nine on the third and fourth rounds, Tiger can be seen leaning on his clubs as if they're canes. He shoots a pair of 78s, the worst scores he's ever recorded at the Masters. The crowd nevertheless cheers his forty-seventh-place finish, and he rewards them with a smile that's part happiness, part relief.

Tiger walks off the course with a feeling "I don't think words can really describe," he tells CBS Sports, "given where I was a little over a year ago and what my prospects were at that time. To end up here and be able to play all four rounds, even a month ago, I didn't know if I could pull this off."

While Tiger's prize money for the 2022 Masters is $43,500, his old clubs go for more than $5 million. On April 10, a fan pays $5,156,162 for nine Titleist 681 T irons and two Titleist Vokey Design wedges stamped TIGER. Though on March 29, Mark Steinberg told *Golfweek* that Tiger still possesses the Tiger Slam–era clubs, Golden Age Auctions attested with "100 percent confidence that these clubs were used by Tiger Woods during his legendary 2000–01 seasons." It's a huge profit for the seller, who'd bought the clubs in 2010 for $57,242.

What's indisputable is that Tiger's latest, and perhaps most inspiring, comeback has further burnished his Hall of Fame legacy.

Chapter 85

The 104th PGA Championship
Southern Hills Country Club
Tulsa, Oklahoma
May 19–22, 2022

The week before the PGA Championship, three members of the ESPN golf broadcast team highlight the lingering image of the 2022 Masters—Tiger's smile.

"Watching him walk off with that smile on his face Sunday at 78 and 78," host Scott Van Pelt says, "that's the first time I would think that 78, 78 on the weekend of a major would be a smile. But I felt like that smile reflected the satisfaction of, man, I got here. I got here. I played well enough to be here on the weekend. Did I play how I wanted? No, but I'm here, man, and I'm playing."

Tiger is forty-six years old, four years younger than Phil Mickelson was last year on May 23, 2021, when he won the 103rd PGA Championship at South Carolina's Kiawah Island Golf Resort. Mickelson was number 115 on the Official World Golf Ranking when, at age fifty—less than a month from fifty-one—he became the oldest player ever to win a major on the PGA Tour.

Mickelson won $2,160,000 that day. "Tiger has been the instigator,"

Mickelson said back in April of 2014, crediting Tiger with the dramatic rise in prize money at PGA Tour events. "He's the one that's really propelled the bus because he's brought increased ratings, increased sponsors, increased interest and we have all benefitted."

But it's no longer enough for Mickelson. On October 27, 2021, came the announcement of LIV Golf, a new professional golf tour named after the Roman-numeral version of 54 (also a nod to the three rounds, or fifty-four holes, of golf allotted to each tournament). Greg Norman was named CEO, with Phil Mickelson and Dustin Johnson rumored to be marquee players in the spring 2022 schedule.

On February 2, 2022, Mickelson was playing in the Saudi International when he ignited controversy by bashing what he called the PGA Tour's "obnoxious greed." On February 17, Mickelson's biographer, Alan Shipnuck, broke the news that although Mickelson dismissed LIV as "sportswashing" on the part of Saudi Arabia's Public Investment Fund (PIF), his involvement in the upstart league was far deeper than anyone suspected.

During a November 2021 phone call, Mickelson had told Shipnuck that launching an offensive against the PGA, the nonprofit organization that had brought him wealth and fame, outweighed his ethical concerns about the Saudi regime.

"They're scary motherf—ers to get involved with," he said. "Why would I even consider it? Because this is a once-in-a-lifetime opportunity to reshape how the PGA Tour operates. They've been able to get by with manipulative, coercive, strong-arm tactics because we, the players, had no recourse" is his rationalization. "The Saudi money has finally given us that leverage. I'm not sure I even want [LIV] to succeed, but just the idea of it is allowing us to get things done with the [PGA] Tour."

Though Mickelson later apologized for his "reckless" choice of words, the damage was done. Sponsors—including Amstel Light, Callaway Golf Company, and KPMG—quickly dropped him, and the PGA Tour quietly suspended Mickelson ahead of the Masters.

Nevertheless, the PGA lists both Tiger and Mickelson in the field in

May of 2022, ahead of the PGA Championship, until Mickelson with-draws, on May 13. Like all PGA Championship winners, Mickelson has a lifetime exemption into the event, but he won't be defending the title he won last year.

"It's always disappointing when the defending champion is not here," Tiger says, but he gives no explanation for Mickelson's U-turn.

When the first LIV Golf event is announced for June, Tiger takes apart its model of guaranteed appearance fees. With $25 million purses, the earnings of even the lowest finisher will rival the winnings of a top-ten finisher at a PGA event.

"I understand different viewpoints," Tiger says, "but I believe in lega-cies. I believe in major championships. I believe in big events, compar-isons to historical figures of the past. There's plenty of money out here. The tour is growing. But it's just like any other sport, you have to go out there and earn it."

The four-time PGA Championship winner (1999, 2000, 2006, 2007) has dedicated the past five weeks to physical conditioning. "The first mountain I climbed was Everest," Tiger says of his endurance test at Augusta National in April. Now "I feel like I can [win] — definitely. I just have to go out there and do it. Starts on Thursday and I'll be ready."

His optimism is short-lived. In the first two rounds, he scores 74–69. On Saturday, the flashes of pain that were visible during the second round noticeably worsen. He limps the six miles around the 7,400-yard course, finishing with a third-round 79, the highest score he's ever recorded in a PGA Championship.

Tiger withdraws from the tournament before the final round. "As much as he's working and trying," Tiger's caddie, Joe LaCava, tells *Golf-week*, "the body just won't cooperate."

The situation is more severe than what's reported to the media. A screw in Tiger's surgically repaired leg came loose and pierced his skin. Further medical treatment is required.

*   *   *

Tiger won't be playing in the RBC Canadian Open, the third-oldest event on the PGA Tour after the British Open and the U.S. Open. Interest is heightened around this second weekend in June because LIV has chosen the same dates for its inaugural event, in England. To Rory McIlroy, who's recently become one of five player-directors on the PGA policy board and who wins the 2022 Canadian Open, LIV's move to attract tour players eager to make a quick buck is not a good look. "The professional game is the window shop into golf," he says of the visibility and influence of elite play.

On June 9, at the Centurion Club, outside London, seventeen PGA players—including major winners Phil Mickelson, Dustin Johnson, and Sergio Garcia—begin first-round play at the first LIV Golf event. They're immediately suspended by the PGA, losing eligibility for tour events and the Presidents Cup. Ten resign their memberships.

According to Greg Norman, CEO of LIV, Tiger was also offered a "mind-blowingly enormous" deal to join the upstart tour. "We're talking about high nine digits." But Tiger's unmoved by the money. On June 10, *Forbes* reports in a headline, TIGER WOODS OFFICIALLY A BILLIONAIRE, NO THANKS TO THE SAUDIS. He's joined a rarefied group—the only other two athletes with a net worth of $1 billion are Michael Jordan and LeBron James. Even in the past year, during which Tiger's largely been recovering from injuries sustained in his 2021 car crash, he earned $68 million from endorsements and other ventures, including golf course design as well as his restaurant and resort business.

His finances are sound, but his body continues to falter. On July 5, Tiger explains why he withdrew from the U.S. Open, citing "some issues with my leg" and saying, "If you asked me last year whether I would play golf again, all of my surgeons would have said no. But here I am playing two major championships this year. I will always be able to play golf, whether it's this leg or someone else's leg or false leg or different body pieces that have been placed or fused. I'll always be able to play. Now if you say play at a championship level, well, that window is definitely not as long as I would like it to be."

The three-time British Open champion (2000, 2005, 2006) won his first two on the Old Course. Returning to St Andrews, Scotland, for the 150th British Open, Tiger leaves nothing to chance. He arrives early, allowing five days of practice.

On July 11, Tiger poses with fellow three-time Open champion Jack Nicklaus—who won the Claret Jug in 1966, 1970, and 1978—on the seven-hundred-year-old stone Swilcan Bridge over the stream between the 1st and 18th fairways. The photo—posted to @TheOpen and captioned simply "Tiger. Jack. St Andrews."—goes viral.

But the fabled history of the place and his past achievements here fail to carry him through the week. Tiger misses the level-par cut by nine strokes.

In respect for the defeated champion, the spectators in the grandstands rise to their feet. Over on the 1st, Rory McIlroy tips his cap.

Tiger returns the gesture, making it his own. Where Arnold Palmer (1995) and Jack Nicklaus (2005) stopped midway over the Swilcan Bridge to tip their caps to the crowd one last time, Tiger crosses over without stopping, his TW cap raised high overhead in greeting.

Some believe that crossing the bridge is an act that connects the past, present, and future of golf. Although he thinks the British Open is unlikely to return to St Andrews before 2030, Tiger hopes he'll be there when it does.

"It was a struggle playing the three events I played this year," he says. "That in itself is something I'm very proud of."

In September of 2022, thirteen-year-old junior golfer Charlie Woods is trying to qualify for the NB3, the Notah Begay III Junior Golf National Championship.

Tiger's good friend Begay—the first Native American to play on the PGA Tour—has made it his mission to bring golf to future generations. He founded the tournament in 2020 in partnership with the Coushatta Tribe of Louisiana, which operates Koasati Pines, at the Coushatta Casino Resort.

The thirty-six-hole qualifier, Last Chance Florida Regional, is held at the Mission Resort + Club, in Howey-in-the-Hills, Florida. On Saturday, September 24, while Tiger was advising the Presidents Cup captain, Davis Love III, by phone, Charlie shot an 80. Today, with Tiger on the bag, he shoots a personal-best 68 that ties him for fourth place.

"Dad told me to stay patient and just play steady golf," Charlie says. "I couldn't have done it without him. Some shots, I would've been so off. He steered me on the right course."

A few weeks later, on November 7, Tiger and Charlie are in the wetlands of southwestern Louisiana among the live oaks and tall pines at Koasati Pines. Fans feel like they've hit the jackpot when they spot Tiger on the bag for his son, wearing a caddie bib that reads WOODS.

Max Homa, six-time winner on the PGA Tour, suspects that Tiger's presence might have the opposite effect on Charlie's competitors. "When I was in Jr high," Homa posts, "I played a tourney with this kid who told me he got his putter from a guy who was on the PGA Tour and I remember being really intimidated for some reason. Not sure I would have handled Tiger caddying in my group too well."

Ten kids in the twelve-and-thirteen division withstand the pressure. Charlie finishes in eleventh place, at 1 under.

The week before Christmas, Charlie and Tiger team up for their third consecutive year at the PNC Championships. During an impressive opening-round 59, Charlie birdies the fourth and delights the crowd by raising his putter with his father's trademark flair.

Tiger, reports golf writer Jason Sobel, made a special request. Could NBC's Peacock streaming service have a camera at the first tee? **After he and Charlie hit their tee shots, they looked into the camera and congratulated Elin, Tiger's ex-wife and Charlie's mom. She gave birth to a baby this past Thursday,** Sobel tweets.

It's Elin's second baby with her boyfriend, Jordan Cameron, a former NFL tight end with the Cleveland Browns and Miami Dolphins. Sam and Charlie also have another half brother, Arthur, born in October of 2019.

Days ahead of Tiger's own upcoming birthday—his forty-seventh—he again takes advantage of the permission to ride a golf cart on the course. As it was during the nine competitive rounds in this year's Masters, PGA Championship, and British Open, his play is marred by leg and back pain. Team Tiger finishes eighth.

To Tiger, the year-end tournament is a lens through which he charts his physical progress. "The first year, I had back surgery and last year I played with a broken leg," he says. "So this year, nothing was broken, but it was good that all the pieces are there again all lined up."

Chapter 86

Genesis Invitational
Riviera Country Club
Pacific Palisades, California
February 16–19, 2023

Forty-seven-year-old Tiger Woods, the player-host of the Genesis Invitational, walks alone on a course where, after thirteen tries, he's never won a tournament. It takes intense concentration to move with the least amount of strain on his back and right leg, which he injured shortly after hosting this tournament two years ago.

Tiger made his PGA Tour debut here thirty-one years ago, playing on a sponsor's exemption in the 1992 Nissan Open. When he looks up to check the current scores, he sees that the leaders, including Jon Rahm and Max Homa, are players who were children back then.

"Because I haven't played a lot in the last few years, there's a tremendous amount of turnover," Tiger tells *Golf* magazine. "I look at the Champions Tour leaderboard"—the top pro golfers over age fifty—"those are all the guys I know. There's a lot of new faces out here that are going to be the future of our tour that I got a chance to see and play with."

Rahm wins, Homa finishes second, and Tiger ties for forty-fifth. Yet he still attracts adoring crowds who keep him hopeful. "Maybe next year," he says.

Tonight, he faces the grueling recovery regimen he undertakes every time he plays a competitive round. "There's a lot of ice going on here," he tells the *Los Angeles Times*. "As soon as I get back to the hotel, it's just icing and treatment and icing and treatment, just hit repeat throughout the whole night. Get ready, warmed up tomorrow, get this big sweat going on, big lift in the morning and stay warm and get off to a good start."

In mid-March, a few weeks ahead of the 2023 Masters, Jack Nicklaus is strategizing about ways in which Tiger, despite his injuries, can prolong his playing career.

"Tiger, you're eligible to take a cart," Nicklaus says, referencing the PGA's disability clause. It's been available for the last twenty-plus years, ever since 2001, when Tiger's Stanford teammate Casey Martin, who had a rare circulatory disorder that causes weakness in his right leg, won his case in the Supreme Court, allowing disabled players such as Martin and, more recently, John Daly to use a cart in competition.

Back then, Tiger had voted against the clause, saying "I think [walking] is an integral part of the game at our level, and I will never take a golf cart until it's sanctioned."

"I'm not going to do that," Tiger says now, but he concedes to Nicklaus, "When I get to the senior tour, I will."

In the Augusta National private dining room on April 4, things are a bit heated—at least on the Champions' Dinner menu, which includes firecracker shrimp, tortilla soup, rib-eye steak, and blackened redfish with jalapeño creamed corn, served in honor of the twenty-six-year-old defending champion, Texan Scottie Scheffler.

The consensus is that the tortilla soup packs too much of a punch. "It had a little bit of kick in it, yeah," says Spaniard José María Olazábal, the 1994 and 1999 winner. "I had to sort of swab the top of my head because it was perspiring," says Sandy Lyle, though the Scotsman, who in 1988 became Great Britain's first Masters champion, admits, "I suppose it's a little bit like when I had haggis. A lot of people didn't know what haggis was." Less understanding is the 1979 winner, Fuzzy Zoeller, who declares, "I about gagged." "Way too hot, too spicy," three-time Masters champion Nick Faldo complains.

The atmosphere itself is rather chilly. Tonight is the first Champions' Dinner since LIV Golf played its inaugural season, in 2022. Phil Mickelson, Sergio Garcia, Patrick Reed, Dustin Johnson, and Bubba Watson may now be ex-PGA, but their Green Jacket status lasts forever. At the Genesis Invitational, Tiger made it clear that the evening was about Scheffler. "Scottie's the winner, it's his dinner. So making sure that Scottie gets honored correctly but also realizing the nature of what has transpired and the people that have left, just where our situations are either legally, emotionally, there's a lot there."

Scheffler forewarns, "I'll definitely get emotional. I wish I didn't but I always do." Dinner otherwise adheres to tradition. As Lyle notes, "Regardless of all the different things that have been said in the last week or so, it went off without a hitch. Nothing from Gary Player or Mickelson."

Faldo observes that three-time Masters winner Mickelson (2004, 2006, 2010) "snuck around next to Gary"—who's also won three Masters (1961, 1974, 1978)—after the group portrait and before dinner.

Player, the eighty-seven-year-old South African who, like many golfers, winters in Jupiter Island, Florida, competed in the Masters fifty-two times; he's attending this year as an honorary starter. He's publicly stated that LIV is "for guys that can't win on the regular tour any more."

The comment is hardly polite dinner conversation. But in his pre-tournament press conference, Tiger reveals that he's wrestling with a similar question. "I don't know how many more I have in me," he tells reporters of his fitness for the Masters.

At the Champions' Dinner, Tiger and Jack Nicklaus take their traditional adjoining seats.

"I'm playing well," Tiger tells his old friend. "I'm hitting the ball great. My short game's great. My putting's good. I just can't walk."

On April 7, the five-time Masters champion, playing his twenty-fifth Masters, ties a record belonging jointly to Player and the 1992 Masters champion, Fred Couples. All three players have made twenty-three consecutive cuts at Augusta National.

The next day, storm clouds burst and temperatures take a dive. Navigating the hills on the course proves a painful struggle. By the time play is suspended for weather, Tiger is at 9 over for an incomplete round—and in last place. A recurrence of plantar fasciitis and arthritis brought on by his foot surgeries forces him to withdraw.

Two weeks after the Masters and six years after back fusion surgery, Tiger undergoes ankle fusion surgery.

At the Folds of Honor Greats of Golf exhibition match on April 29, Nicklaus tells *Golfweek,* "He wouldn't be having the operations if he wasn't interested in wanting to continue to play. He's a very motivated and dedicated young man."

Seventy-two-time LPGA winner Annika Sörenstam, whose own career ended because of injuries, takes "a fan's standpoint" in considering Tiger's ongoing medical struggles. "I think he's in more pain than he lets everybody know. I think it's a lot more serious. But he is so tough. And so courageous."

On July 31, PGA Tour commissioner Jay Monahan receives a forceful letter. It's signed by forty-one PGA players. Two leading the charge are Rory McIlroy and Tiger Woods.

"When Tiger speaks, his voice is very loud," says the 2019 U.S. Open winner, Gary Woodland, one of Tiger's captain's picks in the 2019 Presidents Cup.

The players have serious objections to their lack of agency in shaping the future of their sport. They were blindsided at the surprise reveal on June 6 that the PGA was also in negotiation with the Saudi wealth fund that is backing LIV—the golf league now in its second season—to create an umbrella company that includes the two rival organizations.

The letter writers' common goal is to increase player representation under Tiger's leadership, and on August 1, he joins the PGA policy board as a player-director, altering the balance by a single vote—six to five—in favor of the players.

The shift is significant. "I know he doesn't sleep a lot," says Jordan Spieth, winner of the 2015 Masters, 2015 U.S. Open, and 2017 British Open, "but he's spending most of his waking hours thinking about how to better the PGA Tour for the players. And he doesn't have to do that. He could ride off into the sunset if he wants. We know that's not his personality."

When is Tiger going to play again? In a November 1 interview with Golf Channel's George Savaricas, the 2009 British Open winner, Stewart Cink, drops some clues that the looming question might soon be answered. "He said that he's started practicing, which I think is a great sign," Cink says. "I don't know what he's practicing for, but he said he started practicing, so that means he's in 'go mode' for something."

Savaricas wagers a guess as to Tiger's next competition. "Will he play in December at either Hero World Challenge or PNC Championship?" Savaricas posts after the interview. "My gut PNC Championship best bet."

Golf fans in southwestern Louisiana are out in force the first weekend of November.

Fourteen-year-old Charlie Woods has moved into a more competitive age group in his second Notah Begay III Junior Golf National Championship. The adjustment has him shooting over par.

Like any smart golfer, Charlie knows that a caddie may advise, but it's up to the golfer to execute the shots. "For Dad as a caddie, his reads are hook-bias," Charlie says, "and I don't hook as much as he does. So all of my putts, I miss right. So I have to account for that." Still, the caddie wearing the WOODS bib is the most famous at Koasati Pines. Or any course.

"Tiger is walking like a champ," one fan posts.

But in a post-tournament interview with the Associated Press, Tiger makes it clear that looks can be deceiving. "I'm pretty sore after caddying for four days," he says. "It was a flat course, thank God."

Just as the 2017 spinal fusion surgery repaired his L5 and S1 vertebrae, "where they fused my ankle," Tiger says, "I have absolutely zero issue whatsoever." But the stabilizing interventions have caused a chain reaction of sorts in the interconnected systems. "So you fix one, others have to become more hypermobile to get around it, and it can lead to some issues."

"It's better in the Bahamas" goes a 1992 ad slogan that's remained popular in the Caribbean.

"Hey, guys," Tiger says brightly on a late November day as he walks into the press tent at the Albany Bahamas resort, where he is an investor.

Shortly after Tiger turned pro in 1996 and founded Tiger Woods, Inc., he told *Sports Illustrated* that "I've gone from being a college sophomore to a mini-CEO." Over decades, the empire has expanded, and the role of multihyphenate billionaire is wearing well. Player-host of the Hero World Challenge. Player-director on the PGA policy board. Golf course designer. Restaurateur. Real estate investor. Diplomat.

It "can't happen again," Tiger says of the PGA's secretive negotiations with the Saudi financiers behind the PIF. He speaks with confident authority, though he'd recently weathered the surprise mid-November resignation of his friend and colleague Rory McIlroy, who had tired of the ongoing fluctuations in professional golf.

Stepping in to take his place and maintain the ratio of six player-directors on the PGA policy board is thirty-year-old Jordan Spieth, who praises Tiger's leadership and perspective to the *Athletic*. "He's not stepping in to throw influence anywhere," Spieth says. "It just comes with him when he walks in the door. He's a listener and he has a lot of experience. He's seen the PGA Tour go through a lot of different changes over almost 30 years for him now."

On December 3, 2023, Masters champion Scottie Scheffler wins the Hero World Challenge. Tiger is twenty strokes behind him, placing eighteenth in a limited field of twenty. But he walked all seventy-two holes, banishing the memory of his limping across Augusta National, wielding clubs as canes, before withdrawing from the 2023 Masters.

For 2024, Tiger's set himself an inspiring goal: to play one tournament per month. "Once a month seems reasonable, and it gives me a couple of weeks to recover, a week to tune up," he says. "Maybe I can get into the rhythm of something like that."

The caddie wearing the WOODS bib hands Tiger a freshly cleaned club.

It's not Rob McNamara. The VP of TGR Ventures caddied for Tiger at the Hero World Challenge now that Joe LaCava has teamed with Tiger's fellow PGA policy board member Patrick Cantlay.

"New caddie today!" McNamara declares, joking with reporters who arrived early to cover Tiger's warm-up that he's already been fired.

This debut caddie recently finished fall semester exams for her junior year at the Benjamin School, in North Palm Beach, and wears her long dark hair parted in the center and pulled back in a ponytail. She's sixteen-year-old Sam Woods. **For the first time, Sam Woods is caddying for her father today** ♥ reads a post on the official PGA Tour Instagram account.

Team Tiger 2023 has a third member: Charlie Woods. The fourteen-year-old high school freshman plays on Benjamin's state championship golf team. The squad won—by a single shot—its fourth Florida High School Athletic Association class A title on November 15, with Charlie placing twenty-sixth individually.

The heavy downpour that coincides with the December 16 opening round of the PNC Championship at Orlando's Ritz-Carlton Golf Club is no deterrent to the fans—or the press. "I've stood in the rain for four hours for two people in this world and their names are Taylor Swift and Tiger Woods," a *Golf* magazine reporter posts alongside photos of a smiling, cheering, poncho-clad crowd.

Among them is eighty-four-year-old five-time major winner Lee Trevino, who has some advice for Charlie. For starters, "You got to leave the cell phone at home," Trevino says. "Work on something. . . . You gotta hit a shot. It doesn't have to be a good shot."

"I drove the ball really good today," Charlie says. "Didn't miss a fairway, and still managed to shoot 8-under. We just suck at putting."

His dad agrees. "That sums it up right there."

As caddie, Sam has to be a good driver on a day when the entire field takes carts across the rain-drenched course. "We love you, Sam!" fans positioned next to a tee box shout. She looks down shyly, but Tiger lavishes even more praise on the first-time caddie, who steers Team Tiger to a five-way tie for fifth.

"Sam was fantastic," the proud father says. "For me to have both my kids inside the ropes like this and participating and playing and being part of the game of golf like this, it couldn't have been more special for me, and I know that we do this a lot at home, needle each other and have a great time. But it was more special to do it in a tournament like this."

Chapter 87

Jupiter Island, Florida
January 8, 2024

It's time for a change of uniform, Tiger's decided.

After the PNC Championship, he'd been asked about his FootJoy golf shoes, the brand he wore for the first time at the 2022 Masters. What about Nike? "I'm still wearing their product," he told inquiring reporters.

The partnership with Nike—worth an estimated $660 million to Tiger—has lasted twenty-seven years.

"I'm confident he will be with Nike for the rest of his career" was Mark Steinberg's declaration in 2013, when Tiger's original 1996 contract, extended in 2001 and 2006, was reportedly lengthened ten more years.

"Dr. No" has long been Steinberg's alias, coined for his protective stance toward his top client. But it was Tiger who decided to split with Nike.

Nike answers with a national advertising campaign that rolls out on March 9. "It was a hell of a round, Tiger," runs the caption over a photo of Tiger celebrating his 1997 Masters win, dressed in his iconic Nike red and black.

That historic day at Augusta National, Tiger wore Nike Air Zoom Litany Wingtips. When he returned to the Masters in 2022, following his year-plus recovery from his Los Angeles County car crash, he wore Foot-Joys. And continued to wear them.

"I know beyond a shadow of a doubt that Nike made a thousand pairs of shoes for that guy," says a former Nike brand marketing director. "They cut that FootJoy apart, they used the same leather. I've seen the Innovation Kitchen and they can do miracles. I know Nike bent over backwards to try to make this work."

Tiger announces his Nike breakup with his own bold sign-off: "See you in LA!"

That's where the player-host of the 2024 Genesis Invitational will launch his next, as yet unspecified, venture.

On Monday, February 12—two days after the celebration of the Lunar New Year, ushering in the year of the dragon, and one day after Super Bowl LVIII—forty-eight-year-old Tiger unveils his new apparel line. Its name is Sun Day Red.

The CEO of TaylorMade Golf Company, David Abeles, is one of Tiger's event cohosts. The other is full-time sportscaster and part-time match-maker Erin Andrews. (On her popular podcast, *Calm Down with Erin and Charissa,* Andrews suggested to billionaire singer-songwriter Taylor Swift that she date Kansas City Chiefs tight end and now three-time Super Bowl champion Travis Kelce. "Go on a date with this guy," Andrews told Swift. "Do it for America.")

Tiger and TaylorMade are hoping for another love match...for their international business goals. Sun Day Red is an independent brand within TaylorMade, which also manufactures Tiger's golf clubs. Each of the fifteen points in the logo—a tiger-shaped design at once new and familiar—represents one of Tiger's major championships. The line includes golf wear (shoes and shirts, hats and gloves) as well as lifestyle items such as cashmere hoodies with luxury finishes. The inaugural collection is on display to guests mingling in the elegant, second-floor outdoor party space at the Coach House in prestigious Palisades Village, two miles from the Riviera Country Club, where the Genesis Invitational will be played this week.

Tiger explains the inspiration behind Sun Day Red. "It started with mom. Mom thought—being a Capricorn—that my power color was red, so I wore red as a junior golfer and I won some tournaments. Lo and behold, I go to a university that is red; Stanford is red. We wore red on the final day of every single tournament, and then every single tournament I've played as a professional I've worn red. It's just become synonymous with me."

"It's been full circle for me," Tiger says, offering a nostalgic valentine to Riviera Country Club on Wednesday, February 14. "This is where I played my first tour event and now having my foundation and being in control of that event I hope I figure something out and get in contention."

In the pro-am competition at the Genesis Invitational, Tiger—dressed in a navy-blue sweater, pants, and cap bearing the Sun Day Red logo—teams with Buffalo Bills quarterback Josh Allen and Los Angeles Angels outfielder Aaron Hicks. After a sixth-place finish, Tiger says, "I had an absolute blast today. A lot of talking trash, telling stories...enjoying one another's company."

Reporters amp up the intensity, asking after the fate of the TW logo Nike had created for Tiger's former clothing line. "I don't want it back," he says emphatically. "I've moved on. This is a transition in my life. I moved on to Sun Day Red, and we're looking forward to building a brand that elicits excitement and is transformative."

It's been nearly three decades since Tiger competed wearing clothing *not* bearing the Nike swoosh. Ten months have passed since Tiger withdrew with injuries from the 2023 Masters, but his determination never wavers. "I still love competing, playing, being part of the game of golf," he says. "It's a game of a lifetime and I don't ever want to stop playing."

From the PGA Tour Champions event in Florida, where Notah Begay

III offers commentary for the Golf Channel broadcast team, Tiger's old friend assesses his readiness for tomorrow's challenge. "Ten years ago, 15 years ago, there were no limitations on Tiger Woods. Now he understands, and that's fine. He's not the longest...but he's way above average. So it's just kind of like, can he piece it together at the right time? We'll see."

Tiger walks to the first tee box at Riviera Country Club wearing more clothing from his new Sun Day Red line: a blue cap, white sweater, and white shoes. He drives the ball nearly three hundred yards and birdies the hole. As the round progresses, his play holds steady, ranging between 1 over and 1 under.

Tiger's playing partners in the first two rounds are Justin Thomas and Gary Woodland, who underwent surgery for a brain tumor in September of 2023. Tiger granted Woodland a sponsor's exemption. The fathers share a philosophy of leading by example. "I want to prove to my kids nobody is going to tell you you can't do anything," Woodland told the Associated Press in January. "You can overcome tough, scary decisions in your life. Not everything is easy."

Around the 16th, the now familiar back spasms return—then set in. On the 18th, Tiger drives the ball straight down the fairway 295 yards. Then he hits his second shot into some deep rough to the right of the clubhouse. He recovers from the shank—unusual on the PGA Tour and even rarer for Tiger—sailing the ball between eucalyptus trees, over bunkers, and onto the green. He finishes 1 over par and ties for forty-ninth place.

Still, the crowd rewards their hometown champion with a rousing ovation.

"Oh, definitely I shanked it," Tiger says after the round. "My back was spasming the last couple holes and it was locking up. I came down and it didn't move and I presented hosel [clubhead socket] first and shanked it."

Thirty-one-year-old Patrick Cantlay has a lot in common with Tiger, including hailing from Southern California and serving on the PGA policy board alongside his sporting idol. Today, Cantlay takes an early tournament lead, finishing the first round eight strokes ahead of him.

"You see all the kids emulating Tiger, the game's growing and more rounds are being played than ever before in this country," Cantlay says. "The 10th hole here is the best case study. In the past it was 50-50 whether to lay up. Now, stats show going for the green is worth it. Players are more aggressive today and you almost have to be."

Tiger holds himself to the same standards he set back when Earl was coaching him in the ways of mental toughness. Thursday night, he begins to experience flulike symptoms. But despite having a fever, he's on the range Friday morning, warming up for the second round.

Tiger is uncharacteristically quiet. Gary Woodland notices that he "wasn't himself, just didn't look right."

As in the opening round, Tiger birdies the 1st. Then he bogeys 4 and 5. He's in danger of missing the cut.

But after teeing off on the 7th, Tiger is no longer fit to play. He signals for assistance, and a rules official drives him off the course in a cart. After twenty-four holes, his tournament has ended.

Riviera's Spanish revival–style clubhouse dates to 1928. Fans watch with concern as two vehicles from the Los Angeles Fire Department pull up—an ambulance and a ladder truck. The paramedics deliver the medical supplies urgently needed to treat Tiger.

"The doctors are saying he's got potentially some type of flu and that he was dehydrated," Rob McNamara, VP of TGR Ventures, says. "He's been treated with an IV bag and he's doing much, much better, and he'll be released on his own here soon."

Two hours later, Tiger departs Riviera, a passenger in a red SUV.

Fans stream off the course. Now that they can't watch Tiger play, there's no reason to linger.

The Tiger Effect remains in full force.

100 Rounds

The Benjamin School
Palm Beach Gardens, Florida
March 26, 2024

G olf awards ceremonies are nothing new for Tiger Woods. He's been
smashing records and making history in the sport for almost half a
century.

But he could not be more delighted to attend tonight's ceremony honoring the Florida High School Athletic Association's 2023 state champions. Tiger beams from the audience alongside Elin in celebration of the Benjamin School Buccaneers' win — and their fifteen-year-old son, Charlie, and his high school golf team's impressive accomplishment.

Tiger's logged many hours as a proud spectator at Florida golf courses where the team plays its matches.

"Tiger's been here a lot — it's great to have him watching," coach Toby Harbeck says. "We were playing a match at home, 18 holes, and we finished shooting a course-record 15-under. Tiger's sitting next to me and he goes, 'What did we shoot, coach?'"

Tiger's impressed with the team's score. "Are you kidding me?" he says before congratulating every player on the team, including Charlie, with a handshake.

While Tiger famously intimidates Tour players with 4 a.m. texts high-lighting his incomparable training regimen—I'm in the gym. What are you doing to get better?—Harbeck admires the champion's humble approach to being a golf dad.

"We don't call him Tiger. We call him dad because he's dad," Harbeck says. "And Charlie's not Tiger Woods's son, but he's Charlie, and that's the way they want it to be."

The team receives its championship rings at a ceremony held on Benjamin's upper-school campus. The awestruck players open the jewelry boxes holding the rings marked with a *B* and encrusted with diamonds to catch the light reflected in the brilliant stones.

Harbeck, who's coached the team for four decades, makes an emotional speech. "When you win a state championship, no one can ever take that away from you," he says. "You can be 75 years old sitting in a chair with your grandkids on you and you can tell them, 'I was a state champion.'"

Cameras flash as Charlie puts on his ring and shows it to his dad, who can't make the same statement—for all his honors, Tiger never won a high school state championship.

He's been more spectator than player so far this year. After he withdrew from the Genesis Invitational in February, Tiger's name was also absent from the commitment list for the PGA Tour's flagship event, the Players Championship at TPC Sawgrass, which he's won twice, in 2001 and 2013. But while his aspiration to play one tournament per month in 2024 may have faded, Tiger's diplomatic star has been rising.

On March 6, CBS Sports announced: TIGER WOODS NAMED VICE CHAIRMAN OF PGA TOUR ENTERPRISES.

PGA Tour Enterprises is a new for-profit entity with the stated objective to "continue to build the PGA Tour as the highest level of competition in professional golf."

Tiger is leading the visionary team that's transforming the PGA—and working to bring the best players to the best courses worldwide. The task of his team will be to forge "pathways back" to return the LIV roster to the PGA fold. "Trust me," Tiger says. "There's daily, weekly emails and talks about this and what this looks like for our tour going forward."

Though Tiger's played just twenty-four holes of competitive golf this year, his name is on the player list for the 2024 Masters in April.

As a Masters champion, Tiger's earned a lifetime invitation to the tournament, and the eighty-eighth Masters would mark both his twenty-sixth appearance and the fifth anniversary of winning his fifth Green Jacket and fifteenth major title. "To me," Michael Jordan said after that astonishing 2019 victory, "it was the greatest comeback I've ever seen."

Skeptics question whether Tiger will truly be able to make it to Augusta, but excitement grows when his Gulfstream G550 is tracked to Augusta Regional Airport. On March 30, ESPN's Scott Harig reports that Tiger played a round with Justin Thomas and club chairman Fred Ridley.

The question remains, Can he withstand the physical challenge of walking the several elevation changes on the 6.5-mile course, then repeat the feat each of the next three days? "We're playing on a hillside," Tiger says, "and we're just meandering back and forth across that hillside. So, yeah, it's a long walk."

As Notah Begay III explains during a pre-tournament conference call on April 3, "He's got some constraints . . . He's got zero mobility in that left ankle and really has low-back challenges now."

"I hurt every day," Tiger admits. But he's determined, banking on his familiarity with the course. "I think it's consistency, it's longevity, it's an understanding of how to play this golf course," he says of Augusta National. "There's a lot of knowledge that goes into understanding how to play it."

There's also a record on the line. Though he's more than a dozen Masters cuts away from Jack Nicklaus's record of thirty-seven total non-consecutive cuts, Tiger has made the cut a further twenty-two times since winning his first Green Jacket, in 1997 — in all, twenty-three times *consecutively,* a record he shares with Gary Player and Fred Couples. The only time he's missed a Masters cut was in 1996, the year after making his first cut in 1995, at age nineteen, and winning Low Amateur. He's yet to miss a Masters cut since turning pro.

If he makes it this year, Tiger will take sole possession of the record.

Fred Couples is optimistic about Tiger's chances after they play a nine-hole practice round on April 9. "I don't stare at his gait much," says Couples, the 1992 Masters winner. "But he just hits it so good."

"There he is, there he is," fans murmur when they spot Tiger.

"Boy is he in shape," a spectator from Iowa tells Fox News. "He's buff. He still looks like a defensive back [in the NFL], no doubt about it."

At his press conference, forty-eight-year-old Tiger is filled with nostalgia for Augusta National. "This tournament has meant so much to me and my family," the five-time Masters winner says. "Hugging my dad [after the 1997 win], then a full circle in 2019 [after his fifth Green Jacket] to hug my son [Charlie]."

No matter the outcome this Masters week, he says, "the fact that I'm able to put on a Green Jacket for the rest of my life is just absolutely amazing."

Then comes a prediction only Tiger could make: "If everything comes together, I think I can get one more [Green Jacket]."

"An ideal way to strike your first shot in a major" comes the call from the ESPN broadcast booth.

Tiger tees off at 3:54 p.m. For the first time since 1999, he birdies his first hole.

Heavy rain and forty-five-mile-per-hour wind had delayed the round by several hours, but Tiger is comfortably in the top twenty, tied for seventeenth place with a score of 1 under when darkness falls as he finishes on

13. Tomorrow, he'll need to play twenty-three holes—the five remaining in round 1 and a full eighteen in round 2.

"The body is OK," Tiger tells reporters after Day 1.

On Friday, April 12, Tiger begins prep at 4:30 a.m. He tees off at 7:50 a.m. and plays the five holes held over from yesterday, then signs his round 1 scorecard (73, one over par) at 9:35 a.m., leaving a mere fifty-two minutes before round 2. Team Tiger 2024—agent Mark Steinberg, VP of TGR Ventures Rob McNamara, and new caddie Lance Bennett—are all on hand to support their player.

In a secluded spot on the practice range, Tiger loosens his clothing to reveal a pain patch on his lower back, then covers his trunk and spine with Icy Hot. Thirty minutes until round 2 tee time.

CBS Golf is working with innovative new camera equipment. THE BUNKER CAMERA AT AUGUSTA NATIONAL IS MY NEW FAVORITE CAMERA! posts Omar Villafranca of CBS News.

The lenses capture Tiger protecting himself from the wind that's whipping sand up and out of the bunkers, some blasts lasting up to forty-five seconds.

Tiger makes four birdies—and four bogeys—and pars the other ten holes to shoot 72 and make the cut at one over, tied for twenty-eighth and seven back of the lead. Galleries are stacked deep with fans roaring for Tiger as if they're witnessing a final. It's an emotional moment.

At the post-round press conference, a reporter says to Tiger, "I know it's tough to reflect right after your round, but 24 straight cuts made here at Augusta. What does that mean to you, especially after the quick turnaround between rounds?"

"It means I have a chance going into the weekend," Tiger says. "I'm here. I have a chance to win the golf tournament." His competitive spirit as strong as ever, Tiger jokes with reporters that he plans to "text Freddy [Couples] and give him a little needle" about breaking the consecutive cut record.

"I'm tired," he admits. "I've been out for a while, competing, grinding.

It's been a long 23 holes, a long day. But [caddie Lance Bennett] and I really did some good fighting today."

Saturday's round 3, however, brings pain and disappointment, though Tiger vows to play on Sunday, saying, "My team will get me ready. Kolb [physical therapist Kolby Tullier] has been awesome. It will be a long night and a long warmup session, but we'll be ready."

On the practice range Sunday morning, Tiger watchers are ecstatic to spot a familiar face. Charlie's flown in from Florida—Sam's stayed behind to compete in her high school track and field conference championship—to help his father work on lower-body mobility. The drills look familiar. Footage from 1993 shows Butch Harmon extending a club as Tiger swings, the obstacle forcing him to tighten his arms toward his trunk. Today, Charlie steps into the role of swing coach.

Seeing Charlie Woods on the range giving his old man a lesson...so cool! posts CBS Sports broadcaster Trevor Immelman.

It goes both ways. "I love watching [the younger players] succeed," Tiger said during the pre-tournament press conference. "That's part of the game. We pass on the knowledge. We don't keep it. That's what we do; we pass on the knowledge to the next generation."

Tiger wears his traditional red shirt and black cap for the final round, now from his own Sun Day Red line. It's a powerful image for golf fans.

Tiger Woods in Sunday red at Augusta National just feels right, tweets NBC Sports.

No matter what he shoots in the final round, Tiger is also hitting another notable milestone—today marks his one hundredth round at Augusta. On 16, where in 2005 he made the incredible chip shot that so impressed CBS Sports broadcaster Verne Lundquist, Tiger spots the eighty-three-year-old, who is retiring tomorrow.

"Thank you, Tiger," Lundquist says as Tiger shakes his hand.

"We're gonna be tied at the hip forever," Tiger tells him.

"Pure class," says the *Augusta Chronicle*.

On the 18th, Tiger tips his cap to the admirers who've cheered him through his highs and lows. Though he scores better on his final round than on his third, it isn't enough. "I hoped I was going to shoot something in the 60s. I thought I had that in my system but unfortunately it didn't go that way," he tells Sky TV. Yet completing all four rounds at the Masters opens the way for an even bigger goal. "I think the rest of the majors [this year] is definitely doable for me. Hopefully my body will cooperate."

He's got a plan. "I'm going to do my homework going forward at Pinehurst [U.S. Open], Valhalla [PGA Championship] and Troon [British Open]," he says.

"I'm just going to keep lifting, keep the motor going, keep the body moving, keep getting stronger."

The USGA's national championship, the 124th U.S. Open, is held at Pinehurst No. 2 in North Carolina in June of 2024. On June 12, Tiger is presented with the Bob Jones Award, the United States Golf Association's highest honor, which "recognizes commitment to sportsmanship and respect for golf's time-honored traditions."

Tiger, a nine-time USGA champion—with six amateur and three professional victories—joins Arnold Palmer, Jack Nicklaus, and Ben Hogan in receiving the award. Tiger's career has often paralleled that of Robert Tyre "Bobby" Jones Jr., the greatest amateur to ever play the game. In 1930, Jones won the first—and only—calendar grand slam, which at that time meant the U.S. Amateur, the U.S. Open, the British Amateur, and the British Open. He also helped design Augusta National and cofounded the Masters.

The Bob Jones Award "goes beyond playing performance, recognizing the lasting impact of one person's journey that has forever changed the image and growth of golf," says the USGA CEO, Mike Whan, who foresees Tiger's influence lasting generations.

"His impact on the game is incalculable," adds the USGA president, Fred Perpall, "and there is no doubt that golf would not be the same without Tiger in it."

Notes

The endnotes for this book can be found at https://www.hachettebook group.com/titles/james-patterson/tiger-tiger/9780316438605/.

About the Author

James Patterson is the most popular storyteller of our time. He is the creator of unforgettable characters and series, including Alex Cross, the Women's Murder Club, Jane Smith, and Maximum Ride, and of breathtaking true stories about the Kennedys, John Lennon, and Princess Diana as well as our military heroes, police officers, and ER nurses. Patterson has coauthored #1 bestselling novels with Bill Clinton and Dolly Parton, and collaborated most recently with Michael Crichton on the blockbuster *Eruption*. He has told the story of his own life in *James Patterson by James Patterson* and received an Edgar Award, ten Emmy Awards, the Literarian Award from the National Book Foundation, and the National Humanities Medal.

For a complete list of books by

JAMES PATTERSON

VISIT
JamesPatterson.com

 Follow James Patterson on Facebook
@JamesPatterson

 Follow James Patterson on X
𝕏 @JP_Books

 Follow James Patterson on Instagram
@jamespattersonbooks